Gill NICHOLLS

Learning to

TEACH

A Handbook
FOR PRIMARY & SECONDARY SCHOOL TEACHERS

KOGAN
PAGE

First published 1999, Reprinted 2000 and 2002

Apart from any fair dealing for the purposes of research or private study, or criticism or review, as permitted under the Copyright, Designs and Patents Act 1988, this publication may only be reproduced, stored or transmitted, in any form or by any means, with the prior permission in writing of the publishers, or in the case of reprographic reproduction in accordance with the terms and licences issued by the CLA. Enquiries concerning reproduction outside these terms should be sent to the publishers at the undermentioned address:

Kogan Page Limited
120 Pentonville Road
London N1 9JN

© Gill Nicholls and named contributors, 1999

The right of Gill Nicholls and named contributors to be identified as the authors of this work has been asserted by them in accordance with the Copyright, Designs and Patents Act 1988.

British Library Cataloguing in Publication Data

A CIP record for this book is available from the British Library.

ISBN 0 7494 2865 1

Typeset by Saxon Graphics Ltd, Derby
Printed and bound in Great Britain by Bell & Bain Ltd, Glasgow

Contents

Introduction

Gill Nicholls

Teacher training continues to go through significant changes, the most recent of which has been the response to circulars 10/97, *High Status, High Standards: Requirements for courses of initial teacher training* and 4/98, *Requirements for Courses of Initial Teacher Training*. These circulars have increased the expectations of what it is to be a teacher, and have also set the standards by which future teachers are to be assessed. School-based training has not changed: trainees are still expected to spend the majority of their training time in schools with their mentors. However, Circular 4/98 gives clear categories and standards under which trainees have to demonstrate their abilities; these include:

- knowledge and understanding;
- planning, teaching and class management;
- monitoring, assessment, reporting and accountability;
- other professional requirements.

This book aims to help guide the trainee through each category, with the antici-pated help of their mentor. The underlying principle of the book is that teaching is an art as well as a science. Teaching is one of the most creative and satisfying profes-sions to be involved in. Yet as in any profession there are key elements, skills, prac-tices and standards that have to be achieved, if effective and efficient practitioners are to be developed. This book addresses all the key areas of Circular 4/98. In some chapters this is made more explicit than others; however, throughout it is assumed that trainees will have their own copy of the circular and gain, with the help of the book, a good working knowledge and understanding of the standards required to gain qualified teacher status (QTS).

The book through its tasks and overall design is aimed at helping trainees develop their skills, knowledge and pedagogic practice so that they not only meet the demands of Circular 4/98 but also develop and nurture their own philosophy of teaching.

Every teacher-training course starts trainees on their way. Learning the art and craft of teaching is a process, one that lasts a career – from trainee to newly qualified teacher (NQT) to very experienced teacher. The book attempts to address this learning process by involving the mentor in the trainee's learning. It also shows in later chapters the need to understand what it is to be professional and be involved in continual professional development. The final chapter is specifically aimed at the NQT – taking the trainee from 'trainee' to 'newly qualified teacher'. It allows the NQT to have confidence in what they can do as well as prepare them for the challenges ahead.

Structure of the book

The book is specifically designed to direct trainees at each stage of their learning. Each chapter is designated to a specific task aimed at focusing the trainee on key areas of development. The book is generic in its approach, but all areas and phases of education are catered for through the tasks.

Trainees are expected to use the text as a means of facilitating their learning, within their chosen phase of training. The text highlights key development areas and issues that need to be addressed in order to gain QTS. As such the book can be used as a whole, working through from start to finish, or as a resource that can be dipped in and out of as appropriate to the trainee's learning and development needs. The objectives set in each chapter reflect the demands set in Circular 4/98 as a means of achieving QTS.

The various authors of this text feel that the way the book has been devised allows creativity, motivation and self-development to thrive, while also meeting the highly defined legislative standards required of those wishing to join the teaching profession.

1 An introduction to teaching

James Williams

> Education. . . is the greatest work of all those which lie ready to a man's hand just at present. (T H Huxley, 'A liberal education and where to find it', address to South London Working Men's College, 4 January 1869)

This chapter introduces concepts related to effective teaching and learning. It aims to show the key areas for development and the role the trainee has in developing the skills needed to reach Qualified Teacher Status (QTS). These requirements form part of Circular 4/98, which all trainees should be familiar with.

Objectives

By the end of this chapter the trainee should be able to:

- identify the characteristics of good teaching;
- identify the key areas of development from Circular 4/98;
- understand the basic components of QTS;
- understand the relationship between statutory requirements and personal development.

As long ago as the 1860s, it was recognized that teaching and teachers must have a structure within which they can successfully work. The result was the 1870 Elementary Education Act. This was the first Act to prescribe what should be done in those institutions designated as 'schools'. The Act established the first education authorities, then referred to as school boards, and set up a countrywide system of schools that all children could attend. Thomas Henry Huxley (1825–1895) was a prime mover in the world of Victorian education. When the London School Board was established, it was charged with setting the education agenda of the day.

Huxley campaigned for a place on the Marylebone ward of the Board with, among others, Elizabeth Garrett, the first woman doctor. His influence on education in London and nationally was profound, especially in establishing science in the education framework, or curriculum of the day.

Since that first Act, education has been a central plank of political parties of all persuasions and the inaugural 1870 Act has given way to many others, notably the 1944, 1988, 1996 and, most recently, the 1997 Acts. The basis of all the education Acts for England and Wales is legislation that affects all primary and secondary schools. Over the years the Acts have established the character of English and Welsh education (see Table 1.1 for a brief summary of the main Acts and their prime provisions).

In addition to the education Acts, the Department for Education and Employment (DfEE) has recently set out those standards expected of students who

Table 1.1 The Main Education Acts of England and Wales and their principal provisions. (This is not a comprehensive list of all Acts relating to education provision in England and Wales)

Date	Main Provisions
1870 Elementary Education Act	Establishment of School Boards Allows for Boards to create and enforce by-laws for compulsory school attendance
1902 Education Act	Established the provision of Local Education Authorities (LEAs) Established the provision of county secondary schools
1944 Education Act	The basis of current law on education (repealed and largely replaced by the 1996 Act)
1980 Education Act	Established school governors for primary schools Established the right of parental choice of schools and the right of appeal if a child fails to gain a place at the school of first choice
1981 Education Act	Major changes introduced over the education of children with Special Educational Needs (SENs)
1986 Education (No 2) Act	Reform of school governing bodies
1988 Education Reform Act	Establishment of the National Curriculum Provision for schools to obtain Grant Maintained Status (GMS) Introduction of Local Management for Schools (LMS) Creation of a Standing Advisory Council on Religious Education (SACRE) required of all Local Education Authorities (LEAs) Provision for the establishment of City Technology Colleges (CTCs) Requirement for all pupils in maintained schools to attend a daily act of worship
1992 Education (Schools) Act	Establishment of new provisions for the inspection of schools Creation of Registered Inspectors (for the Office for Standards in Education: Ofsted)

	Outlined the functions and powers of Her Majesty's Chief Inspector of Schools
1993 Education Act	Creation of the Funding Agency for Schools (FAS) Creation of the School Curriculum and Assessment Authority (now part of the Qualifications and Curriculum Authority) Creation of a Special Educational Needs (SENs) tribunal and Code of Practice The Act was repealed in 1996 and replaced with the 1996 Education Act and the School Inspections Act
1994 Education Act	Established the Teacher Training Agency (TTA)
1996 Education Act	A consolidation Act, allowing for regulations and laws relating to schools set up by previous Acts to be covered in one statute. Although many laws have not been altered from earlier Acts those Acts have been repealed, including the 1944 Act which was the basis of much legislation relating to primary and secondary schools for over 50 years
1997 Education Act	Established the position over the physical restraint of pupils and detention of pupils in schools. The 1997 Education (Schools) Act also abolished the assisted places scheme

wish to gain QTS. The standards were introduced as a circular issued by the DfEE in 1997, Circular 10/97. 10/97 replaced a previous DfEE circular, 9/92 that set out the competencies expected of newly qualified teachers (NQTs). 10/97 has itself been superseded with only one minor change to the standards, relating to information and communication technology (ICT) by a new circular, 4/98, which also sets out a National Curriculum for initial teacher training (ITT). This specifies the components of undergraduate degrees leading to QTS and of a Postgraduate Certificate in Education (PGCE) in primary and secondary English, mathematics, science and ICT.

The 1980s and 1990s have been times of major reform in education. Teachers, trainee teachers, their school-based mentors and university/ITT tutors have had to come to terms with new and comprehensive legislation and a great deal of prescription in relation to what is required from those students who wish to qualify as teachers in England and Wales. In addition, the abolished probationary year for NQTs has been reintroduced in a more coherent and comprehensive form as an induction year (see Chapter 13).

But just what are the characteristics of a good teacher? And what are the characteristics of good teaching? In all of the legislation leading up to the Education Reform Act and the establishment of competencies there was no explicit setting out of the qualities that good teachers have or the characteristics of good teaching. In reality, there is no one correct answer to these two fundamental questions. Kyriacou (1997) cites a survey conducted in 1931 designed to ascertain the most important qualities of a good teacher. Teachers, pupils, teacher trainers and others reported the following qualities in order of frequency:

- personality and will;
- intelligence;
- sympathy and tact;
- open-mindedness;
- a sense of humour.

This simplistic view of the characteristics of good teachers is in itself not helpful. Someone with a strong personality and all of the above characteristics will not necessarily make a good teacher. The limitations of such a simplistic categorization was also recognized in the 1930s:

> Education is not so simple a business as is often supposed. It is not enough for the teacher to collect together a mass of knowledge, and retail it to his class. Nor is it enough for his personality to be strong enough to make the children do what he wants them to do ... Education in fact depends both on the school environment and on the response of the children to the teaching as well as on the subject and the teacher. (Board of Education, 1937)

It was clearly recognized then that the complex nature of teaching and education could not be unravelled by a simple categorization of qualities, knowledge and skills, yet that is just what we have today in the form of 4/98. Stones (1992) confirms that despite attempts to come to a consensus on the nature of quality teaching there is none. Just how far 4/98 does define what 'good teaching' and a 'good teacher' are, and how it can assist in the development of quality teaching and teachers, is the subject of this book.

The education of children is a multifaceted process that has a crucial aspect that cannot be ignored: teacher/pupil interaction and the structure and delivery of activities within the classroom. This is the one aspect that legislation cannot prescribe – what actually happens in the classroom. Black (1995) states that 'teaching is both an art and a craft that can be learned through hard work'. There is no doubting that teaching is hard work and learning to teach is not a simple process but recent moves to clarify the requirements as outlined above have clearly identified the areas in which trainees need to be accomplished in order to qualify as teachers.

High Standards: Circular 4/98

In order to be granted QTS by the Secretary of State for Education and Employment, trainees must successfully demonstrate their abilities in four areas:

1. knowledge and understanding;
2. planning, teaching and class management;
3. monitoring, assessment, reporting and accountability;
4. other professional requirements.

Each of these areas will be the subject of more detailed treatment in subsequent chapters. In this chapter we will look at the importance of the first three areas in relation to ITT and the quest for full QTS by trainees and NQTs.

Knowledge and understanding

The government has made explicit its desire to attract highly qualified graduates into teaching. Politicians have made suggestions that the entry requirements for a PGCE course should be set around grades A – C at A level and a 2:1 class honours degree. While these are 'ideal' entry qualifications the nature of graduate supply and the problems associated with shortages in teacher recruitment for some subject areas, notably mathematics and the sciences at secondary level, mean that this cannot be laid down as a requirement for ITT institutions at present. Concern has been expressed that the average points score for entry to undergraduate primary teacher training is far too low, with only 15 per cent of those entering ITT achieving a points score of 20 or above in 1996/7. For some subjects it was lower: zero per cent for those training to teach information technology (*Times Education Supplement*, 1998).

It is specified, however, that during recruitment, it is important for ITT institutions to ensure that 'all trainees possess the personal, intellectual and presentational qualities suitable for teaching' (DfEE, 1998). Where competition is still high for places, for example on primary PGCEs and for subjects such as secondary English, the academic 'targets' can be more easily met. Certain qualifications are mandatory for entry to teacher training. A relevant first degree and GCSE grade A* – C (or equivalent) in English and maths for all teachers and, for those born after 1 September 1979, a GCSE grade A* – C (or equivalent) in a science is required for those wishing to train in primary teaching. Given the variety of routes through the education system and the ever broadening choices made at A level by students, setting out ideal entry qualifications for entrants into teaching is more and more difficult, as is constructing a profile of the ideal candidate.

There is no doubting that having a well-qualified teacher who has secure subject knowledge and the ability to learn new subjects (which is essential in primary teaching where individual subject teaching by specialists is not the norm) is a distinct advantage. In an attempt to raise the standards of those training to teach, the Teacher Training Agency (TTA) introduced National Curricula for primary and secondary courses of ITT in English, mathematics and science. The purpose of the National Curricula is to 'specify the essential core of knowledge, understanding and skills which trainees must be taught and be able to use in relation to English, mathematics, science and information and communications technology' (DfEE, 1998). It will now be a common feature of ITT for students to undergo a series of subject knowledge audits. These audits are not a test of knowledge; rather they are an assessment of the trainees' confidence in their ability to teach elements of the subject National Curricula for pupils. A key phrase in the National Curricula for ITT is that they will 'specify the essential core of knowledge, understanding and skills'.

It would be easy to look at the standards for QTS and the ITT National Curricula subject knowledge requirements and assume in a rather simplistic way that secure subject knowledge and some practical class experience will necessarily lead to quality teaching. Stones (1992) confirms that this simplistic view of teaching is inadequate. He rightly denigrates this surprisingly widely held thesis and contends that insufficient attention is paid to knowledge of the theory of teaching. The ITT National Curricula address this aspect of teacher training with sections on pedagogical knowledge and understanding required by trainees to secure progress in core subjects and effective teaching and assessment methods. Each subject in the National Curriculum for ITT for each of the core subjects (English, maths and science) in primary and secondary education follows the same pattern:

- Section A: Pedagogical knowledge and understanding.
- Section B: Effective teaching and assessment methods.
- Section C: Trainees' knowledge and understanding.

In addition to meeting the standards, trainees must get to grips with pedagogical knowledge and understanding in order to secure progress in their subjects (both primary and secondary) and be familiar with effective teaching and assessment methods for those subjects. The importance of the theoretical aspects of teaching and learning are also emphasized in the standards for both primary and secondary pupils. The standards require that trainees 'are aware of, and know how to access recent inspection evidence and classroom relevant research evidence on teaching primary/secondary pupils ... and know how to use this to inform and improve their teaching' (DfEE, 1998).

The split between pedagogy and subject knowledge has been closed with the publication of Circular 4/98. The split is, however, a relatively recent one. Moon and Mayes (1994) observe that only 100 years ago a central characteristic of pedagogical accomplishment was knowledge of content. They argue that, in the 1990s, research on teaching exposed a lack of emphasis on subject knowledge:

> The emphasis is on how teachers manage their classrooms, organize activities, allocate time and turns, structure assignments, ascribe praise and blame, formulate the levels of their questions, plan lessons and judge general student understanding. What we miss are questions about the content of the lessons taught, the questions asked and the explanations offered. (p 127)

A crucial point raised by Moon and Mayes rests on the transition from expert student to novice teacher. The question, 'How do successful college students transform their expertise in the subject matter into a form that high school students can comprehend?' is central to the section in the standards devoted to knowledge and understanding. This question is not restricted to the transmission of subject knowledge to secondary school pupils. Primary teachers will have much the same problem, though their own subject expertise may be restricted when viewed in the context of the full spectrum of the National Curriculum subjects. Shulman (1986) categorized knowledge in three ways:

1. Content knowledge: the subject-specific knowledge that the teacher possesses.
2. Pedagogic knowledge: how subject knowledge may be used during teaching.
3. Curricular knowledge: knowledge of the whole curriculum, its structure and the materials used.

Given that the role of a teacher is to develop knowledge, understanding and skills in children, how these three act together is important. A teacher must be aware of the relationship between them in order to be effective. A successful teacher has the right balance and provides pupils with opportunities to increase their competence in all three areas. The result is that the pupils are learning. But what is the relationship between the trainees' knowledge and pupil learning? Alexander *et al* (1992) say of the teacher's subject knowledge: '(it) is a critical factor at every point in the teaching process: in planning, assessing and diagnosing, task setting, questioning, explaining and giving feedback'. It is central to teaching.

As an example take the concept of photosynthesis. It is a basic principle in science and a core biological process that pupils have to understand. Plants produce their own food by combining carbon dioxide and water using energy from sunlight to make sugar and the waste gas (for plants) oxygen. In the primary setting at Key Stage 1 pupils need only to know that plants need light and water to grow. At Key Stage 2, this is developed to include the leaf as a food producer and that water and nutrients are taken up through the soil (note the term 'nutrients', not 'food'). By Key Stage 3 the term 'photosynthesis' is introduced in the curriculum for the first time and the final element of the process of photosynthesis is introduced: the gas carbon dioxide. A teacher who did not understand the process sufficiently would be unable to produce an effective teaching scheme that allowed the pupils to understand the process. Even at Key Stage 1 it is important to ensure that the pupils do not carry with them a belief that plants feed from the soil. A common misconception is that the mass of a plant, its biomass, is derived from the soil. It comes in fact from the process of photosynthesis. If a Key Stage 2 teacher held the misconception that plants feed from the soil and inadvertently transmitted this misconception to the pupils, the Key Stage 3 science teacher would have to deconstruct this before being able to progress with the teaching of photosynthesis.

Subject knowledge then is not restricted to knowing and understanding at a level comparable to that of the pupils you will be teaching. To communicate concepts and ideas in a large variety of subjects your subject knowledge must go beyond that of the pupils. As a rough guide you must be at least one Key Stage ahead of them. For primary teachers a broad knowledge up to at least GCSE level would be required for those teaching to the end of Key Stage 2.

Planning, teaching and classroom management

This substantial part of the standards document naturally has three sections: the planning, the teaching and the management of the classroom. Each merits a book in its own right. Again, there is a temptation to divorce planning, teaching and classroom management and simply describe best practice in each. This would be a false view of teaching and of how teachers work. Good teachers produce well-planned lessons, where teaching is effective and class management not an issue as the activities the pupils are engaged in are interesting.

As has been pointed out, planning, teaching and classroom management cannot be divorced from the other areas such as subject knowledge. One of the keys to good teaching is good planning. A well-planned lesson is much more likely to succeed than an ill-prepared and ill-planned lesson. This is common sense: a well-planned journey is more likely to run smoothly than a journey that is mostly chance and intuition.

Planning

There are four stages involved in planning and delivering a successful lesson, as shown in Figure 1.1.

1. *Preparing.* Thorough preparation will involve getting to grips with the subject knowledge required for the lesson and determining the lesson aims, objectives and outcomes. It will involve research on the activities that may be appropriate for the lesson and the required links to the National Curriculum, the school scheme of work (if any exists) and/or syllabus requirements.
2. *Designing.* The design of the lesson is crucial to its success. There should be variety and the lesson must motivate the pupils and maintain their interest.
3. *Presenting.* The delivery of the lesson, its timing, and the way in which you execute your plan will be key contributory factors in its success.
4. *Evaluating.* An often forgotten part of the planning of successful lessons is the incorporation of evaluation points from previous lessons. Evaluating the success of lessons, or the reasons for failure, provides many pointers when designing future lessons. The idea of teachers as reflective practitioners and

professionals capable of learning from their experiences, both positive and negative, should not be undervalued.

Before deciding the activities that pupils will attempt in the classroom, teachers must be clear on the purpose of the lesson. Clear learning objectives and outcomes are needed. It may well be that the lesson being planned is one of a series of lessons that form the scheme of work for the subject or topic under consideration. In the primary setting the topic may form part of a multidisciplinary approach to a theme. In the secondary setting it is more likely to form part of a syllabus for GCSE or a published scheme of work for subjects at Key Stage 3. In nearly all cases it will conform to one or other of the National Curriculum orders. As well as the purpose of the lesson, the planning must take into account the context in which that lesson will be taught, for example as a practical lesson in science, art or music, as part of a syllabus in order to assess pupils against published criteria, or as a theoretical lesson delivering subject knowledge. Lesson planning takes place within the agreed curriculum and schemes of work delivered in schools (see Figure 1.2).

Planning must also have short-, medium- and long-term objectives linked to them. Short-term planning, eg lessons, parts of lessons or short sequences of lessons, will be much of the day-to-day work of the teacher. This must take place within a framework of medium- and long-term planning. The medium term may be a topic or unit of work that will last for part or even the whole of a school term. This, in turn, will be subsumed in the long-term plan that may be based on a Key Stage within the National Curriculum or an academic year. In secondary schools it may be part of the syllabus leading to a recognized certificate or award.

The planning process must also take into account day-to-day information gleaned from the pupils and the teachers' evaluations of their lessons. An

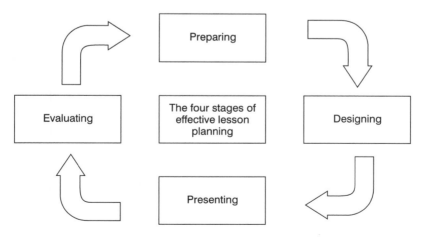

Figure 1.1   The four stages of effective lesson planning

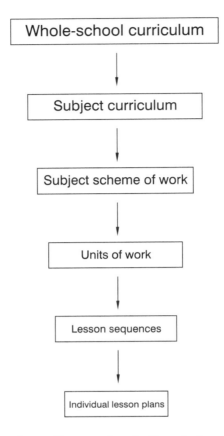

Figure 1.2   The place of lesson plans in the whole-school curriculum

important part of the standards relates to the notion of using assessment infor-mation in the future planning of lessons. During the inspections of ITT by the Office for Standards in Education (Ofsted) this received close scrutiny when inspectors observed trainees in the classroom.

The care taken in planning lessons is more often than not reflected in their success in practice. A poorly planned lesson is rarely successful. It may take place without incident and the pupils may not necessarily run riot in the classroom, but the learning experience for the children will almost certainly be limited and narrowly focused.

Teaching and class management

This is the aspect that trainee teachers often consider to be the most important. Teaching is defined in *The Collins English Dictionary* as 'the art or profession of a teacher'. As a strict definition it is not particularly useful: it gives no real clue as to the actual process. Claxton (1984) defines teaching as 'what one person does to try and help another to learn' (p 211). Claxton's broad definition includes a number of the activities that people most often associate with the act of teaching:

- demonstrating skills;
- giving friendly advice;
- explaining things;
- dictating homework.

Claxton goes on to maintain that a prime consideration for teachers is how learners actually learn. 'If teachers do not understand what learning is, and how it happens, they are as likely to hinder as to help' (p 212). Kyriacou (1997) defines effective teaching as '(that) which successfully achieves the learning by pupils intended by the teacher'. Again the common sense notion of teaching and learning being linked is provided.

For learning to occur there must be order in the classroom and this is where the notion of sound class management comes in to play. The standards recognize that in order for successful learning to take place teachers must establish a safe environment and a purposeful working atmosphere. The creation of a positive learning atmosphere also requires good behaviour on the part of the pupils. The teacher has a key role in setting high expectations of the pupils. Many behavioural problems experienced by teachers may be related to boredom. Pupils will often complain of boredom during lessons. This may be genuine, but it could be boredom generated by lessons that do not engage a pupil's interest. Good teachers are aware of this and will vary their teaching methods to keep pupils engaged in their work. Developing an arsenal of teaching strategies, methods and styles is essential if you are to become an effective teacher.

Monitoring, assessment, recording, reporting and accountability

Marking of pupil work is a core activity of teaching. There are many stereotypical views of teachers and marking – scores out of 10, grading by letter, and any combination of letters and numbers. For marking to be effective it must be clearly understood by the pupils, it must be based on consistent standards and it must reflect agreed criteria. Different schools will operate different marking policies. In all cases schools will take into account any statutory forms of assessment, such as end of Key Stage assessments. For the purposes of monitoring, the marking of pupil work must also feed into the teacher's planning cycle. This will allow teachers to check pupils' understanding, guide the teacher as to where intervention in the pupils' learning is required and chart the progress made by the pupils. Marking then has many potential uses and audiences.

Marking, however, is not the only type of assessment that teachers undertake in the classroom. During lessons, formal question and answer sessions, chatting with individuals or groups of children, teachers are assessing. A key assessment that is made is whether or not the learning objectives for the lesson are being achieved. Knowing this will help teachers to improve on aspects of their teaching. The assessment of pupils, either formally using National Curriculum levels or informally when deciding a pupil's level of understanding of a topic or concept, often presents trainee and newly qualified teachers with one of their most difficult tasks. Accurate assessment is difficult and will only become easier with experience, but by the time trainees gain QTS, they must be able to generate a range of assessments on their pupils which suit the needs of a wide audience.

It is vital that at the start of their teaching career teachers devise and maintain accurate records of pupils' work, progress and attainment. In addition it will be necessary in the secondary school to become familiar with the details of GCSE and A level specifications. During training many trainees are encouraged to shadow the work of experienced teachers when marking, assessing and reporting on pupil progress. With the notion of baseline assessment and value-added being introduced to schools, the assessment role has been widened. 'Value added' is a much-used term in schools and, put simply, it is a measure of the progress made by pupils over a fixed period of time with reference to their starting point. On entry to the school system pupils have a baseline assessment made of their ability. At key points, for example at the end of each Key Stage, the progress made can be compared to either the baseline assessment or the previous Key Stage assessment; this will provide information on the 'educational' value added to that pupil over time. While this may seem to be a simple notion it is really a complex calculation and many factors could play a part in determining the real value added. To illustrate this take the case of a pupil who is assessed as National Curriculum Level 4 in maths at Key Stage 2. It would be reasonable to expect that three years later the pupil should have progressed to, say, Level 6 at the end of Key Stage 3. However, it can be the case that the pupil does not make that much progress and only achieves Level 5. A simple explanation may be that the teaching at Key Stage 3 was not effective. The real reason may be very complex. It could be that the pupil has suffered from prolonged absence due to illness. It may be a curriculum issue in that the breadth of material covered at Key Stage 2 was much narrower than that covered at Key Stage 3. So, a simple cause-and-effect model for interpreting assessment data is not desirable. One aspect of assessment is clearly useful to teachers: the use of target setting to motivate pupils in a bid to raise standards.

Teachers are accountable for the pupils they teach. Their accountability resides in more than just keeping order in the classroom or making sure that work is completed. Teachers will be accountable in many spheres of their pupils' school lives, from health and safety in the classroom, to pastoral issues, personal and social development, academic attainment and others. Being a teacher brings with it many rewards coupled with many responsibilities.

Task 1.1: The characteristics of a good teacher

Describing the perfect teacher is not an easy thing to do and, indeed, it may not be desirable for reasons made clear earlier. For this task, however, you need to have in mind teachers and lessons from your own experience. Think about lessons you attended as a pupil or about lessons run by teachers you have observed. Make two lists of notes: one of those things that you believe made the teacher either memorable and/or successful and the lesson a positive experience, and one of a lesson that was not successful. Now list those features that can be ascribed to one of three categories of influence: the teacher, the pupil and the subject. Now think about the following:

- Who/what has the greatest influence in a classroom?
- How could the proportion of each of the influences (teacher, pupil, subject) in a lesson impact on its outcome?
- Is a totally teacher-dominated lesson successful?
- Does giving pupils autonomy in their learning lead to more highly motivated pupils?

References

Alexander, R et al (1992) Curriculum Organization and Classroom Practice in Primary Schools: A discussion paper, DES, London

Black, P (1995) Curriculum and assessment in science education: the policy interface, International Journal of Science Education, 17 (4), pp 453–69

Board of Education (1937) Handbook of Suggestions for Teachers, HMSO, London

Claxton, G (1984) Live and Learn: An introduction to the psychology of growth and change in everyday life, Harper & Row, London

Department for Education and Employment (1997) High Status, High Standards: Requirements for courses of initial teacher training, Circular 10/97, DfEE, London

DfEE (1998) Requirements for Courses of Initial Teacher Training, Circular 4/98, DfEE, London

Kyriacou, C (1997) Effective Teaching in Schools, 2nd edn, Stanley Thornes, Cheltenham

Moon, B and Mayes, A (1994) Teaching and Learning in the Secondary School, Routledge, London

Shulman, L S (1986) Those who understand: knowledge and growth in teaching, Educational Researcher, 15, pp 4–14

Stones, E (1992) Quality Teaching: A sample of cases, Routledge, London

TES (1998) Agency spotlights training shortfall, 25 September

2 The National Curriculum – a decade of reform

Steve Alsop and Graham Dock

The aim of this chapter is to help the trainee become familiar with the National Curriculum – the compulsory curriculum for all pupils aged 5–16 in state schools in England and Wales.

Objectives

By the end of this chapter the trainee should be able to:

- understand the structure and terminology of the National Curriculum;
- explore key issues in the implementation of the curriculum;
- recognize the role that their specialist subject has in the curriculum;
- appreciate the classroom experiences of school pupils;
- appreciate the role the curriculum has in what is taught.

Introduction

The school curriculum has been a topic of intense debate for many years; in the last 10 years, in England and Wales, the debate has firmly focused on the National Curriculum. In 1988, in over 20,000 UK schools the curriculum changed – this magnitude and type of state intervention in education is unprecedented. It is now 10 years since the Educational Reform Act (ERA) and during these years the curriculum has undergone both major and minor revisions. The implementation of the original proposals was swift: four years after the ERA most significant features were in place. In all state schools in England and Wales, for example, it was possible to identify the subjects and content that all pupils were entitled to receive (ages 5 to 16). In the last six years, the curriculum has congealed and modifications have been of a smaller scale. At the time of writing, reforms are once more gathering pace with the introduction of numeracy and literacy hours, and a curriculum review is underway for the millennium.

What is a curriculum?

It is difficult to reach a consensus over the definition of the term 'curriculum'. *The Collins Dictionary*, for example, defines a curriculum as 'a list of all the courses of study offered by a school or college'. This would seem to place an emphasis on school subjects and, presumably, more specifically the content of these subjects. In this regard, the 'curriculum' contains what should be taught and could look like a syllabus or a list of content – much like a type of revision guideline used for a final examination. A list of what content should be taught in schools is clearly important and in the following discussion we refer to this as 'the subject curriculum'. However, some may argue that a curriculum is more than this and that to restrict a curriculum to a list of subject content would fail to embrace significant considerations such as how courses are taught or the amount of time spent in school or on a particular subject. These are also defining components of school experience – for example, the amount of time spent on a subject carries messages about its importance or perceived intellectual difficulty.

Alternatively, it could be argued that a 'curriculum' should be defined as a product: a description of what is learnt rather than what is taught. In this case it would place greater emphasis on experiences, learning goals, objectives and assessment. Of course, what is taught by a teacher can be quite different to what is learnt by a pupil. As we will indicate, the National Curriculum specifies both the taught content as well as content that should be assessed.

So far, the discussion has considered the assessed subject curriculum; however, a school curriculum will also contain social, personal and health elements – these are commonly referred to as 'the pastoral curriculum'. Furthermore, a balanced curriculum will cover cross-curriculum issues of, for instance, equal opportunities and key life skills, including communication, study, problem solving and information technology. A 'whole-school' curriculum is, at least, comprised of these three areas.

In this chapter, the National Curriculum is outlined – the statutory component of the 'whole curriculum' for state schools in England and Wales. This curriculum has evolved and continues to evolve and as a consequence we outline the curriculum in its current phase. There are plans to revise the curriculum in 2000 and the Qualifications and Curriculum Authority (QCA) has set up a series of meetings and discussion groups to canvas educationalists' opinions about the nature and scope of these revisions. Before outlining this curriculum, a brief historical background to the current legislation is provided.

Background to the National Curriculum

The National Curriculum for England and Wales was just one of a raft of major changes to education brought about by the 1988 Education Reform Act, including Local Management of Schools and the introduction of Grant Maintained Schools and City Technology Colleges. In order to understand the present form of the National Curriculum, it is useful to have some knowledge of the background that led up to what was, in British terms, a revolution. Some of the main political events, ideas and personalities are identified as a means of encouraging further reading.

Considering state education from its inception, say the Forster Act of 1870, it becomes apparent that education in Britain has existed for a long time without anything resembling a National Curriculum. Indeed, for a large part of the 20th century the control of the curriculum by the individual classroom teacher was regarded by some as a pillar of democracy. The important 1944 Education Act, which established secondary education for all as an integral part of the system, paid little attention to the curriculum other than the requirement that: 'it shall be the duty of the local education authority for every area, so far as their powers extend, to contribute towards the spiritual, moral, mental and physical development of the community' (Section 7).

There is not an obvious starting date but certainly the origins of the National Curriculum can be traced to before the Conservative Government of 1988. Furthermore, the events and influences are not confined to a single political party. To justify these last two statements, it is necessary to look at what was being said and written about education during the two decades which led up to the ERA. For the first four years of the 1970s, the Conservatives were in power and Margaret Thatcher was Secretary of State for Education. Raising of the school-leaving age aside, there was little that was revolutionary about government education policy during this period. On the contrary, it continued to maintain and develop policies that had been developed in the 1960s. The rapid growth of comprehensive schools continued. Simon (1988) points out that more schools went comprehensive between 1970 and 1974 than either before or after. The major policy statement of the period took the form of a White Paper in 1972: *Education: A framework for expansion*, that set out a ten-year programme for educational advance involving substantially increased expenditure in five directions: a new nursery programme; a larger building programme for the renewal of secondary, special and primary schools; a larger teaching force to improve staffing levels in schools; a new initiative to improve the pre-service and in-service training of teachers; and the development of a wider range of opportunities in higher education. It is difficult to find the roots of the 1988 Education Reform Act here. Certainly, a National Curriculum and a system of assessment were not part of this 10-year plan.

Within Conservative ranks as a whole, however, there were many who were not happy with the comprehensive 'roller coaster'. One of the most visible manifestations of this dissatisfaction was the series of Black Papers which appeared between 1969 and 1977. Each of the papers consisted of a collection of essays from a wide range of contributors including academics, teachers, MPs and various celebrities. A number of connected themes can be seen running through the publications. There was a conviction that educational *values* and *standards* were threatened by what the authors saw as a growing orthodoxy of progressive education. They argued that the advance of comprehensive schools should be slowed and grammar schools retained to help preserve standards and to provide *choice.* This debate is still very much alive today.

Rhodes Boyson replaced Dyson as co-editor of the Black Papers and, with Cox in 1975, started to advance alternative policies, rather than recommending moderation of prevailing ones. In the final Black Paper, under the heading: 'Letters to Members of Parliament: School Standards' the editors suggest:

> a return of the national inspectorate of HMIs to their original task of the inspection of schools. At the same time the national monitoring of basic standards by examinations for all children at the ages of 7, 11 and 14 or 15 should be introduced. . . The school results of these tests should be available to parents, school governors and the local community. Names of children should not be published, but parents have a right to know the comparative achievement of schools.

There is much in this passage that is similar to aspects of the ERA; particularly striking is the reference to testing at ages 7, 11 and 14 or 15. If this is not a direct antecedent of assessment in the Act, then it can at least be acknowledged that the writing of the Black Papers and the appearance of extracts from them in the popular press helped fuel a growing concern with standards and accountability in schools. In doing so, they were helping to produce a climate that made possible the relatively smooth passage of the 1988 Act.

In both the academic world and in the media, there was, by the mid-1970s, a fierce argument in progress over whether educational standards were in decline. Whether this concern was well-founded or not is not material to the argument here; that the concern existed is very pertinent.

The year 1976 can be regarded as an important watershed. It was the year in which Thameside local authority won its case against the government not to implement comprehensive reorganization and also the year when Fred Mulley, Secretary of State for Education, furnished Prime Minister Callaghan with the HMI

'Yellow Book' that voiced concern about standards in comprehensive schools. It was this document that provided the basis for Callaghan's speech at Ruskin College, Oxford, later that same year. This speech was announced to the media well in advance (CCCS, 1981) and in it the Prime Minister proposed a national debate around several themes:

> There is a challenge to us all in these days and a challenge to education is to examine its priorities and to secure as high efficiency as you can by the skilful use of the £6 billion of existing resources. Let me repeat some of the fields that need study because they cause concern. There are the methods and aims of informal instruction. The strong case for the so-called *core curriculum of basic knowledge*. What is the proper way of monitoring the use of resources in order to maintain a proper national standard of performance? What is the role of the inspectorate in relation to national standards and their maintenance? And there is a need to improve relations between industry and education.

Following the Ruskin speech, the Department of Education and Science organized eight regional one-day conferences under the heading 'Educating our Children' and set in motion what became known as the Great Debate. Discussion centred around the school curriculum 5–16, including the composition of a core curriculum, the assessment of standards, the education and training of teachers and the relation of school to work. Although the concerns are not dissimilar to those addressed by a different government a decade later, the solutions proposed in the subsequent Green Paper (DES, 1977) are different in kind and attention to detail.

The Green Paper points to the need for a 'core' or 'protected' part of the curriculum but seeks to establish a 'broad agreement' with the local education authorities and others on a framework for this. At the same time, it recognizes that a growing need 'for schools to demonstrate their accountability to the society which they serve requires a coherent and soundly based means of assessment for the educational system as a whole, for schools, and for individual pupils'.

The Green Paper did not, of course, bring about immediate tangible changes in schools or in the education system. It did enable and promote the continued discussion about the curriculum and during the next 10 years there appeared a steady stream of documents on the subject from the DES, culminating in *The National Curriculum 5–16: A Consultation Document*, in July of 1987. The Green Paper and the Ruskin speech also brought into open discussion within the education world and in the wider public domain topics which previously appeared to be the sole concern of the educational fringe, such as those writing for the Black Papers. Prominent among these topics were *accountability* and *evaluation*. It is these two topics, together with an increase in parental choice, that form the main political aims of the educational reforms of the 1980s, culminating in the 1988 ERA and the introduction of the National Curriculum.

The plan was to phase in the National Curriculum for the different Key Stages over a four-year period beginning in 1989. It soon became clear that the very detailed curriculum and assessment framework was running into manageability problems within schools. The teaching profession showed their opposition to the nature of this testing and the additional workload it involved by taking strike action. Significant modifications to the design and level of detail of the curriculum and to the approach to assessment were made in 1991. However, these changes were to prove insufficient and in 1993 the Government invited Sir Ron Dearing, Chairman of the National Curriculum Council and of the School Examinations and Assessment Council to carry out a review of the National Curriculum in England. A parallel review was carried out by the Curriculum Council for Wales. The Secretary of State for Education set out four key issues:

1.   the scope for slimming down the curriculum;
2.   the future of the ten-level assessment scale;
3.   how to simplify the testing arrangements;
4.   how to improve the administration of the National Curriculum and the tests.

The reviews, based on wide consultation, were completed during 1993 and the subsequent reports and recommendations were largely accepted by the Government. New orders were introduced in 1995. The range of subjects within the National Curriculum remained unchanged, but there was some reduction in what must be taught outside the core subjects. These changes were most noticeable at KS4 where the reductions allowed for broader choice, including foundation GNVQ courses. This breadth was further enhanced with the introduction of GCSE short courses. The decision was also taken to not apply the 10-level assessment scale to KS4 but rather to retain the GCSE A* to G scale. The 1995 orders used a simplified scale for assessment and there was also some slimming down of the national testing arrangements (eg no national tests for science at Key Stage 1) and a reduction in the overall time spent on testing. The Dearing recommendation was that this version should have a shelf life of at least five years to give the profession some respite from constant change!

Task   2.1: The evolution of your subject

Research what happened to your subject from the introduction of the National Curriculum in 1989 to the 1995 orders. For example, what happened to the content and the number of attainment targets?

An outline of the National Curriculum

The National Curriculum aims to provide pupils with a curriculum that:

- is balanced and broadly based;
- promotes their spiritual, moral, cultural, mental and physical development;
- prepares them for the opportunities, responsibilities and experiences of adult life;
- includes, in addition to the National Curriculum, religious education and, for secondary pupils, sex education.

The Curriculum is composed of 10 subjects that are studied by all pupils. These subjects are well known and have featured in the school curriculum for many years. They are divided into *core* and *foundation* subjects. The *core* comprises English, mathematics, science (and Welsh where the medium of instruction in the school is Welsh); the *foundation* comprises art, geography, history, modern language (for 11–16-year-olds), music, physical education and technology (and Welsh where the medium of instruction in the school is Welsh). These subjects form the statutory curriculum (the minimum entitlement) but schools can extend the curriculum to meet their particular needs and circumstances.

The content of National Curriculum subjects is described using a series of generic terms, namely:

- Key Stages (KS);
- Programmes of Study (PoS); and
- Attainment Targets plus Level Descriptors (ATs).

You need to be familiar with these terms as they are in common use in schools. They are briefly outlined in the following sections.

Key Stages

The National Curriculum classifies school years (ages 5–6) into four Key Stages. A Key Stage corresponds to either two or three years of schooling. Details of these Key Stages, with the addition of the school reception year, are provided in Table 2.1.

In this manner, Key Stages are defined by the age of the majority of children in a particular school year group. KS1 starts at the beginning of the term after a pupil's fifth birthday. Secondary school classes start at year 7 (the beginning of KS3), and finish at year 11, the year of GCSE examinations and the end of KS4. The sixth form, post-16, is now commonly referred to as year 12 or 13 – or in some cases, KS5. School years labelled in this way emphasize continuity and progression from one year to the next.

Table 2.1 The Key Stages and years of the National Curriculum

Age	Description	School year
5 or under	Reception	R
5–7	Key Stage 1	Years 1–2
7–11	Key Stage 2	Years 3–6
11–14	Key Stage 3	Years 7–9
14–16	Key Stage 4	Years 10–11

Programmes of Study

The Programmes of Study specify the compulsory teaching within each subject. In other words, they describe what content, skills and processes should be taught. In each subject, the PoS are separately documented in Key Stages (ie the content for KS1 is followed by the content for KS2, etc). The content is divided into a series of subject *areas* and each area directly matches an assessment attainment target (see the following section). The number of areas differs from subject to subject; as an example, the areas for the core curriculum subjects (English, Welsh, mathematics and science) are listed in Table 2.2.

In some subjects, the content is further divided into sections – a section describing a series of related ideas progressing through the programme of studies. For example: in science, the area 'Life Processes and Living Things' is divided into five sections:

1. life processes;
2. humans as organisms;
3. green plants as organisms;
4. variation and classification;
5. living things in their environment.

However, this subdivision is not clear in all subject areas.

Table 2.2 Areas in the Programmes of Study of the core curriculum

English	Welsh	Mathematics	Science
Speaking and listening	Oral (speaking, listening and viewing)	Using and applying mathematics	Experimental and investigative science
Reading	Reading	Number and algebra	Life processes and living things
Writing	Writing	Shape, space and measures	Materials and their properties
Handwriting and presentation		Handling data	Physical processes

Attainment targets

As well as PoS, each subject in the National Curriculum has one or more attainment targets or ATs (see Table 2.3). These set out the standards of performance which are used as a basis for making judgements about pupils' attainment on particular aspects of the PoS. They do this in terms of either 'level descriptors' or 'end of Key Stage descriptors'.

ATs define the assessment agenda of the National Curriculum (what should be assessed) whereas the PoS define the content agenda (what should be taught).

Level descriptors

Level descriptors exist for ATs in all subjects other than art, music and physical education. Each AT contains eight level descriptors of increasing difficulty. Teachers use their professional judgement to decide which of the descriptors best fits their knowledge of a pupil's performance in the subject over a period of time. The expected range of levels of attainment for the great majority of pupils at the end of a particular Key Stage is as follows:

> KS1   Levels 1 to 3.
>
> KS2   Levels 2 to 5.
>
> KS3   Levels 3 to 7.

Level 8 is available to cater for very able pupils at the end of KS3 and a further descriptor above Level 8 is provided to allow teachers to indicate exceptional performance. Note that the level descriptors do not apply to KS4 where GCSE examinations are the main means of assessing attainment in the National Curriculum.

End of Key Stage descriptors

End of Key Stage descriptors exist for art, music and physical education. They set out the standard of performance expected of the majority of pupils at the end of each Key Stage. End of Key Stage descriptors are similar in style to the level descriptors. Teachers are encouraged to use their professional judgement to decide the extent to which a pupil's attainment relates to the expected standard of performance at the end of a Key Stage. The descriptors correspond roughly to the mid point of the previously cited Key Stage levels. In physical education, additional descriptors are provided to help teachers differentiate exceptional performance at KS3 and KS4.

Table 2.3 The National Curriculum attainment targets (Source: SCAA, 1996)

Subject	Attainment targets			
English	Speaking and listening	Reading	Writing	
Welsh	Oral (speaking, listening and viewing)	Reading	Writing	
Mathematics	Using and applying mathematics	Numbers and algebra	Shape, space and measures	Handling data
Science	Experimental and investigative science	Life processes and living things	Materials and their properties	Physical processes
Design and technology	Designing	Making		
Information Technology	Information Technology capability			
History	History			
Geography	Geography			
Modern Foreign Languages	Listening and responding	Speaking	Reading and responding	Writing
Art (England)	Investigating and making	Knowledge and understanding		
Art (Wales)	Understanding	Making	Investigating	
Music (England)	Performing and composing	Listening and appraising		
Music (Wales)	Performing	Composing	Appraising	
Physical Education	Physical Education			

These subjects have level descriptions

These subjects have end of Key Stage descriptions

Task 2.2: Familiarize yourself with the National Curriculum

Observe a class being taught and identify the content of the lesson. Then use the relevant subject National Curriculum subject booklet to consider the following questions:

- Where does the content appear in the subject's Programme of Study?
- Does the content appear within a given Attainment Target? If so, where?
- Does the content match a level descriptor? If so, which one?
- Does the content appear in one Key Stage only or does it appear at other levels? If so, which?

The statutory framework

As previously noted, the National Curriculum consists of 10 subjects. However, not all these subjects are required to be taught in each Key Stage and there are also significant variations between the curricula for England and Wales. The subjects presently included in the National Curriculum in each Key Stage are shown in Table 2.4. The statutory curriculum for KS4 contains fewer subjects than at other Key Stages. At KS4, secondary schools have the flexibility to offer a range of additional courses to meet students' needs (in line with the 1996 Education Act) and these courses can lead to a range of qualifications including: GCSE, GCSE (short courses), GNVQ, key skills units in information technology and NVQs and NVQ units. Religious education, sex education and careers education are also statutory parts of the KS4 curriculum (QCA, 1998a).

As previously noted, the curriculum is presently under review. Most recently, the White Paper, *Excellence in Schools* (DfEE, 1998b) has highlighted a new set of curriculum priorities and goals. These priorities cover three key areas (QCA, 1998b):

1. breadth, balance and key curriculum principles;
2. literacy, numeracy and key skills;
3. citizenship, personal, social and health education and spiritual, moral, social and cultural development.

The need for flexibility, breadth and balance as well as a focus on the priorities of literacy, numeracy and information technology are reinforced in a range of new statutory and non-statutory arrangements for KS1 and KS2.

To provide flexibility and enable schools to structure the curriculum to meet the needs of individuals and groups of children, from September 1998 to September

Table 2.4   Subjects in each Key Stage for England and Wales

In England	
Key Stages 1 and 2	English, mathematics, science, design and information technology, history, geography, art, music, and physical education
Key Stage 3	As Key Stages 1 and 2, plus a modern foreign language
Key Stage 4	English, mathematics and science (single or double award), design and technology,□ information technology, a modern foreign language,□ physical education
In Wales	
Key Stages 1 and 2	English (except in Key Stage 1 in Welsh-speaking classes), Welsh, mathematics, science, design and information technology, history,* geography,* art,* music,* and physical education
Key Stage 3	As Key Stages 1 and 2, plus a modern foreign language
Key Stage 4	English,(Welsh (except in non-Welsh speaking schools until 1999), mathematics, science (single or double) and physical education
Key:	□ A short course is the minimum requirement. * Separate orders for England and Wales

2000, schools providing for KS1 and KS2 will no longer be required to teach the full PoS in six National Curriculum subjects: design and technology, history, geography, art, music and physical education (with the exception of swimming which remains a statutory requirement). The arrangements for English, mathematics, science, information technology and religious education remain unchanged. Further details concerning the modification of the KS1 and KS2 curriculum can be found in the QCA booklet, *Maintaining Breadth and Balance at Key Stages 1 and 2* (QCA, 1998c).

The recent White Paper clearly highlights the importance of literacy and numeracy for all subjects:

> The first task of the education service is to ensure that every child is taught to read, write and add up. But mastery of the basics is only a foundation. Literacy and numeracy matter so much because they open the door to success across all the other school subjects and beyond. (*Excellence in Schools*, 1998b: para 1.3)

The Government has structured its commitment to promote literacy and numeracy skills at KS1 and KS2 by setting performance targets for 2002 and launching literacy and numeracy strategies to be implemented in September 1998 and 1999 respectively. The National Literacy Strategy (DfEE, 1998c) sets out teaching objectives for Reception to Year 6 pupils in the structural form of a 'literacy hour' (a structured hour of literacy study programme for each day). A similar format will be used for the numeracy strategy (DfEE, 1998d).

In addition to literacy and numeracy, information technology is also considered a curriculum priority. The DfEE publication, *Connecting the Learning Society* (DfEE, 1998a), indicates that developments in information communication technology (ICT) will require a re-evaluation of its status and position within the curriculum. In the recent revision of the KS1 and KS2 curriculum, for instance, the need to use information technology in all aspects of the curriculum is emphasized (QCA, 1998c).

The key skills of communication, problem solving, strategic thinking and working with others have also been highlighted in recent surveys of employers (QCA, 1998b). A consideration of these cross-curricular skills is likely to form a basis for future curriculum revisions, particularly at KS3 and KS4.

Task 2.3: Literacy, numeracy and information technology across the curriculum

Recent education reforms highlight the importance of English, mathematics and ICT across the curriculum. Consult the curriculum booklets for these subjects and consider:

- The importance of these subjects in your teaching.

- How your subject and teaching can be used to help develop skills and competence in these key National Curriculum subjects.

Religious education

Religious education is not part of the National Curriculum but is part of the 'whole curriculum' and is a compulsory part of schooling for all pupils in England and Wales. The Department for Education and the Welsh Office reaffirmed their commitment to RE in two circulars issued in 1994 (Circular 1/94 and 10/94 respectively). These contained recommendations as to the amount of time devoted to religious education at each Key Stage as well as a framework for an agreed syllabus. Religious education syllabuses are agreed through local conferences – the Standing Advisory Councils for Religious Education (SACRE). The School Curriculum and Assessment Authority has produced two model syllabuses for religious education:

1. *Living Faiths Today:* the knowledge and understanding of what it means to be a member of a faith community (SCAA, 1994a); and
2. *Questions and Teachings:* the knowledge and understanding of the teaching of religions and how these relate to shared human experience (SCAA, 1994b).

These models are not statutory nor designed for the classroom, but are intended for use in the agreed LEA syllabus conferences. Nevertheless, they are broadly indicative of local RE school syllabuses.

Cross-curriculum themes, skills and dimensions

Cross-curriculum themes, skills and dimensions were added to the subject curriculum soon after the original 1988 Education Reform Act. They were intended to highlight important components of the 'whole curriculum' that might have been lost in the subject orders. In particular, the National Curriculum Council (NCC, 1990) highlighted:

*   the *skills* of communication, numeracy, study, problem solving, personal and social and information technology;
*   *the cross-curriculum themes:* economic and industrial understanding, careers education and guidance, health education, education for citizenship and environmental education; and
*   *the cross-curriculum dimensions:* personal and social development including a commitment to equality of opportunity and cultural diversity.

The cross-curriculum themes, skills and dimensions are concerned with the 'physical, sexual, moral, social and vocational self' (NCC, 1990: 7) and when combined with religious and sex education they contribute to defining the school's 'pastoral curriculum'.

Although the cross-curriculum elements were included in the original curriculum they have recently become neglected in preference to the assessed subject curriculum. There is little doubt that the introduction of performance indicators, subject-specific Ofsted inspections and league tables have encouraged schools to concentrate more on the assessed components of the 'whole curriculum'.

The cross-curriculum dimensions, themes and skills are now under review as part of a continued commitment to a curriculum that includes 'citizenship, personal, social and health education and spiritual, moral, social and cultural development' (QCA, 1998b). Advisory groups have been set up and are due to report back with recommendations on range of identified cross-curriculum areas that include citizenship, sustainable development and creative and cultural education.

Task 2.4: Moral, cultural and lifelong education

The National Curriculum aims to provide:

- a 'moral' and 'cultural education'; and
- prepare 'pupils for the opportunities, responsibilities and experiences of adult life'.

These elements of the school curriculum are being hotly debated. What do you think these elements encompass and how should they be covered in school? Should they be incorporated within the subject curriculum or in separate lessons? What is citizenship? What is a moral and cultural education?

The National Curriculum in action

As a trainee teacher you are likely to meet the National Curriculum at three levels:

1. *Whole-school polices* – that define, for example, the school timetable.
2. *Schemes of work* – that define, for example, the progression of subject content.
3. *Group and individual pupil activities* – these include, for example, the content of teacher's (and your) lesson plans.

Schools will have *policies* that embrace all aspects of the curriculum, including the non-statutory curriculum, and any individual priorities of the school. A principal aim of these policies will be to secure equality of opportunity and access to the 'whole curriculum' for each pupil. The effective management of the curriculum depends on establishing policies on, for example, attendance, homework, record keeping, pastoral code, codes of behaviour and discipline as well as the drawing up of the school timetable. The Education Reform Act indicates the statutory parts of the curriculum; however, it does not prescribe the amount of time that should be spent on any part of the curriculum. How subjects are timetabled is at the discretion of the school and there are considerable variations between schools.

In secondary schools, the curriculum is usually divided into subjects that have a number of timetable slots in a school week. There is considerable flexibility in the curriculum at KS4 and this flexibility has to be built into the school timetable. In primary schools, the curriculum is less frequently organized by subject, although the recent introduction of the literacy and numeracy hour is likely to result in schools introducing a regular time for these subjects each day.

Task 2.5: The curriculum timetable

Find out, for a particular year group, how the curriculum is organized in your school. Does your school have any curriculum priorities and how are these reflected in the school timetable?

A whole-school approach to planning the curriculum is essential and the school's schemes of work will contain details of the aims and objectives, learning activities, progression and assessment of the curriculum. It is likely that teachers in primary schools will start to plan the curriculum with a cross subject/whole-school approach (often referred to as a 'topic approach') although the literacy and numeracy hour is likely to have a self-contained structure. Recently, the DfEE has published non-statutory schemes of work for science and technology (DfEE, 1998b, 1998c). These should be available to you as a trainee.

In secondary schools, planning usually takes place within a subject department and it is common for members of staff to have responsibility for the curriculum at KS3 and KS4. It will be the responsibility of these staff to liaise with colleagues and construct a scheme of work matched with National Curriculum KS3 requirements and chosen KS4 examination syllabuses.

The PoS provide the basis for what should be taught in each Key Stage as a minimum statutory entitlement. As previously noted, they define the content agenda for the school curriculum. It is up to the school to decide how to teach the PoS and to what depth. The National Curriculum claims to have no implied teaching methodology; however, with the publication of non-statutory lesson plans, particular styles of teaching are increasingly emerging. How the curriculum is structured in terms of pupils and group activities is left up to teachers' professional judgement. Furthermore, teachers can decide whether to augment the specified content with additional materials.

The National Curriculum details the curriculum assessment. Assessment is an integral part of teaching and the National Curriculum provides a framework for day-to-day and end of Key Stage assessment (see Chapter 7). When developing a scheme of work or a lesson plan, attention must be given to the expectations of pupils' progress as represented by the ATs, level descriptors and end of Key Stage descriptors as previously indicated. The subject ATs define the level of experience and how the content should be sequenced. The National Curriculum contains no detail about the mechanisms of day-to-day teacher assessment.

A useful lesson planning sequence, incorporating the statutory requirements, is illustrated in Figure 2.1. Planning and assessing are explored in more detail in Chapters 5 and 7, respectively.

The National Curriculum and continuity and progression

Pupils moving from one school to another have always presented problems to teachers – what has the pupil achieved in the previous school and how to build on this in the new situation? This problem is, of course, potentially much greater when a change of phase is involved, for example from primary to secondary, or middle to secondary school. The resulting secondary teaching group may contain pupils from many different 'feeder' schools.

Prior to the introduction of the National Curriculum, the problem of transferring and interpreting the information was such that it was not uncommon for secondary subject teachers to state that it was more practical to assume that nothing had been done! The potential for reducing motivation because of repetitive or unchallenging work was very real. Research in the 1980s (Galton, 1988) suggested that pupils often regressed in attainment in the first years of secondary school. The National Curriculum is designed to alleviate this problem by providing a clear definition of content in the PoS, common standards in the ATs against which pupils can be assessed, national statutory end of Key Stage tests in the core subjects, and a common vocabulary to help plan for continuity in the curriculum and for describing a pupil's progress.

However, the 1993 Dearing Review suggested that there were still many concerns in this area. Consequently, after the National Curriculum was revised in

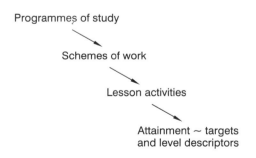

Programmes of study

Schemes of work

Lesson activities

Attainment ~ targets
and level descriptors

Figure 2.1 A National Curriculum planning sequence

1995, SCAA, now QCA (Qualifications and Curriculum Authority), produced booklets giving advice on how to promote continuity between Key Stages and make effective use of assessments (see 'Further reading', below). They have also promoted the development of software designed to reduce the administrative burden of transferring and analysing information.

Task 2.6: Primary-secondary transfer

Find out how your school makes use of information from pupils' previous schools on transfer.

The hidden curriculum

'The hidden curriculum' is a commonly used term to refer to the politics, attitudes and values promoted by school experiences. Much is learned in school that has nothing directly to do with the curriculum content of lessons but is implied by school structures, procedures and organization. For example, the subjects and structure of the school timetable and the mechanisms of school discipline all carry hidden messages. There is much written on the hidden curriculum. Illich (1973), for instance, argues that schools tend to inculcate a 'passive assumption' – an acceptance of the current social order. He goes on to argue that we should do away with schools in their current form and focus instead on providing information to people who want to learn as part of an endeavour to promote lifelong learning. Recently, these ideas have been linked with advances in communication technology and the Internet, which will potentially enable information to be available to larger audiences.

Task 2.7: The hidden curriculum

- What are the hidden messages in your teaching?
- What aspects of the hidden curriculum do you promote?
- Do you agree with Illich's argument that schooling tends to promote an acceptance of the current social order?

Further reading

Useful addresses and Web sites

The National Curriculum is in a state of review. The following Web sites contain up-to-date details about this review and a list of recent policy publications. Many of these publications will be free to trainee teachers.

The Department for Education and Employment (DfEE): http://www.dfee.gov.uk
The Qualifications and Curriculum Authority (QCA): http://www.open.gov.uk/qca
The Office for Standards in Education (Ofsted): http://www.ofsted.gov.uk/ofsted.
   html
The Teacher Training Agency (TTA): http://www.teach.org.uk

Useful general publications

A good overview of the National Curriculum is provided by *A Guide to the National Curriculum,* School Curriculum and Assessment Authority, the Curriculum and Assessment Authority for Wales and the Teacher Training Agency (1996), HMSO, London.

Individual subject booklets are also available from HMSO publications, for example, *English in the National Curriculum,* DfEE (1995), HMSO, London.

Recent policy documents

At KS1 and KS2

Department for Education and Employment (1998) *The National Literacy Strategy,* DfEE, London
DfEE (1998) *The National Numeracy Strategy,* DfEE, London
DfEE and the Qualifications and Curriculum Authority (1998) *Information Technology – A teacher's guide: Scheme of work for Key Stages 1 and 2,* QCA, London
DfEE and QCA (1998) *Science – A teacher's guide: Scheme of work for Key Stages 1 and 2,* QCA, London
QCA (1998) *Maintaining Breadth and Balance at Key Stages 1 and 2,* QCA, London

At KS3 and KS4

Qualification and Curriculum Authority (1998) *Key Stage 4 Curriculum in Action,* QCA, London

References

Centre for Contemporary Cultural Studies (1981) *Unpopular Education: Schooling and social democracy in England since 1944*, Hutchinson, London

Department for Education (DfE) (1994a) *Religious Education and Collective Worship*, Circular 1/94, DfE, London

DfE (1994b) *Code of Practice of the Identification and Assessment of Special Educational Needs*, Circular 10/94, DfE, London

Department for Education and Employment (DfEE) (1998a) *Connecting the Learning Society*, HMSO, London

DfEE (1998b) *Excellence in Schools*, HMSO, London

DfEE (1998c) *The National Literacy Strategy*, DfEE, London

DfEE (1998d) *The National Numeracy Strategy*, DfEE, London

Department for Education and Science (DES) (1969) Black Papers, HMSO, London

DES (1977) *Education in Schools: A consultative document*, HMSO, London

Galton, M (1988) The implementation of innovation in primary education at the local level, *Western European Education*, **20** (3), pp 323–44

Illich, I (1973) *Deschooling Society*, Penguin, Harmondsworth

NCC (1990) *Curriculum Guidance 3: The whole curriculum*, NCC, York

Qualification and Curriculum Authority (QCA) (1998a) *Key Stage 4: Curriculum in action*, QCA, London

QCA (1998b) *Developing the School Curriculum: Advice to the Secretary of State on the broad nature and scope of the review of the National Curriculum*, QCA, London

QCA (1998c) *Maintaining Breadth and Balance at Key Stages 1 and 2*, QCA, London

SCAA (1994a) *Religious Education Model Syllabuses – Model 1: Living faiths today*, SCCA, London

SCAA (1994b) *Religious Education Model Syllabuses – Model 2: Questions and teachings*, SCCA, London

SCAA (1996) *A Guide to the National Curriculum*, SCAA, London

Simon, B (1988) *Bending the Rules: The Baker 'reform' of education*, Lawrence and Wishart, London

3   Children's learning

Margaret Cox

The aim of this chapter is to introduce the trainee to the nature of pupils' learning and development. It considers a variety of learning theories and a range of views on how these theories can be implemented in the classroom, as well as inform teachers on how pupils may learn more effectively. Consideration is given to pupils' learning and the context in which pupils may learn. These contexts are then discussed with a view to making teaching and learning more effective.

Objectives

By the end of this chapter the trainee should have an understanding of:

- a variety of learning and developmental theories;
- how these theories can be used to enhance pupil learning;
- how these theories can inform teaching strategies;
- how pupils can be motivated;
- how pupils learn.

Introduction

There have been many theories developed and studies done about the nature of learning with both children and adults and there continues to be a range of views about which theories are closest to the reality. From years of research and teachers' experiences in schools we now know that children's learning is also affected by their everyday experiences in the world, giving them ideas some of which seem to conflict with those we are trying to teach. We also know that children don't learn in isolation but that their learning is influenced by collaborating with other children, interacting with the teacher and with their environment. How they feel about themselves, their abilities and position among their peers also has an effect on how well they learn. Teaching children is not, as is sometimes assumed, pouring knowledge into an empty vessel; it is about helping them to build ideas about the world and to understand how they learn. All of these factors and many more need to be considered when devising effective strategies for teaching.

In this chapter I start by briefly explaining some of the most widely known theories of children's learning and the many other issues such as the learning context, pupils' attitudes and social position which also affect the ways in which children learn. This is followed by a discussion of where teaching and learning activities have been influenced by these theories, leading to ideas for tasks that will help you make use of this knowledge.

How do children learn?

We begin by considering the learning theories which have influenced the world of education and which often form the basis for teaching strategies and curriculum materials. It would be impossible here to include all the theories which have been proposed over the years, so I am only presenting briefly theories most commonly used and discussed in education.

Skinner

One of the earliest theories of learning which is still used today by many educators but has been widely criticized by many others was proposed by Skinner (1974), a US behaviourist psychologist, who did extensive research, mainly with animals. For example, his early research involved rewarding animals with food if they 'learnt' how to open doors. Behaviourism, which is a theory based on empiricism, assumes that knowledge is primarily acquired by the evidence of the senses (Nussbaum, 1989). Knowledge is what is confirmed through careful observations and logic. From his research results, Skinner concluded that the award principle governed all behaviour including that of human beings.

When Skinner applied his results to the teaching of children in the earlier part of this century, he believed that teachers were not making use of effective 'schedules of reinforcement' in the classroom. He argued that formal education was usually based on negative reinforcement. For example, when children behaved inappropriately in lessons the result was sometimes punishment by the teacher with language or behaviour which was intended to humiliate, instead of the teacher showing interest about the formation and reinforcement of responses to be learned. He saw lessons and examinations as a means of showing what pupils do not know and cannot do, rather than revealing and helping them to construct the material they know. He argued that children's behaviour was not formed effectively by negative reinforcement, the learning was not appropriate and often the learnt material was quickly forgotten. Concerned with the application of his theory to education, Skinner designed the first 'learning programs' for use on teaching machines, the forerunner of drill and practice programs and integrated learning systems using IT, which are discussed in the next chapter.

In today's teaching, this theory of behaviourism is reflected in the rote learning of, for example, verbs or multiplication tables where it is expected that if the pupils work through an exercise enough times they will memorize and learn the facts being taught. Behaviourists believe that the way to achieve pupils' 'correct' learning is through the procedure of careful and systematic teaching where each stage is monitored and where children are given regular feedback to confirm what they have learnt. As we know there are still many examples of such teaching strategies today, but this theory did not take account of the stages in the intellectual development of all children nor the effects on learning of such factors as the learning context and the social milieu.

Piaget

It was Jean Piaget, a Swiss psychologist who studied the development of children for more than 40 years (Piaget and Inhelder, 1969), whose theory presents, in detail, specific universal stages in human development and provides a possible explanation connected with when and how a child is ready to learn or develop specific forms of knowledge and understanding. In his theory, action and self-directed problem solving are basic factors in learning and development. While learners are interacting with their environment, they discover how to control it. He proposed that in human beings, the basic principle of thinking is formed when they learn how to act in the world and discover the consequences of their actions.

According to Piaget, in the development of intelligence certain processes are happening behind all learning, whether it is in simple organisms or in human beings. The two essential processes are:

- adaptation to the environment; and
- organization of experience (in terms of action, memory, perceptions, or other kinds of mental activities).

As children become older, they adapt to a sequence of environments and at the same time they organize their experiences in a more complex way. According to Piaget (1926), 'Attempts to teach the products of a "later" stage before previous stages have been passed through cannot facilitate development nor can it foster understanding'. This means that what children can learn will depend on the mental stage of development they have reached, which can vary a lot at any age from one child to another.

Piaget and Inhelder (1969) distinguished three main periods in which cognitive development is quantitatively different. The first of these is the period of sensori-motor intelligence, which extends from birth until the appearance of language, approximately during the first 18 months of life. The second period, that of concrete operations, extends from this time until about 11 or 12 years. Here, children can think in a logically coherent way about objects that do exist and which have real properties, and about actions or relations that are possible. The third period, that of formal operations, begins at about 12 years and is fully developed roughly three years later, when children are able to think in a more abstract and complex way. It involves the development of higher-cognitive skills, such as classification, analysis, synthesis, deduction and drawing of inferences. According to Piaget, children develop through the same sequence of stages before they achieve mature, logical thought. At each stage there are four main aspects of development during school years, which Piaget has defined as:

1. the directive function of language;
2. the formation of concepts;
3. translation of concrete experiences into verbal and symbolic terms; and
4. the evolution of logical thinking.

Piaget uses the terms 'schemas' or 'schemata' for well-defined sequences of actions. Although they may have a different nature or complexity, their main characteristic is that they are organized wholes which are frequently repeated and which can be recognized easily among other various and different behaviours. When new objects or experiences are incorporated into existing schemas, it is called 'assimilation'. Children assimilate experiences into a sequence of cognitive schemas; put more simply, when children are taught something new this is added to their existing knowledge which is reorganized to include the new knowledge.

The term 'accommodation' describes the process of modifying schemas in order to solve problems arising from new experiences within the environment. During the interaction of the two intellectual processes, children assimilate new experiences into their existing schemas and accommodate their schemas by extending or combining them (when meeting new situations). For example, children pushing toy bricks along a slippery table may form a mental model of the rate of movement relating to their pushing effort. When they try to repeat the process but this time pushing the bricks on a carpet, they will find that the effort required is considerably greater. To assimilate this new experience will require modifying the previous mental model to include the effect of friction representing the influence of the nature of the surface across which the bricks were being moved. To accommodate new knowledge children's schemas are very flexible and although they are extended or modified, they keep their property of being organized wholes. Through these procedures individuals develop an adequate amount of schemas to deal with the events they meet and in doing so they become adapted to their environment; but it is a temporary adaptation only and is modified as the environment changes or as the individuals act in a variety of ways.

Most of children's thinking in any one stage or period is characterized by a structure. This structure of children's thinking at each stage is distinct, the same for all children at this stage and different from other children or adults at other stages. As children grow older, the structure built at a younger age develops gradually and becomes an integral part of the structure of the following stage. For example, the idea that an object is a permanent thing, which is learnt gradually in the first period, is necessary to the notion of conservation of quantity, which is learnt in the period of concrete operations. Similarly concrete operations form a basis for the system of formal operations that follows them; for example, to understand proportionality in adolescence, children must first learn to compare any two quantities or to equalize them, as they do in the period of concrete operations. The more complex and abstract hypothetico-deductive thinking is therefore generally developed in adolescence.

The periods of development appear to follow a constant series: there is a sequence as one structure appears to follow another. Though all children pass through these distinct sequential stages, they pass with different speed. Thus, the age at which a stage is distinguished cannot be fixed, because it is always relative to the individual characteristics of the child and the environment that may encourage, restrict or prevent its appearance. A stage may appear fairly early or late according to the relevant situation for each individual child. Thus, children who have not entered the stage of concrete operations may not be able to understand certain basic mathematical concepts, for example. Or, in the stage of concrete operations, they may not be able to understand certain kinds of scientific thinking. As the nature of young children's thought affects what they can learn, it often limits their learning. It may result in a restriction of the knowledge they can hold, even if the range of the educational experiences offered is quite broad. This means that in a class of 11-year-olds some pupils may be reaching the formal operations stage and be able to grasp quite difficult topics while others in the same class may not, despite careful and well-organized lessons. One of the hardest things to learn about teaching is that you cannot conduct your lessons at the pace of the least able because the progress of the whole group may then be too slow, but there are strategies you can adopt which will help all pupils progress to an improved understanding. Figure 3.1 shows a diagrammatic representation of the stages in Piaget's theory of learning.

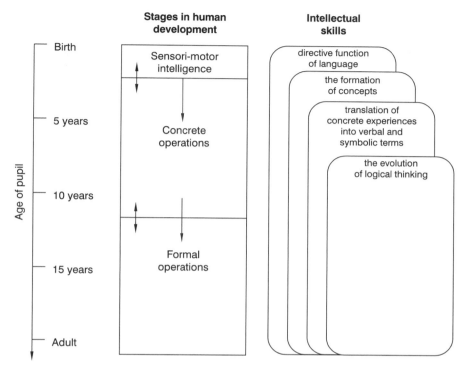

Figure 3.1 Piaget's stages in human development and intellectual skills

Piaget also observed that children learn faster when they co-operate with others; this co-operation develops and improves their formal thinking. For example, adolescents who show more socialization can exchange their ideas and discuss their different viewpoints, and this verbal communication is seen as a way to enrich their thinking. According to Beard (1969) collaboration:

> has the effect of leading children to a greater mutual understanding and gives them the habit of constantly placing themselves at points of view which they did not previously hold. Consequently they progress to making use of assumptions. In addition, discussion gives rise to an internalized conversation in the form of deliberation or reflection.

The role of language in Piaget's theory is similar to that of visual perception. Language is a system of symbols used by the individual to represent the world, and is distinct from actions and operations that lead to thinking. Yet, as will be shown later, pupils' linguistic abilities will strongly affect their reasoning and other mental activities.

Although Piaget wrote very little about the educational implications of his theories, many psychologists and educators explored the educational directions of Piaget's theory and transformed it into curricula, approaches to teaching and a whole philosophy of education (Wood, 1988). A very important part of these developments has been the studies on the effects of the context on children's learning.

The learning context

Many researchers have developed Piaget's work further to include the effects of the environment in which pupils are learning. One particularly well-known Russian researcher was Vygotsky, who claimed that pupils' learning is also affected by the culture of the learner and participation in society. He regarded these developmental interactions as a relationship between nature and culture. He maintained that learning can be enhanced through collaboration with others including through an adult tutor. He defined this influence as:

> the distance between the actual developmental level as determined by independent problem solving and the level of potential development as determined through problem solving under adult guidance or in collaboration with more capable peers. (Vygotsky, 1978: 86)

This he called the 'zone of proximal development' and it has widely influenced teaching strategies at all levels of education. However, his theories mainly focused on the effects of the social environment on cognitive development, excluding the effects of pupils' understanding of the social world itself, their perceptions of themselves, how colleagues perceive them and their role and position within the class, the school and their own communities (Durkin, 1997: 381), all of which will play a part in the way they respond in lessons and their general behaviour.

From theory into practice

The theories discussed above provide useful foundations supported by an enormous amount of educational research into how children learn. Using these theories educators have considered the implications for teaching and learning for a range of aspects of education. The following are important to consider if our pupils are to achieve effective learning:

- stages in cognitive development;
- ages and education levels of pupils;
- existing preconceptions;
- prior knowledge;
- influence of the learning environment;
- social influence and cognition;
- children's attitudes towards learning, fellow pupils and themselves;
- influence of literacy and numeracy skills.

Whether you are involved in primary or secondary teaching, in order to take account of all the aspects listed above you need to know your pupils. This is easier at the primary than the secondary level. The following sections provide more information about these aspects with ideas about how to include them in the planning and delivery of your teaching.

Stages in cognitive development

Piaget's theoretical arguments about the nature of thinking, cognitive development and the relationships between what is seen, heard and understood have direct consequences for teaching and its effectiveness:

> Attempts to question, show or explain things to children before they are mentally 'ready' cannot foster development, though the child may learn some 'empty' procedures. Indeed, premature teaching and questioning may demoralize or frustrate a child who can't begin to understand what is being 'taught'. A teacher can provide appropriate materials and contexts for development, and organize time and space so that children are free to act upon the world with objects and tasks that serve to foster the emergence of operations and an understanding of invariance. (Wood, 1988)

Although the educational applications of Piaget's theory and the pedagogical implications of children's' cognitive development continue to be discussed, there are some general teaching recommendations which all the experts seem to agree on. These particular recommendations may be grouped into three broad categories (Brainerd, 1978):

1. the sequencing of curriculum material;
2. the content of curriculum material;
3. the methodology of teaching.

These recommendations are described briefly here but more detailed information about planning lessons is given in Chapter 5.

Sequencing of curriculum material

This category is concerned with when to introduce certain topics into your teaching programme. Piaget's theory emphasizes the readiness of pupils to be able to learn and understand the materials. Firstly, the material taught to children should be in accordance with their present stage of cognitive development. Secondly, you should not try to force your pupils' progress through the material on a given subject. The third mentions that you should try, where possible, to teach children new concepts in the same order that these concepts appear during spontaneous cognitive development. In a Piagetian curriculum, teaching is always a two-stage process of diagnosis followed by instruction in the concepts for which the child is ready. It is therefore important to identify the present cognitive stage of each of your pupils when planning the curriculum.

The content of curriculum material

This category is concerned with which specific topics should be part of the curriculum and the detailed content. For example, for primary pupils more of the curriculum should involve practical activities that depend upon concrete operations rather than more formal abstract reasoning. The content of your curriculum materials can also include activities that involve pupils working in groups to facilitate learning through peer interaction. Not only should the stage of cognitive development of each pupil with regard to the subject being taught be considered, but also the developmental stage of the language used by the pupils, which is discussed later in this chapter. For example, there are many examples of curriculum materials designed for use by pupils of a particular age group that are at a language level way beyond the abilities of those pupils.

The methodology of teaching

This category is concerned with the strategies that you should adopt when dealing with children. There are three aspects relating to the theories discussed earlier. Firstly, consider the central role that children play in their own learning and try to make learning experiences as active as possible. Secondly, try to follow pedagogical strategies that make children aware of conflicts and inconsistencies in their ideas. Finally, you could make use of the child's peers for the facilitation of learning building on the work of Vygotsky discussed earlier. The following task is to examine how well existing class and/or homework activities reflect these stages of development and how you can improve on these activities.

Task 3.1: Relating the learning tasks to cognitive development

This activity is based on the topic 'energy', which can be included in science, applied mathematics and technology. A similar approach can be used for other subject areas with an appropriate topic. Depending upon the complexity of the lessons this activity can be carried out at either primary or secondary level.

- Collect different homework and lesson activities already existing in your school on a particular topic for the year group which you plan to teach or are already teaching.
- Write out a list of all the concepts and skills you can find which are involved in these activities, in three columns.
- Put in column 1 all the concepts relating to the subject topic, for example, if the topic was conservation of energy, the concepts would include: temperature, heat, warmth, heat sources, heat gains, heat losses, etc.
- In column 2, note the concepts you think could be taught corresponding to the concrete operational stage (by providing simple experiments which pupils can do in the classroom to learn those energy concepts).
- In column 3, list the concepts that you think require more advanced abstract reasoning skills.
- Revise the activities into new assessment tasks which start with the easiest ones relating to the concrete operational activities followed by more advanced activities for pupils who may have reached the formal operational stage.

In most cases planning assessment tasks for a group of pupils will vary with the age and the level of the pupils as given in the National Curriculum as well as their actual cognitive development. It is often the National Curriculum requirements that are uppermost in teachers' minds rather than the specific stages in cognitive development, and there are clear differences among the different National Curriculum subjects relating to the pupils' ability to reach a particular level according to their level of cognitive development.

Ages and education levels of pupils

The current requirements of the National Curriculum allow for pupils to be at different levels of attainment for a particular subject within the same class. Teachers are expected to progress their pupils through these levels to reach higher levels of achievement. When the National Curriculum was first launched in the late 1980s, primary school teachers were, in theory, expected to assess each of their pupil's achievements for over 260 attainment targets. In 1995 the National Curriculum (DfEE, 1995) was deliberately slimmed down to reduce this number to a much more manageable level but it is still difficult to know how to measure what pupils have learnt which corresponds to these levels. Assessing pupils' achievements is discussed more fully in later chapters. Here it is important to recognize that being clearly aware of the ages and levels of achievement of pupils through assessment will give you insights into their relative cognitive and social development and how this will influence what they learn.

Existing preconceptions

Pupils frequently come to lessons with preconceived ideas about how the world works, particularly in science and applied mathematics. Extensive research by educators and psychologists has shown that before children are taught many topics in school they have acquired some knowledge about these through informal experiences. This knowledge is characterized by ideas sometimes different from the formally accepted ones, and moreover these ideas can be held strongly and be resistant to change. For example, in science education, researchers have found that pupils' prior ideas are an important factor in their understanding of school science and pupils whose observations and inferences about phenomena differ from the scientifically accepted ones, have different interpretative schemes.

The fact that children have their own scientific ideas that often differ significantly from the generally accepted ones and that children often use their own words in everyday language about scientific phenomena, may reflect their current stage of cognitive development. Having a certain cognitive ability, pupils may not yet be able to understand and use the specialized language of some curriculum subjects and therefore they express themselves in their own words. It is therefore important, particularly if you are teaching science, mathematics or technology, to know what are the common informal ideas children have.

Researchers have identified an extensive background of children's conceptions about the natural world, and at the same time teaching strategies have been proposed in order to help them develop more scientist-like ideas. The proposals for teaching science, which apply to many other school subjects as well, take into account the way in which an improvement of pupils' knowledge can be achieved. In order to teach effectively it is safest to assume that your pupils have an existing conceptual scheme that is used in interpreting and making sense of new situations and phenomena. As a teacher, it is then important to acknowledge and build on these conceptual schemes. According to Piagetian theories, the learner relates the newly-met concept to the pre-existing cognitive structure. Knowledge and skills acquired during one stage of cognitive development form the basis for the knowledge at the next stage. In this way, pupils' prior conceptions become an important factor in their understanding and therefore their prior ideas and assumptions and their willingness to use them have to be considered as a starting point for effective teaching.

When children are dissatisfied with their present viewpoints, it does not necessarily mean that this is an adequate reason for making them change their view. If children need to change their view, they must have access to a new and better idea that will replace the old one. According to Posner *et al* (1982) this new idea needs to be intelligible, plausible and fruitful:

> intelligible, in that it appears coherent and internally consistent; plausible, in that it is reconcilable with other views the pupil already has; and fruitful in that it is preferable to the old ideas on the grounds of elegance, parsimony or usefulness in daily life and school situations.

By asking pupils questions and getting them to volunteer their ideas about a topic you can get some insights into their present viewpoints.

Prior knowledge

It should be clear from the discussion in the previous section that pupils' prior knowledge has a very important part to play in their learning. This prior knowledge is not restricted to preconceptions about the topic being taught, but extends to knowledge acquired from lessons already given on the same topic, or on related topics previously studied, or knowledge related to the subject but from another domain, such as mathematics for reading maps in geography.

One of the most fundamental problems which pupils have in learning is that of transfer: the transfer of knowledge between domain and/or contexts. There are two well-known teaching approaches to help with transfer. The first is to teach children very specific strategies for solving specific types of tasks. Brown (1981) found that this sort of teaching produced little transfer. However, more recently Cristafi and Brown (1986) found that when there was some variety in the original teaching materials, and the teaching included a specific generalization element that emphasized the underlying target (the reasons that make the strategy useful), then pupils showed a reasonable degree of transfer, within the specific type of problem.

The second approach has been to teach general learning strategies, relevant to those that are usually applied across a wide variety of types of problems (Feurstein, 1980). More recent studies have shown that pupils can learn more complex skills and processes in a context with which they are very familiar than when they are learning in a formal academic subject in the school curriculum. When devising schemes of work it is then helpful to select activities which help pupils build on knowledge derived from other contexts. You need to identify what knowledge you expect the pupils to have already in the subject being taught and related subjects, including numeracy and literacy skills, and what particular conceptual weaknesses you might expect. A good scheme of work will also have lists of objectives and outcomes so that progression can be based on prior knowledge from each previous lesson and the learning outcomes achieved.

Influence of the learning environment

As was mentioned earlier, pupils' learning is influenced by the environment in which the learning takes place, which includes how the class is organized, what resources are available and whether the lesson is being taught in a relevant physical context. For example, in the case of using IT, pupils are often taken to another room full of computers for a geography, history or science lesson away from their normal classroom, which according to some studies produces an unreal context for the topic being studied (Watson, 1990).

In the previous sections most of the discussion is about pupils as individual learners, yet in the classroom situation there are often opportunities for pupils to work in pairs or groups where they benefit from sharing their expertise, challenging each others' knowledge and assumptions and contributing different views about topics and practical activities. Getting pupils to work in groups is also a way of finding out more about what they know through the conversations they have and the collaborative work they do. The main factor in co-operative learning is 'positive interdependence': pupils working together toward mutual goals in a way where the work is shared and members of the group must depend upon each other. Skills such as leadership, conflict resolution and decision making are taught and practised in a co-operative learning situation. When working with ICT (explained more fully in the next chapter), students frequently form groups of various sizes. Straker (1989) observed that work with computers can contribute to the development of group skills, such as communication skills, study and observation skills, problem solving skills, personal and social skills.

Building on the research of Eraut and Hoyles into group work with computers (1988), the following task can be carried out to help you decide whether or not to put pupils into groups for the teaching of any topic with or without ICT.

Task **3.2:** Relating the learning tasks to group work

Select a particular set of learning objectives relating to a particular topic and the National Curriculum level of the pupils. Write out a lesson plan, and show how it answers the following:

- For what types of learning goal is group work most appropriate?
- What is its potential contribution to the learning activity?
- What kinds of tasks can be designed which facilitate group work?
- Is it possible to identify criteria for task design, group management and their interrelationships for effective group work to be established?
- What kinds of grouping is best for achieving particular learning goals?
- How will the group work be prepared, implemented and evaluated?

Task 3.2 also needs to take account of the composition of the pupils in the class, the range of abilities, their ethnic mix and the opportunities available to them outside formal lessons. Issues of race, gender and class may also affect the way in which pupils can respond to the learning environment and to the influence of their fellow students (Cole *et al*, 1998). When planning the organization of your lessons you need to consider the learning objectives not only in terms of the topic being taught but also in terms of the broader objectives of fostering an enthusiasm for learning and pupils developing into socially responsible adults. Some of these issues are discussed in the next section.

Social influence and cognition

Most of the issues discussed above have focused on the cognitive development of pupils' learning, how well they come to understand a topic and what issues affect this growth in understanding. Yet there is now a large field of research into pupils' social cognition; the development of their understanding about the human world in which they live, themselves, their position among their peer groups, their standing in the community and their future prospects as an adult (Durkin, 1997). Pupils' preconceived ideas about their peers can have a positive or negative effect on their attitudes and performance. For example, a study of boys working in pairs showed that:

> the boys who had been forewarned that their partner was a bit of a trouble maker were less friendly towards them, talked less and put less effort into the joint task. For their part the alleged problem kids found the task less enjoyable, judged their day as not doing so well, and took less credit even for good performances. (Durkin, 1997: 343)

This study shows that if you can foster mutual respect among your pupils they are more likely to maintain good social relationships leading to fruitful collaborations in the classroom.

Being aware of the social and psychological influences on pupils should help you to understand the difficulties pupils face and how these may affect their learning progression. This also applies to pupils coming from different social backgrounds and different cultures. For example, when planning a learning task for a class of pupils of different ethnic backgrounds try and include resources that relate to the different pupils' culture and family experiences. Pupils who show signs of a lack of interest in a topic may be feeling left out of the peer group or alienated from the culture in which the topic context is based. There are many activities described by other authors (see Durkin, 1997 and Cole *et al*, 1998, for example) which show teachers how to help pupils develop socially as well as academically through their educational experiences. Pupils' social awareness and cognition will also influence their attitudes to education, their fellow pupils and themselves. These social aspects clearly have an important influence on the pupil's ability to learn topics within the National Curriculum and to maintain an interest in education.

Children's attitudes towards learning, fellow pupils and themselves

The attitudes children have towards themselves, their fellow pupils and their own abilities can have a strong influence on their motivation to study and learn. When designing lessons or other learning tasks it is important to recognize the distinction between pupils' positive motivation encouraged by success in achieving specific tasks and greater self-esteem, and negative motivation caused by a fear of failure. In the latter case this might lead to avoidance of engaging in particular learning tasks, for example, using IT, for fear of failing.

Motivating activities were once mainly considered to influence such emotions as pride, shame, guilt and a general self-concept of the ability to achieve specific goals. Through the influence of Vygotsky and others, it has been recognized in recent years that the degree of motivation of individual learners is also influenced by social values and the context in which the learning takes place. Hence the desire of learners to do better than their colleagues, rather than improve their previous level of personal achievements. This aspect of motivation has implications for co-operation versus competition, and internal versus external rewards.

Ames (1992) analysed the work of many researchers into motivation to develop a framework for motivation relating to a belief in oneself and the ability of pupils to do better through long-term goals. She defined two types of motivation goals: mastery goals and performance goals, which involve different ways of thinking about oneself. Mastery goals relate to the belief that effort and outcome are interdependent. With such goals there is a motivation to learn by developing new skills, trying to understand the tasks, improving the level of competence and achieving a sense of mastery based on self-referenced standards. Achievement of mastery goals is therefore likely to lead to a longer-term high quality involvement in learning compared with achieving performance goals of particular tasks.

Performance goals on the other hand focus on one's ability and sense of self-worth. 'Especially important to a performance orientation is public recognition that one has done better than others or performed in a superior manner' in achieving specific goals (Ames, 1992). These goals are directed towards achieving success in relation to the achievements of one's colleagues. Research by Ames has also shown that:

> tasks that involve variety and diversity are more likely to facilitate an interest in learning and mastery orientation. Students are more likely to approach and engage in learning in a manner consistent with a mastery goal when they perceive a meaningful reason for engaging in the activity.

This supports the earlier discussion about the importance of making the purpose of the teaching clear to the pupils and fostering positive self-esteem among your pupils.

Fostering positive self-esteem can be achieved by a careful balance between performance and mastery goals. The ideal teaching objective is to help pupils achieve mastery goals by developing their knowledge and skills across a wide range of subjects that provide them with the ability to progress. Performance goals can be introduced through assessment tasks, specific lesson activities and particular learning objectives, although care needs to be taken that pupils who regularly perform less well than their peers do not lose motivation and interest in their education. You need to devise a range of lesson and homework activities which help the least able to perform well in at least some aspects of the task.

Influence of literacy and numeracy skills

The effective learning of pupils across a range of subjects and ages requires a sound basis of good literacy and numeracy skills. These have very recently been emphasized through the Government's introduction of a range of new requirements including both a literacy and a numeracy hour for all primary pupils, and the mathematics and English core within the initial teacher training compulsory curriculum (DfEE, 1998). Competency in English and mathematics affects the pupils' abilities to learn other subjects well. For example, pupils are sometimes assumed to be poor at mathematics until the teacher realizes that it is because they can't understand the language of the work-sheets or exercise books they are using. On the other hand, pupils with weaknesses in numeracy and mathematics more generally will also be handicapped in other subjects such as science, geography, technology and IT.

Gilbert *et al* (1982) have observed patterns of pupils' understanding connected to their conceptions in mechanics, which have implications for all curriculum areas and relate to pupils' literacy skills. The types of understanding the researchers have observed represent:

- The use of everyday language: when a term/word is connected to its everyday interpretation it is easier to understand. For example, children may use the words 'push' and 'pull' that appear commonly in their everyday vocabulary and experience instead of the term 'force'.
- A self-centred and human centred viewpoint. Phrases and situations are considered in terms of human experiences and values. For example, in the system bicycle-cyclist, children may indicate forces applied to the bicycle indirectly, through the cyclist's actions (such as pedalling).
- The endowment of objects with the characteristics of humans or animals. Objects may have the characteristics of feeling, will or purpose, and these words are often used without metaphorical meaning. For example, an object/box sliding on a slope may want to stand up and resist its motion.

As children use words from everyday situations, it is necessary for you to know the correspondence of children's views to the formal ones – what formal term children mean when they use particular words. In addition, examples from everyday situations (in which reference to children's 'terms' is made), seem to facilitate pupils' understanding of many topics. The situation is even more complicated if the pupils' first language is not English. For example, for pupils originating from some African countries, there is no equivalent word for 'velocity' to distinguish it from 'speed', whereas for pupils coming from Inuit regions there are more than 10 different words for 'snow'.

The importance of pupils' numeracy and literacy skills for learning all subjects throughout their formal education and beyond cannot be overemphasized. Both Piaget's and Vygotsky's theories of learning, discussed earlier, stress the importance of language in the development of thinking skills; when a pupil has to study in a second language or has other language difficulties it can inhibit satisfactory progression in many National Curriculum subjects. By using a range of different teaching methods, including IT, it is possible to overcome some of these difficulties through pictures, icons, graphs and models.

Pupils' learning about learning

Research in recent years has shown that pupils' learning can be improved if they are helped to think about the way they learn and to develop methods of making their learning explicit (Adey and Shayer, 1994). There are several techniques that can be used to help learners organize their knowledge such as Knowledge Venn diagrams, advance organizers, lesson outlines and concept maps, but the work of Adey and Shayer (ibid) has been widely recognized as causing a learning revolution across the UK in the last eight years. Applying the CASE (cognitive acceleration in science education) teaching methods has resulted in pupils consistently gaining higher GCSE results, not only in science but in other subjects as well. As a result of this the CASE team has developed an extensive in-service teacher-training programme to train teachers how to teach cognitive acceleration in science and mathematics (CAME).

Another technique to help you develop teaching plans that prevent pupils' 'misunderstandings' involves constructing and using concept/proposition maps to make clear what is to be taught and to identify possible areas of 'misunderstanding' by pupils. The maps should be constructed according to concept hierarchies and cover the content of a microschema or unit. These maps are diagrammed facts, concepts, propositions, attitudes, processes and physical skills that need to be taught during the presentation of a taught unit. Arrange the information diagrammatically to show the interrelationships among the content. After the content of the unit has been mapped, the information can then be reviewed in each area of knowledge to locate potential 'misunderstandings' that pupils held before or during the teaching-learning process.

To help pupils think about the way they learn, encourage them to describe their own views, verbally and pictorially, and help them express these ideas clearly, in order to recognize what they can and cannot explain. If such activities result in pupils' dissatisfaction with their existing ideas and the teacher provides additional experiences which will lead to further dissatisfaction, then this will probably cause conceptual conflict. Nussbaum and Novick (1982) suggest that this conflict must be sufficient to persuade pupils to recognize that their existing views require modification. Accommodation develops when pupils search for a solution to their conflicting ideas. Using this approach, concept learning is achieved by exposing alternative frameworks, creating conceptual conflict, and encouraging cognitive accommodation.

Task 3.3 helps you to develop strategies for helping pupils to think about the ways they are thinking and learning. If you choose to question the pupils orally it is important to ensure that over a period of time all pupils are volunteering answers. Written questions can help overcome this problem.

Task 3.3: Helping pupils question their ideas

This task presents ways of helping pupils think about what they know when you are teaching a lesson.

- Plan a lesson that includes questions relating to the learning objectives.
- At the beginning of the lesson, question the pupils either orally, or hand out a prepared sheet of questions to find out the ideas which children bring to the problem situation.
- Write the pupils' responses on the board so they can all see them.
- Ask the children to hold their ideas in their heads, and then present other possibilities which the children will evaluate later.
- Explain the 'new' idea by linking it to the pupils' existing ideas.
- Refer to the old ideas for comparison, with each other and with the new idea.
- Ask the pupils to explain which ideas they think are the right ones, and if they have changed them find out how their thinking led to this new knowledge.

Summarizing the above, the types of teaching strategies which have been suggested by various researchers as facilitating conceptual change and helping pupils think about their learning include:

- providing opportunities for pupils to express clearly their own conceptions about the topic so that they can be examined in detail;

- presenting examples that challenge children's prior ideas;
- using strategies that enable pupils to consider and evaluate alternative conceptions of presented phenomena;
- providing opportunities to use new conceptions; long-term accommodation of a person's conceptions is not likely to happen if new schemas are not seen as useful;
- giving pupils opportunities to become aware of their own conceptions and how they change.

Influence of ICT skills

There is substantial research evidence of the effects of ICT on pupils' learning and its impact on the curriculum itself. In the last year the Government has announced two major programmes for the development of the use of ICT in education which have been widely claimed as the biggest investment in education, amounting to over £1.3 billion, since World War II. It is therefore crucial that all teachers should know about what will be expected of them as well as the ways in which ICT can actually contribute to pupils' learning. The uses of ICT in different curriculum areas and teaching IT as a subject are discussed in more detail in the next chapter.

Conclusions

This chapter has discussed some of the theories about children's learning and presented ideas for accommodating these in your teaching. Table 3.1 shows a summary of the most important issues associated with these theories.

Table 3.1 Issues relating to how children learn and acquire knowledge

Issues	Explanations
Stages in cognitive development	Sensori-motor → Concrete operational → Formal operational. Pupils may be at different stages within the same class. Until they have passed one stage they will struggle with tasks that require higher level cognitive developmnent. Teaching and learning tasks should relate to the pupils' stage of intellectual development

continued overleaf

Table 3.1 *continued*

Issues	Explanations
Ages and education levels of pupil	Key National Curriculum stages, intellectual levels of achievement. The nature of any learning task needs to match the intellectual level of the individual pupil. Achievement goals within one subject level descriptor of a National Curriculum level may include goals which are at different intellectual levels so that pupils may not be able to achieve all aspects of any level. National Curriculum programmes and levels should be examined and chosen to fit the intellectual levels of the pupils concerned
Existing preconceptions	Pupils' everyday informal experiences outside the classroom will influence how they can assimilate new knowledge within the lesson. Regular informal experiences can lead to entrenched misconceptions particularly in science and mathematics. Efforts should consistently be made to find out pupils' informal knowledge and misconceptions
Prior knowledge	The robustness of the prior knowledge the pupils have about a topic will influence how well they can understand the new topic being taught. Prior knowledge in a different but relevant area will also determine how readily pupils are able to acquire new knowledge. Some pupils will remember and retain topics and concepts covered in previous lessons better than others. Knowing and taking account of pupils' prior knowledge will help all pupils progress to their maximum potential
Influence of the learning environment	Whole-class, group work or individual work will all affect the ways in which the pupils learn. Group work can sometimes produce better learning outcomes than individual pupils working on their own
Social influence and cognition	The social background, different cultures and/or ethnic origins of the pupils will influence their ability to learn in different groups and particular lessons. It is important to know about the backgrounds of all your pupils and to vary the lessons and curriculum materials to help pupils benefit and enjoy their learning
Children's attitudes towards learning, fellow pupils and themselves	Pupils already have well-established attitudes and personality traits before they come to school. Within a class there will be those who are confident and co-operative and those who are negative about themselves, their school and their teacher resulting in a lack of co-operation and aggressive behaviour. Organize tasks and lessons which help foster the achievement of mastery and performance goals
Influence of literacy and numeracy skills	Pupils who have literacy problems may underachieve in science for example. Pupils whose first language is not English may need additional help in lessons that involve substantial text or oral presentations. Pupils with numeracy problems may need additional help with other subjects such as science, technology and geography as well as with mathematics
Influence of ICT skills	Pupils' ICT skills and experience will affect their ability to grasp subject concepts and may enhance or inhibit learning (see Chapter 4)

Although the issues discussed in this chapter may be daunting for the student teacher, it is encouraging to remember that in spite of all the differences between individual pupils and the additional difficulties this presents when planning and preparing lessons, pupils usually start school wanting to learn and have an amazing resilience to the difficulties and problems they meet through their formal schooling. At the end of the day, although you cannot assume that each and every pupil learns in the same way nor at the same pace nor even consistently over time, given an interesting, committed and enthusiastic teacher, who tries to take account of the issues discussed here, most pupils will respond with co-operation, dedication and determination to do well in their education.

References

Adey, P and Shayer, M (1994) An exploration of long-term far transfer effects, *Cognition and Instruction*, **11** (1), pp 1–29

Adey P, Shayer, M and Yates, C (1990) *Better Learning: A report from the Cognitive Acceleration through Science Education (CASE) project*, Centre for Educational Studies, King's College, London

Ames, C (1992) Classroom goals, structures and student motivation, *Journal of Educational Psychology*, **84** (3), pp 261–71

Beard, R (1969) *An Outline of Piaget's Developmental Psychology*, Routledge & Kegan Paul, London

Brainerd, C (1978) *Piaget's Theory of Intelligence*, Prentice-Hall, Englewood Cliffs, NJ

Brown, C (1981) The implementation of curriculum change by schools, in *The School Curriculum in the 1980s: Aspects of education*, ed G Elliot, **26**, The University of Hull, Hull

Cole, M, Hill, D and Shan, S (1998) *Promoting Equality in Primary Schools*, Cassell, London

Cristafi, M and Brown, A (1986) Analogical transfer in very young children: combining two separately learned solutions to reach a goal, *Child Development*, **57**, pp 953–68

Department for Education and Employment (DfEE) (1995) *The National Curriculum*, HMSO, London

DfEE (1998) *Teachers Meeting the Challenge of Change*, Stationery Office, London

Durkin, K (1997) *Developmental Social Psychology: From infancy to old age*, Blackwell, Oxford

Eraut, M and Hoyles, C (1988) Groupwork with computers, ESRC Occasional Paper, in TER/3/88, University of Lancaster, and *Journal of Computer Assisted Learning*, **5** (1), pp 12–24

Feurstein, R (1980) *Instrumental Enrichment: An intervention program for cognitive modifiability*, University Park Press, New York

Gilbert, J, Watts, D and Osborne, R (1982) Students' conceptions of ideas in mechanics, *Physics Education*, **17** (2), pp 62–66

Nussbaum, J (1989) Classroom conceptual change: philosophical perspectives, *International Journal of Science Education*, **11**, special issue, pp 530–40

Nussbaum, J and Novick, S (1982) Alternative frameworks, conceptual conflict and accommodation: Toward a principled teaching strategy, *Instructional Science*, **11**, pp 183–200

Piaget, J (1926) *The Language and Thought of the Child*, Routledge & Kegan Paul, London

Piaget, J and Inhelder, B (1969) *The Psychology of the Child*, Routledge & Kegan Paul, London

Posner, G *et al* (1982) Accommodation of a scientific conception: toward a theory of conceptual change, *Science Education*, **66** (2), pp 211–27

Skinner, B (1974) *About Behaviourism*, Vintage Books, New York

Straker, A (1989) Different ways of learning mathematics, *Local Education Authority Primary Schools: Mathematics in schools*, **18** (3), pp 10–12, May

Vygotsky, L S (1978) *Mind in Society: The development of higher psychological processes*, Harvard University Press, Cambridge, MA

Watson, D (1990) The classroom or computer room, *Computers and Education*, **15** (1–3), pp 33–37

Wood, D (1988) *How Children Think and Learn*, Blackwell, Oxford

Using information and communication technologies (ICT) for pupils' learning

4

Margaret Cox

> If we didn't have computers life would be very difficult because they help a lot with all difficult subjects and make you understand the 'problem' better. (13-year-old boy, cited in Cox, 1997)

This chapter introduces the trainee to the requirements and standards set for information and communications technology (ICT) following Circular 4/98 (1998a) and the National Grid for Learning. The trainee is taken through what ICT means, its nature and provision in school, and how this affects the trainee's own learning. ICT is a key issue in the classroom, with a clear expectation that teachers will play the leading role in promoting it. This is part of the trainee's role.

Objectives

By the end of this chapter the trainee will have an understanding of:

- the new policies for ICT;
- the implications of ICT for their teaching;
- the need for pupils to participate in ICT;
- the need to continually develop their own ICT skills.

Introduction

What is the difference between information technology (IT) and information and communication technologies (ICT)? There is considerable confusion among many educators about IT and ICT, especially in schools where, for example, many have now replaced the IT co-ordinator by the ICT co-ordinator. It is therefore important to be clear about the distinction especially as both are so important in teaching and learning.

Information technology is the design, study and use of processes for representing physical, hypothetical or human relationships employing the collection, creation, storing, retrieving, manipulation, presentation, sending and receiving of information. IT is one of the National Curriculum subjects to be taught at all school levels, but the current National Curriculum orders (DfE, 1995) do not provide any guidelines as to whether or not it should be taught as a separate subject.

Information and communication technologies are electronic and/or computerized devices and associated human interactive materials that enable the user to employ them for a wide range of teaching and learning processes in addition to personal use. ICT is being included in many new government initiatives that will be discussed later on.

ICT includes computers, videos, televisions, connections with other computers, sensors, switches, interface boxes, the Internet which links computers globally together, telecommunications, satellite connections, and all the software and materials which enable us as teachers to use them to teach our pupils. Just as a television would be useless without visual and audio material reaching it through an aerial, video or cable, which we can then watch and hear, so a computer needs software to make it communicate with us, the user. These devices have an important place in education in all school subjects.

The development of IT and ICT in education

It is only in recent years that the phrases 'information technology' and 'information and communication technologies' have come to be used in society and in education. Before that the most common phrases for IT and ICT in education were 'computers in education' and perhaps 'microelectronics in education'. The use of computers in schools goes back many years, long before the requirements of the National Curriculum and there have been a series of government programmes since as early as 1974, with an investment of over £250m to support the use of computers and more recently ICT in education. More recent programmes and centres include:

- the Education Support Grants (ESG, during the 1980s and early 1990s) for the appointment of advisory teachers and the provision of hardware, more widely known as the Grants for Education Support and Training (GEST);
- the British Educational and Communications Technology Agency (BECTa)

(1997 – present) formed from a restructuring of the National Council for Educational Technology (NCET) but with a greater focus on ICT, and with special responsibility for the National Grid for Learning.

Evidence from research studies has shown that these and many other initiatives have had an impact on education, through extending learning opportunities (Mellar *et al*, 1994), improvements to children's learning (Watson, 1993) and enhanced motivation (Cox, 1997). Among these and many other research studies there is substantial evidence about the value of IT and ICT to teaching and learning, with improvements that cannot be achieved through other means.

In May 1998 the government announced new programmes that would amount to new funding of over £1.2 billion towards the National Grid for Learning, ICT for all initial teacher trainees and an ICT training allocation of £450 for every practising teacher. However, in spite of the initiatives described above, government surveys show that ICT is not yet used substantially in most National Curriculum subjects.

With all the changes that have taken place in the school curriculum over the last 15 years since the introduction of the National Curriculum it is understandable that many teachers, if not the majority, are still unwilling or unable to use ICT in their subject teaching. In fact, according to the government survey of ICT in schools in 1997/98 (DfEE, 1998b) less than 10 per cent of science, mathematics, foreign language and English teachers reported making substantial use of ICT in their subject teaching. Not surprisingly, most of the more substantial uses of ICT were reported by teachers of information technology, business studies, design and technology and music.

In May 1998, the new national curriculum for initial teacher training (DfEE, 1998c) was published. It includes 14 pages of ICT requirements for *all* teachers of *all* subjects aimed at 'equipping every newly qualified teacher with the knowledge, skills and understanding to use ICT effectively in teaching subjects'. These include a wide range of skills from being able to 'successfully connect up ICT equipment, including input devices, eg touch screens, overlay keyboards, . . . to the use of CD-ROMs, the Internet, information from weather stations. . . computer based modelling'. Although these requirements may seem overwhelming to most teachers it is not expected that pupils will spend their entire time in front of a computer screen but only that ICT should be used where it will enhance pupils' learning. There are five main aspects of ICT/IT use in schools:

1. teaching IT as a subject which involves studying the concepts, skills, processes and applications of IT;
2. using ICT to enhance learning of all subjects;
3. pupils using ICT to support their private study and assessment tasks;
4. using ICT to manage pupils' learning programmes and progression; and
5. using ICT for teachers' personal use and administration.

The focus in this chapter will be on the second aspect involving contributions of ICT to pupils' learning although the other aspects are also important for the improvement of education.

The IT curriculum

The purpose of teaching IT, which takes some of its topics from computer science, is to teach pupils how to design systems, generate and communicate ideas in different forms, give direct signals and commands that produce a variety of outcomes, create and use IT-based models or simulations to explore processes and real situations, etc. The main themes of the IT National Curriculum are:

- systems, their components and functions;
- communicating information;
- handling information;
- controlling and measuring; and
- modelling and simulations.

These curriculum themes provide opportunities for pupils to learn new skills and concepts that will influence their learning in other curriculum areas. Many aspects of the IT curriculum embrace the ICT skills and processes that are expected to be included in all subjects. Although you may not be expecting ever to teach IT as a subject, there are many schools that are still trying to teach IT through other subjects even though this approach has so far proved to be very difficult and unsuccessful (Goldstein, 1997). Schools are also combining IT with ICT, thinking that this is the same educational requirement. In most primary schools IT is 'taught' across the curriculum, so for any new teacher it is important to know what is involved in the IT curriculum and which IT skills and processes help pupils to use ICT in other curriculum areas.

There are two publications that provide a good starting point to find out what the content of the IT curriculum is. For primary schools, the Qualifications and Curriculum Authority has published a curriculum book on teaching IT in primary schools (QCA, 1997), and for secondary schools the National Association for Co-ordinators and Teachers of IT has produced an informatics pack for Key Stage 3 (ACITT, 1999). Other useful reference materials are listed at the end of the chapter.

There is a widely held misconception among teachers, pupils and parents alike that teaching IT is simply about pupils learning how to word-process, create spreadsheets and use the Internet, yet it is interesting to note that not one specific application package nor item of hardware is mentioned in the IT National Curriculum orders (DfE, 1995). It is not possible to provide details of all the elements of the IT curriculum in this chapter, but two examples are discussed briefly below to show the kinds of IT knowledge and skills which should be part of the IT National Curriculum.

In primary schools pupils should be taught at Key Stage 1, to 'use a variety of IT equipment and software, including microcomputers and various keyboards' and at Key Stage 2, 'they should be given opportunities to use IT to explore and solve problems in the context of the work across a variety of subjects' (DfE, 1995). Often the IT experience pupils are given is limited to irregular use of word-processors. However, ICT equipment can include sensors, switches and graphics tablets (more commonly called concept keyboards) which enable young children to interact with the technology in a very simple way. The important education objective is that the pupils should understand the purpose for using IT, therefore the first stage would be to identify a problem such as 'How can we find out how cold the classroom gets during the night when the heating is turned off?' The task for the pupils is then to think of a temperature gauge which could be connected to a computer that would record the temperature every hour, for example. This simple activity would involve the pupils in planning the investigation, hypothesizing, estimating, collecting and analysing information, measuring, controlling equipment and so on.

Research into pupils learning science has shown that if pupils engage in conducting experiments which enable them to confront their own misconceptions, they come to a better understanding of the processes and concepts involved (Brna, 1990). There are many different activities involving this process which can be undertaken in the IT curriculum.

Learning about the function and uses of IT equipment and software can be introduced at all stages in the curriculum and in many different curriculum areas. Task 1 for the teacher will help you think of ideas for teaching the systems aspect of IT. For more advanced A level IT activities see, for example, Mott and Leeming (1998). Use Task 1 to identify a range of IT equipment and/or software that can help pupils understand the impact of IT on society. The activities can be undertaken in preparation for a lesson, getting pupils to record information about machines in their homes, or as part of individual or collaborative work in the lesson itself. The complexity and language level of the activity will depend upon the Key Stage of the pupils and their previous IT knowledge.

Task 4.1: Using IT equipment

Many aspects of our lives depend upon access to IT.

1. List three pieces of equipment found in the home which contain microprocessors/computers, eg a washing machine.

Task *continued overleaf*

Task *continued*

2. Write down the tasks that you think each one performs, eg operating the washing machine.
3. List all the things it will have to measure, eg water level, temperature, stage in the washing cycle.
4. List how these would be done without a machine, eg filling up a bowl with hot and cold water, using your eyes or hands to tell when you have enough water and whether the temperature is right for the clothes.
5. Prepare a table for the whole class listing the different machines they or you have thought of, their tasks and the manual equivalent, and discuss how they supplement or replace human activities.

This task will encourage pupils to think of the relationship between the many different machines which we use, and the manual processes which IT can now control or replace. Extending these kinds of tasks to include pupils thinking about cause and effect and how such mechanistic processes work, can help them develop causal reasoning skills. Studies of the use of problem-solving activities involving causal relationships (Mellar *et al*, 1994) have shown that pupils develop higher order thinking skills and autonomy of learning. The IT curriculum also involves many of the skills required to use ICT in other subjects.

When teaching IT or even using ICT within another subject teachers often discard their best teaching practice and 'throw the baby out with bath water'. It is not the case that pupils using IT within a subject should be put in front of computers for the whole of a lesson. At least half of the timetabled IT lessons should involve pupils discussing ideas, drawing up plans, sequences and models on paper, collecting data and so on away from the computer.

It would be an amazing breakthrough if the IT curriculum could be successfully taught within other subjects instead of as a separate subject. Many schools have adopted this approach to save money and to avoid the sensitive issues of changes in staffing and timetabling. However, recent Ofsted (Office for Standards in Education) reports have shown that in the majority of schools where IT is taught across the curriculum the coverage is superficial with most pupils only reaching levels 4 to 5 in Year 11 and many schools not having any IT at all at Key Stage 4 (Goldstein, 1997). The reality is that pupils are losing out on an important part of their learning because of the difficulties schools face in delivering the IT curriculum. However, with the next government initiative, planned to last from 1999 to 2002, which is to provide the equivalent of £450 for every state school teacher to obtain additional training in the use of ICT in their teaching, hopefully many more teachers will be able to make productive use of ICT to promote pupils' learning. Ideas for how ICT can promote pupils' learning are discussed in the next section.

ICT to promote pupils' learning

A useful framework to consider regarding the contribution of ICT to pupils' learning is the one based on the earlier work of Kemmis *et al* (1977) who proposed four paradigms for computer-assisted learning that are still relevant to today's technology. These paradigms are: instructional; revelatory; conjectural and emancipatory.

The instructional paradigm

The instructional paradigm applies to a learning task that can be broken down into a series of sub-tasks, each one involving its own prerequisites and objectives. These separate tasks are then structured and sequenced to form a coherent whole. ICT software that fits this paradigm is usually given names like 'skill and drill', 'drill and practice' and 'instructional dialogue' and is mostly based on Skinnerian theories of learning. Within this paradigm are included integrated learning systems, first devised by Skinner himself in the late 1960s, but which are now extensive programmed learning systems involving graphics, colour, sound and moving images, promoted vigorously by a few hardware companies and increasingly adopted by schools which have often obtained poor academic results. However, most of the evidence from research into this kind of software is that it is of limited value to pupils' learning and relates mainly to short-term performance goals rather than more substantial understanding.

The revelatory paradigm

The revelatory paradigm relates to ICT environments that involve guiding a pupil through a process of learning by discovery. The subject matter, and its underlying model of the associated theory, are gradually revealed to the pupils as they use the program. This would include simulations of processes and situations. but not modelling. The use of simulations provides the pupil with the opportunity to investigate a scientific experiment that, for example, may be too expensive in materials and equipment, or take too long to be practicable, or cannot be undertaken in the laboratory because it is dangerous. The computer may facilitate the building or imagining of models or systems that are too complex to be understandable in any other way. When the pupils carry out simulated experiments that would be impossible to undertake under other conditions, allowing them to alter and experiment with variable factors, they take a greater part in controlling the direction of their investigations. When the calculation process is entirely managed by the computer, users can concentrate more easily on thinking (eg making hypotheses about why things are happening), and this has been found to be a very effective stimulus to discussion when the activity happens in small groups. The skills promoted by the use of simulations are both practical and intellectual, involving reasoning, experimenting, and interpreting.

The educational philosophy of most simulations is based on Piagetian theories of learning where the pupils can challenge their existing schemas by exploration and build on these through practical observation of the results of their hypotheses and actions. An early example of a simulation is 'Indian Farmer', from the Computers in the Curriculum (CIC) project 1988, which simulates the life story of a Hindu family living in a hypothetical agricultural village on the Ganges Plain. The software displays pictures for each family member, their names and ages, the numbers of fields of rice and millet planted, and the amount of grain available for planting at the beginning of each year in a simple bar chart. An example of one screen display is shown in Figure 4.1.

Figure 4.1 A family after the harvest and their grain store

The program allows the pupils to make decisions, as though they were part of the family, about how many fields of rice and millet they should grow and whether to buy a bullock or not. The family story then varies according to those decisions, revealing the long-term social aspects of life in a poor agricultural community.

Although this simulation was designed for secondary pupils of all ages, it can be used with Key Stage 2 pupils to stimulate an appreciation of the problems faced by other societies and cultures and by the weather.

During the period from 1973 to 1995 hundreds of useful simulations were produced in the UK. Many of them are still available today, updated to run on current machines, although more resources are needed to make more of these programs compatible with today's technology since the educational design of many of them is relevant to the current curriculum. Simulations include history, geography, economics, role playing, and educational games as well as many in science and technology. Research by the Impact project (Watson, 1993) among others provides convincing evidence of the positive contribution of simulations to pupils' learning.

The conjectural paradigm

The conjectural paradigm relates to increasing the pupils' control over the computer by allowing them to manipulate and test their own ideas and hypotheses. The range of programs which relate to this paradigm include modelling where pupils can propose and construct relationships and then test them against real processes. Modelling programs include programming languages such as LOGO, for which there have been widespread claims for many years about the contributions to pupils' learning. Papert (1980), who invented LOGO, found in his research studies during the 1980s that pupils using LOGO developed higher order thinking skills, including problem solving, hypothesizing and logical reasoning, which could be applied across a range of subjects.

Although there is conflicting evidence from research studies about the value of modelling in learning particular concepts, one commonly agreed finding is the importance and value of modelling in education because it facilitates and extends investigations, exploration and confrontation of one's own conceptions in an inter-active and immediate environment.

There are two types of modelling activities generally referred to in education: quan-titative and qualitative modelling. Quantitative modelling involves pupils constructing mathematical relationships of real-life processes, while qualitative modelling involves rule-based logical relationships using, for example, Boolean Logic.

Although you can build your own models through the use of general purpose software such as the spreadsheet package EXCEL, or the data-handling package

ACCESS, there are very comprehensive modelling packages available that have been developed specifically for education. A Window's based modelling system, Model Builder (Booth and Cox, 1997) has been designed to be used with pupils aged from 9 years up to adulthood and includes a simple modelling language (incorporating natural language). Using this environment, learners can explore the models provided with the pack or build models themselves. Models can include pictures, diagrams, graphs and tables, and can vary from very simple models with only two or three parameters to very complex models, involving sub-models and different modes of operation. Some ideas for using this kind of modelling software are described below.

At the primary level, pupils can explore models such as HOUSE.MDL, shown in Figure 4.2, which performs a simple calculation of the heat gains and losses in a home, or they can build their own models of their home showing how it gains and loses heat and how to save energy by starting with HEATING.MDL, shown in Figure 4.3.

Similar kinds of investigations can be carried out using the spreadsheet package EXCEL as shown in the Energy Expert curriculum pack (Cox and Webb, 1993). Each

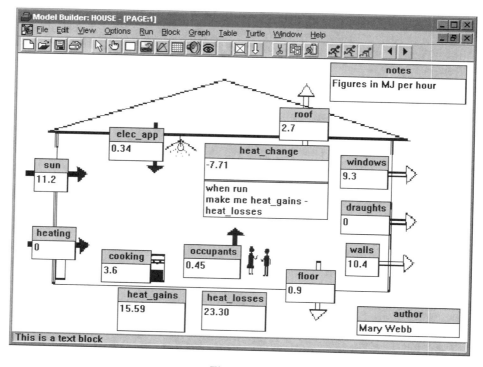

Figure 4.2

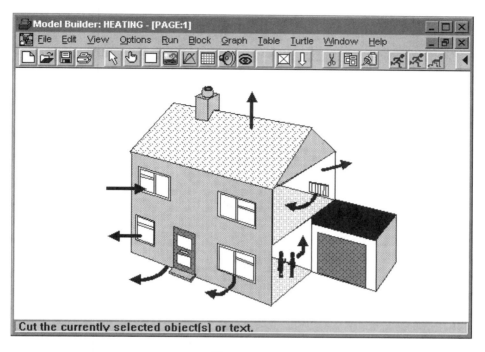

Figure 4.3

modelling application, eg Model Builder, EXCEL, has its own set of metaphors for the way the information is displayed on the screen. It is important when choosing which one to use, that you consider the level of IT skills of the pupils and their ability to use different types of commands and interpret the information. For example, for Key Stage 1 pupils, EXCEL is not easily usable since pupils are not yet capable of understanding a tabular format which allows text, numbers and relationships to be inserted into any cell.

Model Builder or EXCEL can both be used to help pupils build simple mathematical models, such as the relationship between the volume of a cube and its dimension, or simple everyday models such as MONEY2. MDL, in Model Builder. Figure 4.4 shows a model that can be constructed by Key Stage 2 pupils to investigate the relationships between their income, expenditure and savings.

At the secondary level there is a whole range of models provided with Model Builder, enabling pupils to investigate, for example, the processes of the carbon cycle and the amount of carbon dioxide produced in the atmosphere by the industrial combustion of fossil fuels, also taking into consideration the rate of absorption by plants and the oceans. Figure 4.5 shows the model CCYCLE.MDL, which can be investigated or extended to enable pupils to understand the uses, advantages and disadvantages of this particular modelling technique in studying the way human

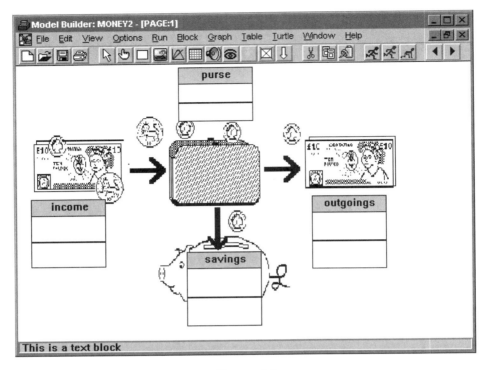

Figure 4.4

behaviour affects our global environment. Pupils at Key Stages 3 and 4 can build similar models either working in small groups to create sub-models or using sections from the sample models provided in the pack.

For GCSE and GNVQ projects there are many ideas within Model Builder and the curriculum pack Energy Expert (Cox and Webb, 1993), suitable for longer activities which involve the pupils gathering data and building a model of a topic relevant to a range of subjects. For example, pupils can follow Activity 10, Designing a Home, described in the Energy Expert curriculum pack. This students' guide provides a series of staged tasks involving: initial ideas, research, evaluating your own ideas, the detailed design, evaluating the design and presenting your design.

Similar kinds of modelling activities can also be achieved with software such as EXCEL, but using a more formal mathematical language for building the models. Figure 4.6 shows the sample model FORECST2.XLS, built by pupils using EXCEL (Cox and Webb, 1993) which enables pupils to forecast energy demand by consumers, dependent on the outside temperature, the inside temperature, hourly energy use and weighting factors. This model can be built and evaluated by pupils to compare their own home energy use with that forecast by their model. This

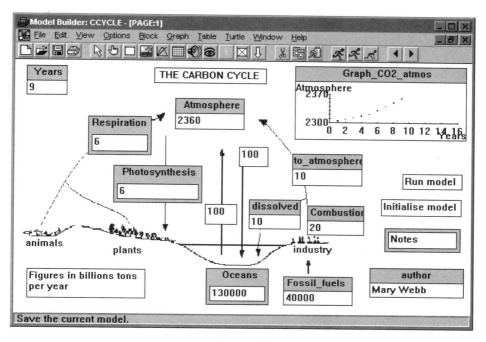

Figure 4.5

Figure 4.6

	A	B	C	D	E	F	G	H
1								
2				Gas Consumption Forecasting				
3								
4	Base Temperature		20.0 °C			Energy Factor	0.8	
5								
6	Date	Outside Temp.		Degree Day	Smoothed De	Hourly Energy Use		Weights
7	1	7.0 °C		13.0 °C				1
8	2	10.0 °C		10.0 °C				2
9	3	11.5 °C		8.5 °C				3
10	4	12.0 °C		8.0 °C				4
11	5	13.0 °C		7.0 °C	9.1 °C	7.2 KwH		
12	6	12.5 °C		7.5 °C	7.9 °C	6.3 KwH		
13	7	10.0 °C		10.0 °C	7.6 °C	6.0 KwH		
14	8	12.5 °C		7.5 °C	8.5 °C	6.8 KwH		
15	9	12.0 °C		8.0 °C	8.2 °C	6.6 KwH		
16	10	11.0 °C		9.0 °C	8.2 °C	6.6 KwH		
17	11	13.5 °C		6.5 °C	8.5 °C	6.8 KwH		
18	12	14.0 °C		6.0 °C	7.7 °C	6.1 KwH		

Figure 4.6

model can then be extended to suit different weather patterns, different types of communities and longer periods of time.

Activities using modelling software, such as those described above, enable teachers to include computer-based modelling in many different areas of the National Curriculum, from Key Stage 1 to above Key Stage 4, not only in IT, but in design and technology, science, mathematics, geography, physical education, economics and business studies. With the tools now available, modelling can be applied to almost any curriculum area.

The modelling packages referred to above are principally designed for quantitative model building through algebraic relationships. Qualitative tools, such as the expert system shell, Expert Builder (Booth *et al*, 1994) have been developed to allow the learner to construct a logical network of phrases in the form of questions, facts, rules and advice, displayed on the screen as boxes linked together through logical connectors. While the model is being constructed, it can be interrogated by the pupils to test their logic and reasoning behind the model. This kind of system is based on formal logic and inference rules. Figures 4.7a and b show an example of a model, CREEPY.EBD built by secondary, Key Stage 4 school pupils for the classification of insects and other animals. This model is constructed through typing in characteristics of an animal in each box, then linking them together in logical sequences.

A simpler version of this could be built by younger pupils at Key Stages 2 or 3, with pupils bringing in small insects and other animals, or visiting the local museum or zoo to collect data to help construct their animal classification system. Expert Builder can also be used to create or explore fault-finding procedures for devices in technology, conditions for the development of a town in history, dietary factors and healthy eating in food technology and biology, human behaviour leading to desertification in geography and conditions for illnesses in biology.

Using modelling software and simulations enables pupils to investigate their own ideas about different subject processes and concepts, at the same time as learning ICT skills about model building and graphical representations, and using computers for simulating complex physical, economical, or geographical processes. There is also no in-built teacher control except for the constraints imposed by the modelling framework. The subject and level of understanding are determined by the learner and not the software developer.

Computer models can also be built using any programming language such as BASIC, LOGO, PASCAL, Prolog and Smalltalk, although the use of some of these in the classroom is still very rare. An additional difficulty in using most programming languages is that the routines for the input and graphical displays have to be created as well as for the model itself. Data analysis software also enables pupils to study the relationships between sets of experimental data and to perform statistical analyses, thereby engaging in many of the processes of modelling. The types of software that can be used for simulating and modelling are almost limitless and

(a)

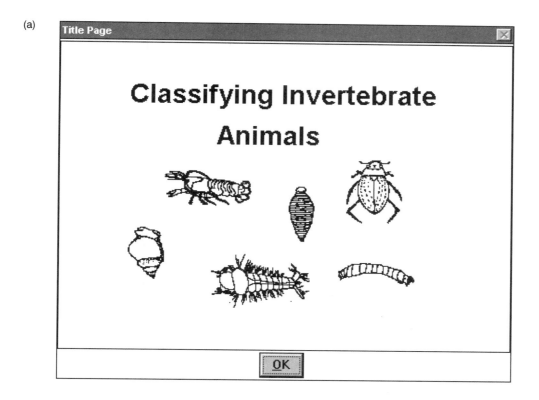

(b)

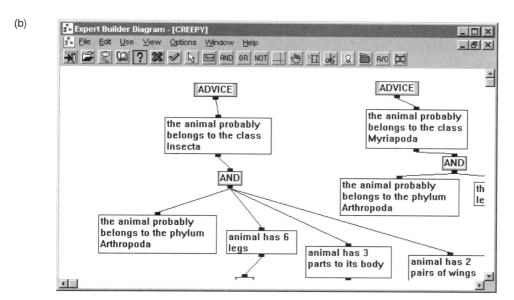

Figure 4.7

include many activities now available over the Internet. Examples of these are discussed in relation to the emancipatory paradigm.

Chapter 3 explains that a major contribution to pupils' progression in learning is made by helping pupils think about how they learn. The interactive nature of modelling using ICT enables them to do this through, for example, the creation of a model of a process where the pupils can see an immediate result of their model in relation to the outcomes of a real process.

The emancipatory paradigm

The fourth and final paradigm suggested by Kemmis and MacDonald means being emancipated: the learners have more control over the computer and use it as and when they want as an aid in the learning process. It involves the use of ICT as a 'labour-saving device', to perform calculations, to plot graphs, to retrieve information, to manipulate text and, in general, to deal with some given task. In this type of ICT use, the information handling abilities of the computer are exploited so as to improve the quality of the learning experience by taking the monotony out of some kinds of tasks.

By using an 'information retrieval' program, pupils can store their own information on a computer, they can display this information, and they can access specific items of information for themselves. An information retrieval program allows the person using it to form a database. This can be defined as 'an organized collection of related data, where the structure of the data is independent of any particular application'. Data handling and analysis are a major part of the IT curriculum and also a major ICT activity relevant to science, history, geography and many other curriculum areas at both primary and secondary levels.

Data analysis packages have some strong advantages in particular curriculum applications. They enable pupils to recognize patterns or tendencies in the data they are examining. When there is the need to consider a large quantity of data or a wide range of observations, the use of a database package facilitates the organization or management of information. Data processing is one way for pupils to develop a more systematic approach to problem solving, especially in cases where, for instance, planning, categorization and formal reasoning are demanded. When the computer generates results of simulated experiments, pupils may analyse the results to discover the underlying operating relationships. Moreover, they have more time to interpret patterns of data and results from investigations, and to gain confidence when they summarize information.

Data-handling skills are perhaps one of the most important range of skills which pupils need to be taught today because of the expanding growth of information in our society and of the method of access through the Internet and other telecommunication systems. A recent study by Cox and Nikolopoulou (1997) investigated the strategies and skills of pupils aged 13–15 who were using a computer-based data analysis package compared with similar classes of pupils who used sets of data on paper cards. They found that the pupils using ICT outperformed the control group and developed important data-handling skills, previously only found among older pupils.

This study and previous ones have shown that the following skills and understanding are promoted by the use of database software:

- formulating queries;
- using Boolean logical operators (and, or, greater than, less than, equal to);
- conducting single and multiple condition searches;
- performing two parallel logical reasoning tasks;
- classifying and interpreting data;
- specifying ranges of numbers;
- recognizing patterns in unfamiliar data.

Although data handling is a cross-curricular activity it usually takes place within a subject-specific context. The skills mentioned above can be promoted in many different curriculum applications. For example, in history, census schedules are commonly used to encourage enquiry learning through pupils formulating and testing their own hypotheses. In biology pupils are required to develop the skills of classifying insects and other animal forms, and in chemistry pupils use and construct chemical databases to speculate about conceptual links, about correlations and trends in chemical behaviour, and about causal relationships.

Underwood (1985) evaluated the investigations undertaken by teachers and pupils using computer-based information handling packages in 18 primary and secondary classrooms, across a range of subjects, and compared the expressed objectives/ intentions of teachers using databases against recorded classroom outcomes. Types of teachers' intents included:

- skills and knowledge (cognitive, communication, computer) acquired from the exercise;
- teaching and learning strategies employed (eg emancipation, motivation);
- social and psychological climate of the classroom; and
- societal issues (eg life skills).

Although not all the recorded transactions and outcomes matched the teachers' intentions, the results of these 18 case studies showed that computer-based information handling packages can be beneficial to pupils' learning. Teachers were aware of the wide range of skills and knowledge which could be stimulated by database use, and the emphasis in the transactions and outcomes was very much towards the cognitive skills (in particular formulating hypotheses and questions), communication skills, and the organization and management of the classroom. The data-handling skills and attainment levels of the National Curriculum are shown in Table 4.1.

Table 4.1 Levels of difficulty in data-handling skills

Elementary skills Levels 2,3,4 (ages: 7–11)	Intermediate skills Levels 5,6,7 (ages: 11–14)	Advanced skills Levels 8,9,10 (ages: 14–16)
• collect data • select data • retrieve data • sort & classify discrete data • compare & contrast (observe similarities & differences) • ask questions	• select relevant information • formulate & test hypotheses • classify (against 1 or 2 criteria) • interpret (graphics, relationship) • predict relationships • make decisions • organize & analyse data • analyse patterns • draw conclusions	• analyse results to test a hypothesis • compare & contrast • identify patterns • interpret evidence • make predictions • evaluate information • analyse complex information

Task 4.2: Relating data-handling tasks to the National Curriculum

From Table 4.1, choose a data-handling curriculum task that would require an ICT package for the data to be entered and analysed within two lessons.

1. List the number of fields for the data; eg height, weight, name.
2. Write down the number of records (a record is all the information for one item).
3. Write a set of procedures to enable the pupils to follow through the data-handling activity.
4. Identify the skills from Table 4.1 involved in the task you have devised.

The second example of an ICT activity that relates to the conjectural as well as the emancipatory paradigm is communicating information.

Communicating information involves understanding what information is, the different forms of information and how it can therefore be communicated. For example, in the primary classroom pupils might be asked to bring in different kinds of information sources, such as leaflets, labels, bus tickets, posters, letters or post-cards and then to examine them for their content, the audience, the purpose of the information, its design, the time it might be accessed and so on. The next stage would be to consider what kinds of information might be enhanced with the use of a word-processor or desktop publishing program, planning the design to take account of the purpose, the message and the audience.

Schools that have access to the Internet could include an activity involving downloading and printing out a few Web pages to examine the different ways in which information is presented. Figures 4.8a, b and c give three very different types of Web pages showing the different emphases the Web designer has placed on the information provided. Lessons can be planned around an evaluation of these Web pages, why they were produced, what kind of information they hold and how this differs from paper-based information.

The teaching of general information-handling skills without computer use seems to be organized according to pupils' experience and development. Piaget and Inhelder (1969) assert that the mastery of basic operations like seriating and classifying is important to cognition and a prerequisite for success at later cognitive tasks. To these can be added instruction in comparing, contrasting and observing, which come prior to teaching more complex skills such as analysing, synthesizing and evaluating.

When using a computer for information handling, tasks also need to be structured and sequenced. Hunter (1987) suggested that pupils should start with activities that develop prerequisite skills, such as locating, classifying and interpreting information, before they take on tasks requiring more complex skills (like analysing, formulating hypotheses, evaluating). Parker (1986) states that the lower order thinking skills with database work might include entering data into the database, retrieving factual information, and using databases to organize lists. Higher order thinking skills might include determining the information needed to test an hypothesis, reorganizing and synthesizing data to test ideas and find non-obvious relationships, selecting between relevant and irrelevant information, and drawing inferences.

In the examples above, ICT uses have involved using stand-alone or networked computers without any peripheral equipment except printers, yet one of the most important aspects of ICT is the use of sensors, switches and other alternative devices which enable pupils to collect a wide range of scientific and other data, directly or remotely. According to Joseph Deken, technology curator at the California Museum of Science and Industry (Deken, 1990), measurement and control devices form the main components of robotics, 'a new and universal medium, which will certainly make obsolete all the primitive machines and computers of the 20th century'.

There are many experiments that are difficult or impossible to carry out in the classroom without the use of measurement and control devices because the time-scales required are either very short, such as measuring the speed of a falling object, or very long, such as measuring the rate of change of humidity in the air. Frost (1994) has provided many examples of how sensors and switches can be used by pupils to collect simple scientific data. For example, pupils can measure the speed of a moving object by the computer recording the exact time it passes through two light gates. Using sensors pupils can collect accurate information and then compare their own results with their own theories of the process. It also enables them to see

(a)

(b)

Figure 4.8

(c)

Figure 4.8 continued

the results immediately and avoid the sometimes laborious process of recording the data by hand then carrying out calculations. Barton and Rogers (1991), who researched into pupils using motion sensors and light gates to measure the movement of objects, found that in both cases 'the immediate presentation of data connects the investigation and the results. This has the effect of freeing pupils to spending most of their time analysing, interpreting and predicting skills which are at the heart of scientific investigation.'

Practical examples of measurement and control activities include:

- pupils measuring their pulse and changing their rate of physical activity to investigate the relationship between pulse rate and human exertion;
- measuring the variation in temperature levels over a period of several days in various locations in the school, using remote sensors to determine the highest sources of heat loss;
- measuring the levels of infrared radiation as a detector of human presence to trigger an alarm.

Task 4.3 provides ideas for introducing measurement and control concepts to pupils. A visit to a local canning factory or car manufacturing plant provides very stimulating insights into how important measurement and control devices are in our lives.

Task 4.3: Measurement and control devices

This task can be used for either primary or secondary pupils; the detail will depend upon the intellectual stage of the pupils.

1. Organize a visit with the pupils to the local supermarket.
2. At the supermarket get the pupils to record all the devices they can see which measure things or might be controlled (eg automatic doors, bar code readers at the checkout; lighting, car park gates, fridges, burglar alarms).
3. Get the pupils to make a second list of the different types of food and produce in the supermarket (eg fresh, canned, non-foods).
4. In the following lesson, with the pupils in small groups, ask them to identify the kinds of sensors these devices might have (eg light, sound, position). For younger pupils, this might need ideas from the teacher.
5. List their results on the board and discuss the reasoning of their results.
6. For more advanced work provide a list of questions for the pupils for homework for them to propose what kinds of sensors and switches might be needed in providing the food in the different types of containers. (For example, what sensors and switches might be needed in a machine that fills coke cans and then seals them?)

The examples in this chapter of ICT uses are just the tip of the iceberg in terms of resources and different curriculum applications. New ideas and resources are arriving on the World Wide Web every day and a few useful Web sites are given at the end of the chapter. The overwhelming ICT resources available on the Internet make it even more difficult to decide what to include when using ICT in one's teaching. The final section explains some of the issues that might help with these decisions.

Organizing ICT in one's teaching

Since the publication of Kemmis *et al*'s paradigms in 1977 the ICT environment has changed almost beyond recognition, although the Internet was around then and computers look the same from a distance! Most software on sale today is now very versatile and dynamic with pictures, icons, sound and moving images. The Internet and the material available through it is profoundly changing society and education. The teacher of today has the difficult task of trying to organize a powerful resource into subject lessons and into a crowded timetable. For example, one CD ROM designed for use in teaching geography, Distant Places, has enough material for pupils to spend hours longer on geography than on other topics, so the teacher has to decide how to plan a series of useful lessons without having to leave out many other skills and concepts also included in the National Curriculum.

The main issue that has to be considered when planning to include ICT in one's teaching is how to relate the ICT activity to the learning aims and objectives of the curriculum. Ten golden rules to follow when planning and using ICT in the curriculum will help you in ensuring that it is used to enhance pupils' learning:

1. Identify the learning aims and objectives for the pupils that can be enhanced by the use of ICT.
2. Select appropriate ICT resources to meet the learning aims.
3. Ensure that the pupils have enough ICT skills to be able to carry out the activity.
4. Plan the timing of the activity to include non-ICT tasks such as question and answers, group work, pupils' discussions.
5. Plan enough lessons to enable the activity to be completed.
6. Decide on the groupings of the pupils – they do not always have to work alone.
7. Introduce the lesson to all the pupils first before working on any ICT.
8. Intersperse the ICT activity with whole-class guidance and direction.
9. Allow enough time for the pupils to reflect and evaluate their achievements at the end of the lesson.
10. Allocate homework or other assessed work in which the pupils extend their thinking about the activity, and through which you can find out what they have learnt.

It would be impossible to address all the Teacher Training Agency's new requirements for teachers using ICT in schools (TTA, 1998) in this chapter, although it is important to bear in mind that Ofsted will be including assessment of the uses of ICT in their school inspections more extensively in the future. There is now a list of new approved training providers to train the teachers already in schools and this list went out to schools in March 1999 together with information about conducting a needs assessment of every teacher in the school and how to plan for the training.

Conclusions

ICT is becoming one of the most important aspects of education today. Some people have claimed that this is a bigger revolution than the industrial one. New government programmes require all teachers to use ICT widely in their teaching and it will no longer be an optional activity. The range of ICT skills required of teachers makes the numeracy and literacy skills pale into insignificance, yet the time needed to acquire all these new teaching skills is rarely available to the over-worked teacher. The important point to remember is that it is not necessary to change or discard all the pedagogical practices used with more traditional resources since most of these are relevant to teaching with ICT.

The first reason for being a teacher is to help pupils learn. The most compelling reason for using ICT is that there is convincing evidence that children can learn some things more effectively with the use of ICT and that its uses can motivate pupils who have been disillusioned with education. Denying pupils the opportunities to use ICT in their learning will impoverish their education and make their education less relevant to today's world of new technologies. Using ICT in lessons makes it fun to teach as well as to learn!

Further reading

British Computer Society (1998) *A Glossary of Computing Terms*, 9th edn, British Computer Society, London

Mott, J and Leeming, A (1998) *Information Technology for Advanced Level*, Hodder and Stoughton, London

School Curriculum and Assessment Authority (1996) *Information Technology: Exemplification of standards*, The Stationery Office, London

Useful Web sites

The Association of Science Education – http://www.ase.org.uk/
BECTa – http://www.becta.org.uk/
Department for Education and Employment – http://www.dfee.gov.uk/dfeehome.htm
The Education Market Place – http://www.education-net.co.uk/
The Guardian – http://www.guardian.co.uk/
The IT Network – http://www.becta.org.uk/gen-sheets/itnetwork/
Journal of Computer Assisted Learning – http://www.lancs.ac.uk/users/ktru/jcaljrnl.htm
Museums in the UK – http://www.mda.org.uk/vlmp/)
The National Association of Co-ordinators and IT Teachers – http://www.acitt.org.uk/
The National Grid for Learning – http://www.ngfl.gov.uk/ngfl/index.html
The Qualifications and Curriculum Authority – http://www.qca.org.uk/
The Virtual Teachers Centre – http://vtc.ngfl.gov.uk/vtc/index.html

References

ACITT (1999) *Informatics at Key Stage 3*, National Association of Co-ordinators and Teachers of IT, Barking and Dagenham LEA, The Westbury Centre, Barking

Barton, R and Rogers, L (1991) The computer as an aid to practical science – studying motion with a computer, *Journal of Computer Assisted Learning*, **7** (2), pp 104–13

Booth, B *et al* (1994) *Expert Builder (qualitative modelling software environment)*, The Modus Project, Harpenden

Booth, B and Cox, M J (1997) *Model Builder*, The Modus Project, Harpenden

Brna, P (1990) A methodology for confronting science misconceptions, *Journal of Educational Computing Research*, **6** (2), pp 157–82

Cox, M J *et al* (1993) *Energy Expert*, The Modus Project, Harpenden

Cox, M J (1997) *The Effects of Information Technology on Students' Motivation: Final report*, NCET/King's College, London

Cox, M J and Nikolopoulou, K (1997) What information handling skills are promoted by the use of data handling software?, *Education and Information Technologies*, **2**, 105–20

Deken, J (1990) Robotics; computers the next step, Inside Science No.38, *New Scientist*, 29 September

Department for Education (1995) *Information Technology in the National Curriculum*, The Stationery Office, London

Department for Education and Employment (DfEE) (1998a) *Requirements for Courses of Initial Teacher Training*, Circular 4/98, DfEE, London

DfEE (1998b) Survey of information and communications technology in schools, *1998 Statistical Bulletin*, 11/98

DfEE (1998c) *Teachers Meeting the Challenge of Change*, The Stationery Office, London

Frost, R (1994) Computer software for science teaching, *School Science Review*, **76** (287), pp 19–24

Goldstein, G (1997) *Information Technology in English Schools: A commentary on inspection findings 1995–1996*, Falmer Press, London

Hunter, B (1987) Knowledge-creative learning with databases, *Social Education*, **51** (1), pp 38–43

Kemmis, S, Atkin, R and Wright, E (1977) How do pupils learn?, *Working Papers on CAL, Occasional Paper 5*, University of East Anglia: Centre for Applied Research in Education, Norwich

Mellar, H *et al* (1994) *Learning with Artificial Worlds: Computer-based modelling in the curriculum*, Falmer Press, London

Mott, J and Leeming, A (1998) *Information Technology for Advanced Level*, Hodder and Stoughton, London

Papert, S (1980) *Mindstorms: Children, computers and powerful ideas*, Harvester Press, Brighton

Parker, J (1986) Tools for thought, *The Computing Teacher*, **14** (2), pp 21–23

Piaget, J and Inhelder, B (1969) *The Psychology of the Child*, Routledge & Kegan Paul, London

Qualifications and Curriculum Authority (1997) *Teaching Information Technology in Primary Schools*, QCA, London

TTA (1998) The use of ICT in subject teaching (Annex B of DfEE Circular 4/98), DfEE, London

Underwood, J (1988) An investigation of teacher intents and classroom outcomes in the use of information-handling packages, *Computers in Education*, **12**, pp 91–100

Watson, D M (ed) (1993) *The ImpacT Report – An evaluation of the impact of information technology on children's achievements in primary and secondary schools*, King's College, London

5 Plan and prepare to be an effective teacher

Mike Waring

This chapter introduces the trainee to the nature and context of planning and preparation. Following the standards set out in Circular 4/98, it shows the trainee the importance of planning and the role it has to play in becoming an effective and responsible facilitator of learning. A variety of planning models are considered, with each model highlighting areas of possible development for the trainee. Pedagogical and subject knowledge are discussed with respect to planning aims and objectives. Preparation is considered from the perspective of being a successful and competent teacher.

Objectives

By the end of this chapter the trainee should understand:

- the need for planning and preparation;
- the mechanics of planning and preparation;
- standards and the planning process;
- the relevance of pedagogic and subject knowledge to the planning process;
- the need to specify educational objectives;
- the need to organize learning activities;
- successful preparation.

Irrespective of the subject, phase or ability of the pupils being taught, regardless of the nature of government reforms in ITT and despite the erosion of time for all teachers, planning and preparation remain the fundamental components in the facilitation of an effective and progressive learning experience for all pupils (and for that matter trainees).

Good lesson planning translates school policies and subject guidance into informed classroom practice; it identifies learning objectives, making provision for the different learning needs of pupils, and specifies the activities to be pursued in the lesson, the use of time, the resources, any assessment opportunity and any link to cross curricular themes and spiritual, moral, social and cultural development. (Ofsted, 1998: 78)

It should be no surprise therefore, that some of the criteria used by the Office for Standards in Education (Ofsted) inspectors for judging teaching quality and effectiveness (Ofsted, 1993), and a significant portion (section B.2.a-e)[1] of those standards for the award of qualified teacher status (QTS) as outlined in Circular 10/97 and which form the statutory assessment of trainee teachers in ITT, refer specifically to planning.

So why plan?

In addition to the need to satisfy the standards as part of the statutory requirements as outlined in Circular 10/97, trainees need to plan in detail for a number of other reasons, even though these may not initially appear to be those driving the trainee (McIntyre, 1997). Teachers need to provide themselves with a well-constructed guiding framework provided by sound planning. This will ensure that they remain focused not only on the immediate learning outcomes, but also the way in which these progressively contribute and relate to medium- and long-term learning objectives and outcomes. The whole process of writing things down allows trainees to articulate the desired pupil learning in the lesson. It also allows them to explore the necessary organization and management of the environment in which to facilitate those desired learning outcomes. In so doing, the teacher has explored and generally appreciates, prior to delivery, the optimal amount of time to devote to particular portions of the lesson and the associated differentiation of each activity. Added to this is the essential identification, association and subsequent progression of each portion of the lesson. Planning allows the teacher to take into account pupil differences and the necessary teaching and learning activities that might be appropriate to combat any problems linked to ability. Importantly there has to be a degree of flexibility in planning. Flexibility is an important factor and should not be ignored. The degree of flexibility will grow with the expertise and experience of the teacher.

As Williams (1996: 29) has identified:

Student teachers are given the responsibility for teaching classes normally taken by a qualified teacher. The teacher remains accountable, at the end of the day, for the achievements of pupils. It is therefore reasonable for the teacher to have evidence of adequate preparation. While this may also be provided by talking to the student, a written plan can show quickly and simply whether likely eventualities have been planned for.

Thorough planning also plays a role in minimizing potential problems, especially in the initial periods of learning to teach. Not only can potential problems be recognized and to a great extent eliminated, but planning also allows teachers to focus on the finer points of their delivery in that it reduces the amount of thinking that they have to do during the lesson. For example, being secure in the knowledge that the necessary resources have been selected, prepared and organized prior to the lesson, along with being confident that there is appropriate progression in the content, is something that can only be adequately achieved prior to the lesson through planning.

Evaluation of the learning by the pupils and by the teacher in each lesson is an essential part of the process of teaching, if there is to be progression in learning for both parties. On the basis of this evaluation, the nature, structure and content of future lessons can be appropriately enhanced. Therefore, planning has to exist as a prerequisite around which this developmental process can consistently evolve.

The critical association between planning and preparation needs to be dealt with. Simply put, planning leads onto preparation of the materials, resources and props that will be needed in the lesson. If these materials are prepared prior to the lesson, the teacher is in a much better position to successfully differentiate the activities, as well as to cope with maintaining the smooth and effective progress in learning throughout the lesson for all pupils.

The value of the reduction in stress and anxiety for the teacher that comes from identifying and minimizing potential problems before entering the teaching context is one outcome of effective planning that cannot be overestimated. Such room for manoeuvre and the associated increase in confidence allow the teacher to organize alternative resources, tasks and styles if the initial ones do not appear to facilitate the learning outcomes the teacher may have intended. This is supported by Clark and Yinger (1987: 88) when they state three main purposes to planning:

- planning to meet immediate personal needs (eg reduce uncertainty and anxiety, to find a sense of direction, confidence and security);
- planning as a means to an end of instruction (eg to learn the material, to collect and organise materials, to organise time and activity flow);
- direct uses of plans during instruction (eg to organize students, to get an activity started, to aid memory, to provide a framework for instruction and evaluation).

Planning and preparation can be seen as essential components of effective teaching for a myriad of interrelated reasons. Not least of these is that they minimize ambiguity for the teacher and pupils, thus forming the foundation on which realistic and effective assessment, recording and reporting can be based.

Numerous authors have attempted to articulate the progression of elements to be addressed in effective planning. Table 5.1 provides a simple summary illustration of a selection of these. Highlighted on the left is Tyler's (1950) linear, rational, objectives-based planning model. Such a model has been advocated as an appropriate approach for teachers to use when planning their teaching (Mawer, 1995). Others, such as Taylor (1970) have proposed an alternative model that sees the content being taught and the teaching context as the primary considerations,

Table 5.1 The suggested elements of effective planning and their progression

	Tyler (1950)	Kyriacou (1986)	Kyriacou (1991)	Leask & Davison (1995)	Kelly & Mayes (1995)	Williams (1996)	Taylor (1970)
1	Specify objectives	General aims and specific educational outcomes	Decision about objectives	How do pupils learn?	Who am I teaching?	What are pupils going to learn?	Content being taught and teaching context
2	Selection of learning material	Take account of the context	Selection and scripting of lesson	Require-ments of the curriculum	What am I teaching?	What tasks are going to be set during the lesson and in what order?	Pupil interests
3	Organization of learning activities		Preparation of all props to be used	Most appropriate methods of teaching the topic and resources available	How can I teach it?	How will teacher help the pupil answer the task? What organization issues are there?	Aims and objectives of course: course philosophy
4	Specification of evaluation procedures	Monitor and evaluate	How to monitor and assess	Evaluations of previous lessons		How will teacher assess pupil learning?	Criteria for evaluation

rather than objectives. This variation in planning is considered to be a consequence of the relative experience of the teacher. Table 5.1 identifies other models that are variations on this theme.

Do as I say not as I do. . .

Critically, bound up in the relationship between the trainee teachers and their mentors are the potential tensions of any novice-expert exchange. In relation to the development of planning for the trainee teacher, it is essential to remember that the notion of an objectives model of planning (eg Tyler, 1950) is only one of a number of variations, as illustrated in Table 5.1. However, as with the increasing range of teaching styles a teacher can adopt and practise with, as well as more 'effectively' adapt through their increasing exposure to them, so they are able to *internalize* elements of the planning process:

> While student teachers on teaching practice are usually required to make explicit lesson plans, experienced teachers more often rely on their extensive experience to form a mental framework of how they want the lesson to proceed. This does not necessarily mean that the lesson plans of established teachers are any less detailed than those of beginning teachers, simply that the lesson plans have become internalised through repetition. (Kyriacou, 1991: 17)

On a superficial basis it might appear to the external observer that such internalization constitutes neglect by the experienced mentor/teacher[2] of certain aspects in the planning process such as the pre-specification of objectives and evaluation procedures. This would be an unfortunate misreading of the situation. The fact is that they have rehearsed their planning so many times that they can afford to redirect the bulk of their overt attention to aspects in the process other than the objectives and evaluation procedures. This is certainly not to state that they are no longer important in the process – they are. They remain fundamental even to the experienced teachers' thinking, although not externally acknowledged. As Borko and Niles (1987) argue, supported by the research literature on teacher planning (Mawer, 1995), pre-service and inexperienced teachers should still approach planning through the pre-specification of objectives and evaluation procedures, because they have not yet attained the breadth and depth of experienced teachers (Mawer, 1995).

Consequently, in order to appreciate and begin to 'internalize' the planning process it is important, especially for the trainee and novice teacher, that they adopt an objectives model of planning. Inevitably this will mean that mentors should expect trainees to adopt different models of planning to themselves. Both parties need to be aware of the reasons for this. Within the context of this chapter the objectives model of planning will be explored to highlight the most significant aspects of effective planning.

Bearing this in mind and considering the predominantly school-based model of ITT which exists in the UK at present, it is essential that trainees, mentors and tutors are able to share in a common translation of an objectives model of planning as it relates to Circular 10/97 section B2 (planning), because this is part of the basis on which all trainees work and are assessed regarding their QTS.

Standards and the planning process

Table 5.2 identifies on its left-hand side an example of an objectives model of planning with each stage numbered, as in Table 5.1. Listed and labelled to the right-hand side are each of the statements on planning in Circular 10/97. The numbers written centrally suggest those elements of the objectives model which might correspond to that particular statement in Circular 10/97.

Pedagogical content knowledge

Before exploring an objectives model of planning in more detail, it is necessary to consider the foundation on which it has to be built. If trainee or novice teachers are to plan effectively over any kind of time-frame, where do they start? Yes, they need to look at the objectives; however, it is important to understand and appreciate the context in which these will apply. Shulman (1986) coined the term 'pedagogical content knowledge' as a way of conceptualizing the essential knowledge required to be able to teach subject content knowledge. Cochran *et al* (1993: 263) have extended this by stating that:

> Pedagogical content knowledge (PCK) differentiates expert teachers in a subject area from subject area experts. PCK concerns the manner in which teachers relate their subject matter knowledge (what they know about what they teach) to their pedagogical knowledge (what they know about teaching) and how subject matter knowledge is a part of the process of pedagogical reasoning.

Table 5.2 The potential relationship between elements of an objectives model of planning and the planning portion of the standards for the award of qualified teacher status (Circular 10/97, B2)

		Elements of model corresponding to standards	*Planning standards (Circular 10/97–B2)*	
	An objectives model of planning	1, 2, 3, 4	Identifying clear teaching objectives and content, appropriate to the subject matter and the pupils being taught, and specifying how these will be taught and assessed	2(a)i
1	Specify objectives	2, 3	Setting tasks for whole-class, individual and group-work, including homework, which challenge pupils and ensure high levels of interest	2(a)ii
2	Selection of learning material	1, 2, 3, 5	Setting appropriate and demanding expectations for pupils' learning, motivation and presentation of work	2(a)ii
3	Organization of learning activities	1, 4	Setting clear targets for pupils' learning, building on prior attainment, and ensuring that pupils are aware of the substance and purpose of what they are asked to do	2(a)i
4	Specification of evaluation procedures	2, 3 4, 5	Identifying pupils who: have SEN, including specific learning difficulties; are very able; are not yet fluent in English; and know where to get help in order to receive positive and targeted support	2(a)v
5	Preparation of materials, resources and props	1, 2, 3, 4	Providing clear structures for lessons, and for sequences of lessons, in the short, medium and longer term, which maintain pace–motivation and challenge for pupils	2(b)
		2, 4	Making effective use of assessment information on pupils' attainment and progress in their teaching and in planning future lessons and sequences of lessons	2(c)
		1	Planning opportunities to contribute to pupils' personal, spiritual, moral, social and cultural development	2(d)
		1	Where applicable, ensuring coverage of the relevant examination syllabuses and the National Curriculum Programmes of Study	2(e)

Consequently, a great deal of background knowledge needs to be generated by the teacher regarding the learners, the curriculum and the context of teaching the activity prior to specification of learning objectives. This requires familiarization with:

- the National Curriculum for the particular subject area (as well as others regarding cross-curricular dimensions);
- the activity areas to be taught;
- the particular school and departmental context;
- the pupils;
- resources.

Once this foundation on which to construct the more overt planning process has been achieved, teachers can then consider the nature of the learning experience they want the pupils to have.

Kyriacou (1986: 115) states that when planning one must ensure that the learning experience fulfils three psychological conditions necessary for pupil learning to occur:

> – *attentiveness:* the learning experience must elicit and sustain pupils' attention;
> – *receptiveness:* the learning experience must elicit and sustain pupils' motivation and mental effort;
> – *appropriateness:* the learning experience must be appropriate for the educational outcomes desired.

Cohen's (1987) concept of 'instructional alignment' is one that supports Kyriacou in relation to the need for certain elements to be complementary. 'Instructional alignment' basically means that there is a close affiliation between the intended learning outcomes for the pupils and the tasks which facilitate them, and finally that the assessment of the learning or achievement supports both of them. If this cohesion is to be achieved, trainees must have a sound knowledge of the activity they are about to teach.

However, limited depth and breadth of knowledge across the subject area is an area of concern consistently reported by those involved in the ITT process (Hardy, 1996; McIntyre, 1997). This is a significant factor in the planning process (a) for the trainee due to the amount of time and energy it can involve, and (b) for the mentor and tutor facilitating this process. The consolidation and enhancement of the trainees' subject knowledge base, in conjunction with all the other knowledge they have to gather in order to prepare to plan (eg concerning the context of the department and school, knowledge of the pupils and resources), are extremely time- and energy-consuming. For many trainees this can also be a demoralizing portion of the planning process, as they realize they only have the material with which to build, and not the building. However, if a trainee does realize this it is certainly a significant movement along the road to internalization of the planning process. The challenging and exciting part of the planning process – ie the manipulation of the subject and pedagogical content knowledge to achieve instructional alignment – still has to be addressed.

Having outlined some of the necessary background information and knowledge required to develop the objectives model of planning, each of the elements involved in planning using an objectives model will now be discussed.

An objectives model of planning

1. Specifying educational objectives

The identification of clear educational objectives has consistently been seen as an essential feature in planning (DES, 1985, 1988; Ofsted, 1993, 1998). It gives teachers a structure and purpose to their planning. However, it is essential that each objective describes an aspect of pupil learning, hence the term 'objective' is often used interchangeably with 'learning outcome'. Describing an aspect of pupil learning does not mean stating what the pupils will be doing: it involves a description of what is to constitute the learning. For example, correctly expressed educational objectives would be: to understand the implications of taking non-prescription drugs as an elite athlete; or to gain knowledge of vulcanicity. Inappropriately expressed ones would be: working through an exercise on non-prescription drugs and elite athletes; or to draw a map of a volcano. The potential for confusion, especially for trainees, is generated by a belief that planning is merely the organization of activities, something that is reinforced by their imprecise thinking about the educational objectives.

The structure of the National Curriculum can be used to highlight the varying degrees of specificity of educational objectives within planning. The attainment targets state the knowledge, skills and understanding that various pupils are expected to develop within each subject area. More refined and specific objectives exist within the activity-specific statements within programmes of study (PoS) for each area within each Key Stage. Finally there will be those objectives for each individual lesson which will tend to be even more specific.

This emphasizes the essential concept of continuity in pupil learning over time through different phases of planning: long, medium and short term. In other words, this refers to a scheme of work, a unit of work and a lesson plan, respectively. A scheme of work is drawn from the National Curriculum subject PoS and contains what is planned for the pupils over a Key Stage or a year, regarding the knowledge, skills and processes required for each activity area. A unit of work represents a teacher's medium-term planning covering a shorter block of time (eg a few weeks or a term). A unit is derived from a scheme of work. The number of units may vary between areas and the number of lessons in each unit may vary from school to school. A unit should introduce pupils to a new aspect of learning; build on previous learning; identify the most appropriate teaching styles to be used; and identify available resources/facilities and how they might be used. Sometimes the terms 'schemes of work' and 'units of work' are used interchangeably – this is not a problem as long as the concept of continuity and progression in pupil learning is acknowledged and maintained through increasingly more specific planning.[3]

> The need for continuity and flow in your teaching is most important, not only through one lesson, but also from one lesson to another and throughout a whole unit of work. Continuity and progression can be achieved if you have carefully thought out your objectives for the lesson and for the unit and if you constantly work towards these objectives, both in your planning and teaching. (Capel, 1997: 27)

Importantly, the trainee must appreciate that what *is* to be learnt needs to be linked with what *has* been learnt, if planning is to be effective. This means that the process of planning is far from linear in its organization. It should be considered more as a spiral so that elements can be practised and consolidated to support effective learning for pupils. The formulation of learning objectives for a future lesson will be dependent on the trainee's interpretation of the pupils' background and the evaluation of the achievement of learning objectives in previous lessons.

2. Selection of learning material

Kyriacou (1986) makes an important distinction between 'content' and 'lesson organization' when referring to the selection of learning activities. The selection of learning material can come under the banner of 'content'. Even with the National Curriculum framework and the need to adhere to the PoS for the area, there is still a great deal of autonomy for teachers when selecting learning material. Fundamentally, teachers must know what the pupils already know, so that they can extend their knowledge and understanding from 'where they are now'. As with the establishment of learning objectives, when selecting appropriate learning materials the teacher must ascertain the pupils' present knowledge, understanding and skills related to the area of study, but must also ensure that these, or a development in them, can satisfy the learning outcomes established for the lesson.

It is the whole planning process which allows teachers to consider the best breakdown of conceptually appropriate steps in order to achieve the desired educational objectives for the particular pupils in the given context. However, this is also one of the most challenging and daunting aspects of planning for trainees. Not only does it require them to select content, but also to separate the topic into sections that are progressive, meeting the needs of all the learners in achieving the learning outcomes. This is a complicated and interrelated process for any teacher, but especially the trainee. Therefore, what are the repertoire of demands placed on the trainee to achieve this? Once again good content knowledge is essential, along with an awareness of how to sequence elements of the topic relative to the needs of the pupils.

3. Organization of learning activities

Lessons can be structured in a wide variety of ways depending on the nature of the subject, as well as the particular focus within it. If one considers what is probably the most basic organization of a lesson, it would be one that has three reinforcing components. The first would be the introduction to the lesson, in which the topic would be outlined. The second component would comprise the main learning activities. Finally, there would be a review of the learning that has occurred in the lesson. It is essential when deciding on the structure of the lesson that it is considered in an holistic manner. In other words, what is the total experience the pupils will receive and will it achieve the intended learning outcomes?

Whatever the organization of the lesson and the learning activities, they must sustain the interest, attention and motivation of the pupils. In order to do this there has to be variety in the activities. This equates to the use of a variety of teaching styles which help to facilitate different ways of learning in conjunction with opportunities for pupils to practise, give and receive feedback, read, and listen to theory about how to do it. The selection of elements and the amount of time that teachers spend on the activity and the way in which they organize it in the given context will be significant in terms of influencing the tone and atmosphere of the learning environment.

Everyone can have difficulty in planning for differentiation, not just trainees. However, if all pupils are to learn effectively, then differentiation is important. Table 5.3 identifies a variety of ways in which one could differentiate an activity which can and should be incorporated in planning to assist pupils to achieve personal learning targets, including those pupils with special needs. (One must remember that special needs equates not only to the less able but also to the very able.)

Table 5.3 Different forms of differentiation

Differentiation through:	
Outcome	in which the teacher may set tasks that are appropriate for the pupils' starting level, or pupils might answer the task as set according to their level of ability
Content	appropriate tasks – differentiation may be achieved offering a range of more difficult tasks in which pupils may choose to enter the learning situation, or in which different individuals or groups may have different roles or responsibilities. Pupils should have the opportunity to experience all of these roles
Pace	the pace at which pupils perform may well be a function of physical fitness and capacity as well as cognition or concentration (eg, PE)
Level	this may be related to differentiation through pace. Where task cards are progressive, perhaps through setting increasingly demanding and complex tasks, pupils may be working at different levels as well as at a pace appropriate to their abilities
Teaching Style	use of a range of teaching styles and approaches can elicit different responses from pupils. Some of these responses will match individual's preferred learning styles better than others
Grouping	appropriate pupil groupings (eg, by friendship, ability, group or individual activities). The majority of groupings are selected by the teacher to maintain safety and differentiate; however, some contexts allow pupils to choose whether they work alone, in pairs or in larger groups and may also accommodate individual differences and preferences
Resources	do all pupils have to have the same resources or is there potential for some variation dependent upon ability? Appropriate equipment for different levels of ability (eg, different size/weight of ball, varying target size/height, varying distances from the target, increased size of work cards)

Adapted from Williams (1996) and Mawer (1995)

4. Specification of evaluation procedures

In order to determine whether the lesson is effective in terms of being able to achieve the learning outcomes, a teacher needs to monitor and assess pupils' progress and attainment. Concurrently, the teacher will be receiving feedback on what aspects of the original plan are satisfactory or may require modification in order to achieve learning outcomes. As Kyriacou (1991) identifies, 'this requires more than just being responsive and reactive to feedback'; it means the teacher needs 'to be active, and to probe, question, check whether the progress and attainment intended are occurring.' Therefore, there is a great deal of forethought required by the trainee. For example, the bridging organization or transitions within lessons are ideal times to involve the whole class, small groups or individuals in questions and evaluation of the learning outcomes so far. This is an ongoing approach in lessons. There is also the more formal assessment of homework and tests, which can assess certain learning outcomes.

Integral to this process is the self-reflection of the trainees/teachers with regard to their planning and teaching performance. As a consequence of the pupils' responses teachers need to alter and modify schemes and units.

> Without a well thought out and structured self-reflection strategy, it is easy to drift aimlessly into a limited form of reflection based purely on aspects of teaching that cross your mind at a particular moment in time. A well-structured self-reflection strategy worked out in advance ensures that all aspects of your teaching performance are reflected upon during the unit of work. (Mawer, 1995: 89)

There are a myriad of questions that could be asked about numerous elements of the lesson when a trainee comes to evaluate it. Therefore, it is important to maintain some kind of progressive focus. But on what? If one considers three categories of questions regarding the pupils, the material and the teacher, certain questions can be asked of the trainee, such as:

Pupils
- How many pupils had difficulty learning the tasks set? Which pupils?
- How many pupils found the tasks too easy? Which pupils?
- Did the class always understand the explanations? If not, how could this be improved?

Materials
- To what extent were the lesson objectives achieved?
- To what extent were the activities appropriate for the age and ability of the pupils?
- How successful were attempts to differentiate activities during the lesson?

Teacher
- How will you modify your learning activities and objectives in the light of the answers to the above questions?
- What aspects of the lesson caused most time to be wasted? Why?
- How effective were the teaching approaches used? Were they appropriate for the objective for the lesson, the pupils and the activities being taught? If not, how will you modify your teaching approaches in the light of the answers to the other questions?

(Adapted from Mawer, 1995.)

So many questions could be asked after each lesson; however, the important point is that there is a focus to the evaluation and self-reflection by the trainees and their mentors and that it is relevant to the trainees' understanding and stage of development. In fact the focus of the lesson evaluation should be a follow-up from a previous lesson to see how the established targets have been developed. Of course new elements will be highlighted and identified in terms of targets, but at this point it is the notion of development and progression that needs to be understood and facilitated collaboratively by the mentor and trainee.

5. Preparation of materials, resources and props

The preparation and organization of the teaching environment and the equipment required are essential if the lesson is to be successful and fulfil the learning outcomes planned for. Preparation also includes the need to prepare assessment materials. Such materials need to be built into the planning of lessons both generally and specifically, and a formal note made of pupils' performance. When doing this the teacher needs to be clear about the realistic number of assessments to be made in a lesson, as well as the procedures that will be adopted. Plans will also be required for how records are to be made and kept, especially when one considers that a variety of assessment materials will be used and types of responses given (eg direct observations of pupils' behaviour, questioning in verbal and written form, paper and pencil texts, and information derived from normal coursework, including homework) (Kyriacou, 1991).

When preparing any materials it is essential that they are of a good quality and care has been taken to present them in the best manner possible. The time and effort taken to prepare them is likely be reflected in their positive reception by the pupils. For example, why should pupils read a scrap of scruffy paper when it is clear it has just been thrown together at the last minute, they can't read it all, and it contains errors? A colourful, laminated and word-processed task card with bold images on it is much more stimulating and motivating and creates a much more positive working environment.

When using equipment or materials of any kind for a practical session or experiment, it is important that teachers undertake some form of rehearsal to familiarize themselves with the equipment and identify potential problems that may occur. Another reason is that the equipment might be different to what the teacher has used before. It is important to note that such rehearsal by the teacher should also include an evaluation from the perspective of the pupil. So when the equipment or material are arranged, one needs to ask, is it user-friendly for the pupils? Regardless of the length of time spent preparing, and the belief that nothing could go wrong, the trainee should always have an alternative available that will be able to deliver the lesson's learning outcomes.

Any materials produced or purchased as part of the preparation for a lesson must always be appropriate to the learning outcomes that are intended for the lesson. It should not be the case that the resource was selected merely because it was readily available to purchase.

Prepare to be successful

The planning process is extremely complicated and has numerous interrelated aspects. Consequently, it is a process that is constantly developing and evolving for trainees as they increase their experience and understanding. This movement towards *internalization* of the planning process, and increasing understanding and facilitation of the concept of instructional alignment, is important, but it will vary from trainee to trainee. However, there are some common strands and these have been highlighted and simplified in this chapter. One thing always remains the same: in order to be successful in achieving the desired learning outcomes for a lesson there has to be effective planning and preparation.

Planning is therefore an essential feature of pedagogical thinking and reasoning. Planning appears to mediate between a teacher's basic knowledge of the subject being taught and his or her ability to teach the subject effectively, because it brings into play the teacher's general pedagogical content knowledge. This includes knowledge of theories and principles of teaching and learning, knowledge of the learner, and knowledge of the techniques and principles of teaching such as class management. The plan for a lesson, unit or course is the result of a considerable degree of thinking on the part of the teacher. (Mawer, 1995: 55)

This is a continual and evolutionary process towards internalization for every teacher. The nature of the framework that guides it fundamentally remains the same. However, it is the emphasis placed on certain elements at certain times which focuses the attention of trainee teachers in their quest to facilitate the most effective pupil learning.

Task 5.1

With your mentor discuss the topic areas you are expected to teach and the learning outcomes you intend to achieve. Before planning your lessons and schemes of work find out the following:

- What has been taught on the topic area already?
- What is the time-scale for you to teach the topic area?
- What resources will you need and what will the school supply?
- How much of the work will be assessed?
- How will you monitor and report pupil progress?

Task 5.2

With your mentor collaboratively plan a unit of work which includes at least six lessons with one class. Discuss with your mentor how you will ensure continuity and progression within and between lessons, clearly identifying how you will achieve the learning objectives.

Notes

1. In its entirety Section B is headed: Planning, Teaching and Class Management. The fact that planning has been highlighted in this chapter should certainly not detract from the essential interrelationship that exists between planning and class management in achieving learning objectives.
2. The term 'teacher' has been used here as well as 'mentor' because, within the mentoring process, trainees will not only work with their assigned mentor within their particular subject department, but they must also experience the approach, work, etc of other members of the department so that they can appreciate the essential individuality they will ultimately generate in their teaching approach and style. The crucial thing here is the timing of this process relative to the experience and needs of the trainee.
3. The term 'progression' here is taken to refer to the planned development of knowledge, skills, understanding or attitudes over time (Capel *et al*, 1997).

References

Borko, H and Niles, T (1987) Description of teacher planning, in *Educators' Handbook: A research perspective*, ed V Richardson-Koehler, pp 167–87, Longman, White Plains, NY

Capel, S (ed) (1997) *Learning to Teach Physical Education in the Secondary School: A companion to school experience*, Routledge, London

Capel, S, Leask, M and Turner, T (eds) (1997) *Starting to Teach in the Secondary School: A companion for the newly qualified teacher*, Routledge, London

Clark, C M and Yinger, R J (1987) Teacher planning, in *Exploring Teachers Thinking*, ed J Calderhead, pp 84–103, Cassell, London

Cochran, K F, De Tuiter, J A and King, R A (1993) Pedagogical content knowing: an integrated model for teacher preparation, *Journal of Teacher Education*, **44** (4)

Cohen, S (1987) Instructional alignment: searching for the magic bullet, *Educational Researcher*, November, pp 16–20

DfEE (1997) *High Status, High Standards: Requirements for courses of initial teacher training*, Circular 10/97, DfEE, London

DfEE (1998) *Requirements for Courses of Initial Teacher Training*, Circular 4/98, DfEE, London

Fink, J and Siedentop, D (1989) The development of routines, rules and expectations at the start of the school year, *Journal of Teaching in Physical Education*, **8** (3), pp 198–212

Hardy, C (1996) Trainees' concerns, experiences and needs: implications for mentoring in physical education, in *Mentoring in Physical Education: Issues and insights*, ed M Mawer, Falmer Press, London

Kelly, L, Whitehead, M and Capel, S (1997) Lesson organization and management, in *Learning to Teach Physical Education in the Secondary School: A companion to school experience*, ed S Capel, Routledge, London

Kelly, T and Mayes, A (1995) *Issues in Mentoring*, Routledge, London

Kyriacou, C (1986) *Effective Teaching in Schools*, Blackwell, Oxford

Kyriacou, C (1991) *Essential Teaching Skills*, Stanley Thornes, Cheltenham

Leask, M (1995) Taking responsibility for whole lessons, in *Learning to Teach in the Secondary School: A companion to school experience*, ed S Capel, M Leask and T Turner, Routledge, London

Leask, M and Davison, J (1995) Schemes of work and lesson planning, in *Learning to Teach in the Secondary School: A companion to school experience*, ed S Capel, M Leask and T Turner, Routledge, London

McIntyre, D (ed) (1997) *Teacher Education Research in a New Context: The Oxford Internship Scheme*, Paul Chapman Publishing, London

Mawer, M (1995) *The Effective Teaching of Physical Education*, Longman, Harlow

Shulman, L (1986) Those who understand: knowledge growth in teaching, *Educational Research*, **15** (2), pp 4–14

Taylor, P H (1970) *How Teachers Plan Their Courses*, National Foundation for Educational Research, Slough

Tyler, R W (1950) *Basic Principles of Curriculum and Instruction*, University of Chicago Press, Chicago, IL

Williams, A (1996) *Teaching Physical Education: A guide for mentors and students*, David Fulton, London

6 Teaching and classroom management

Mike Waring

This chapter will guide the trainee through the requirements and development of classroom management skills. It shows that to reach the required standards trainees, with the help of their mentors, need to constantly reflect and reconsider what they do in the classroom in order to minimize disruption and create effective learning environments. The emphasis is on the trainee understanding the relationship between pupil behaviour and classroom management skills, by focusing on issues such as rules and routines, positive climates for learning, relationships, motivational aspects and strategies for monitoring classroom behaviour.

Objectives

By the end of this chapter the trainee should understand:

- the need to establish effective learning environments;
- the need to establish rules and routines with pupils;
- the relationship between good planning, preparation and classroom behaviour;
- the need to create motivating and positive classroom environments;
- the need to establish monitoring strategies for classroom behaviour.

Introduction

Teaching and Classroom Management (Section B.2.f-n) forms the second portion of Section B in Circular 10/97 in addition to 'Planning'. This is a significant point for the trainee and mentor to consider and consistently reflect upon, as there is a fundamental interrelationship between these two aspects, each impacting on the effectiveness and development of the other. The emphasis may be different between phases, but the underlying principles remain the same.

Under the heading of 'Teaching and Classroom Management' in Circular 10/97 there are a number of statements outlining those components that each trainee has to satisfy in order to gain QTS. These are shown in Table 6.1.

The intention in this chapter is to identify some of the key aspects of teaching and classroom management which will allow the trainee and mentor to explore the meaning and underlying processes associated with them and in so doing enhance their development as effective teachers.

What is meant by 'teaching and classroom management'? A simple but effective definition provided by Capel *et al* (1997: 78) is:

> Effective classroom management is essential to effective learning. Classroom management refers to the arrangements made by the teacher to establish and maintain an environment in which learning can occur, eg effective organization and presentation of lessons so that pupils are actively engaged in learning.

Good planning and preparation allow trainees to develop many areas of their teaching, not least their confidence. However, when trainees are attempting to create and maintain an 'effective learning environment' in their lessons, one of the biggest concerns they have is related to class control, management and organization (Hardy, 1996).

Establishing an effective learning environment

Establishing an effective learning environment requires the trainee to understand that there is a difference between managing behaviour and managing learning. Each requires a different set of skills that trainees should develop with the help of their mentor. It is important that the trainee has a sound grasp of the fundamental class management skills to facilitate and maintain appropriate behaviour because it is on this foundation of management, facilitated by good planning, that effective learning is based and can be developed. Therefore, the establishment and sustainability of an effective learning environment is due to a number of predominantly proactive rather than reactive decisions made by the teacher.

Table 6.1 Teaching and Classroom Management (Circular 10/97, B2)

Ensure effective teaching of whole classes, and of groups and individuals within the whole-class setting, so that teaching objectives are met and best use is made of available teaching time.	2(f)
Monitor and intervene when teaching to ensure sound learning and discipline.	2(g)
Establish and maintain a purposeful working atmosphere.	2(h)
Set high expectations of pupils' behaviour, establishing and maintaining a good standard of discipline through well focused teaching and through positive relationships.	2(i)
Establish a safe environment which supports learning and in which pupils feel secure and confident.	2(j)

Use teaching methods which sustain the momentum of pupils' work and keep all pupils 2(k) engaged through:
(i) stimulating intellectual curiosity, communicating enthusiasm for the subject being taught, fostering pupils' enthusiasm and maintaining pupils' motivation;
(ii) matching approaches used to the subject matter and pupils' being taught;
(iii) structuring information well, including outlining content and aims, signalling transitions and summarising key points as the lesson progresses;
(iv) clear presentation of content around a set of key ideas, using appropriate subject-specific vocabulary and well chosen illustrations and examples;
(v) clear instruction and demonstration, and accurate well-paced explanation;
(vi) effective questioning which matches the pace and direction of the lesson and ensures that pupils take part;
(vii) careful attention to pupils' errors and misconceptions, and helping to remedy them;
(viii) listening carefully to pupils, analysing their responses and responding constructively in order to take pupils' learning forward;
(ix) selecting and making good use of textbooks, IT and other learning resources which enable teaching objectives to be met;
(x) providing opportunities for pupils to consolidate their knowledge and maximising opportunities both in the classroom and through setting well focused homework to reinforce and develop what has been learnt;
(xi) exploiting opportunities to improve pupils' basic skills in literacy, numeracy and IT, and the individual and collaborative study skills needed for effective learning, including information retrieval from libraries, texts and other sources;
(xii) exploiting opportunities to contribute to the quality of pupils' wider educational development, including their personal, spiritual, moral, social and cultural development;
(xiii) setting high expectations for all pupils notwithstanding individual difference, including gender, and cultural and linguistic backgrounds;
(xiv) providing opportunities to develop pupils' wider understanding by relating their learning to real and work-related examples.

Make effective use of assessment information on pupils' attainment and progress in their teaching and in planning future lessons and sequences of lessons.	2(l)

Rules and routines within class management

Brophy's (1983) term 'proactive problem prevention' is one which highlights the need for advanced planning and detailed consideration by trainees regarding the kind of learning environment they wish to establish and maintain not only in each individual lesson, but over a period of time.

What are the rules and routines in the context of class management? Rules identify general expectations for behaviour that cover a variety of situations (Siedentop, 1991: 95). Mawer (1995) develops this further by stating that a rule defines general expectations of acceptable and unacceptable behaviour that will cover different situations; for example, expecting pupils to be quiet and attentive when the teacher is talking (p 93). Rules must remain flexible, so that they can be altered effectively to the changing circumstances of the context – that is the interrelationship between the teacher, pupil and classroom. However, the teacher must endeavour to enforce rules on a continual basis. Teachers also need to consider the extent to which they intend to specify consequences for rule violations. Once again these decisions will have a bearing on the way in which the relationship between the teachers and the pupils will be framed and maintained and consequently the nature of their planning.

Routines may be considered to be a compromise between procedures established by the school, the pupils' expectations from other classes, and the teacher's own values and ideas. More specifically Siedentop (1991: 95) identifies routines as procedures for performing specific behaviours within a class, particularly those behaviours that recur regularly. Consequently, routines have to be established from the very beginning of those encounters between the teacher and the class and need to be reassessed and reapplied throughout the year. The effective use of routines can save a great deal of learning time and minimize disruption within the context of the lesson. However, if they are to be effective, routines need to have the consent of the pupils. This consent is facilitated by a clear rationale shared between the teacher and the pupils. A learning environment that is governed by accurately planned, open and well-understood routines is more likely to be a productive one.

The distinction between rules and routines has fundamental implications for the way in which a trainee and mentor will work towards developing the teaching and classroom management competencies of the trainee. A rule attempts to specify a generalized behaviour which can occur in a number of differing situations, whereas a routine is a constant procedural matter specific to the context. This means that the management of the situation will require different skills and techniques to initiate and maintain a positive and effective learning environment.

What do these 'rules' generally relate to? When one considers the nature of rules they tend to relate to the following areas (adapted from Mawer, 1995; Siedentop, 1991):

- respect for others, pupils and teacher;
- respect for the learning environment;
- safety;
- support for the learning of others/attitude to work rules.

In every classroom, whether it be Reception or Year 11, teachers have to set classroom rules that are relevant, positive and that the pupils can relate to. Creating a positive atmosphere requires the teacher to use rules that highlight what is acceptable as opposed to that which is less desirable. This is something that Cohen and Manion (1989) acknowledge, along with 'relevance' and 'meaningfulness', as part of their rationale for the recommendation that rules should be kept to a minimum. It is possible to identify some simple guidelines that a trainee and mentor can consider in order to create the most appropriate class rules:

- Keep the rules 'short and sweet' and very much to the point.
- State rules positively, providing mainly positive, but also negative examples.
- Ensure that the terminology used for the rules can be understood by those they apply to.
- Ensure that the rules are supported by and consistent with school-wide rules.
- Identify and consistently apply consequences to rules, ensuring that you are willing to enforce them.
- Do not provide too many rules to be applied and remembered in any given context – a maximum of six.

Routines need to be established if trainees are to be successful in their classroom management skills, that is:

- managing work and movement (getting pupils on-task);
- managing relationships and reinforcing expectations of attitudes and behaviour (firm, fair and friendly);
- gaining attention – for pupils and the teacher (verbal and non-verbal cues).

Kelly *et al* (1997: 79) develop these three areas when they outline the organizational issues associated with: the teacher (being organized and the presentation of self); the environment/working space (preparation before lessons, establishing authority and expectations); the pupils/equipment (planning and strategies for organizing); and the timing of the lesson (planning and progression). The teacher is a role model and must therefore set a good example in being prepared and organized prior to the lesson. Once again the issue of planning consistently highlights itself as a significant foundation on which to be an effective teacher. Kelly *et al* (1997: 80) offer a checklist to organize the start of the lesson; this is shown in Table 6.2.

Table 6.2   Checklist for trainees to organize the start of a lesson

Prepared the lesson:	Learning outcomes clearly identified in advance
Marked homework:	Meeting deadlines and positive, useful feedback; associated with motivation of pupil
Checked the working space:	Is it available and safe to use?
Checked and counted all equipment:	Is it readily available and in good order?
Established entry into the classroom:	Orderly and quiet
Established routines:	Attending to such tasks as coats and bags and handing out books
Taken the register:	This needs to be done without wasting too much time (eg, during organization of books, etc)
Established routines:	Organizing the taking out of equipment

Have resources ready to use in the appropriate place (eg, visual aids, work cards, additional materials, etc)

Such a checklist supports the identification of various routines offered by Mawer (1995) when he explores Fink and Siedentop's (1989) five different kinds of routines adopted throughout a lesson:

1. *Preliminary routines* – entering/leaving the classroom; introductory activity; pupils' method of gaining teachers' attention; teachers' method of gaining pupils' attention and request for quiet.
2. *Transitional management routines* – pupil dispersal (eg to the work area); pupil gathering (eg for demonstrations); equipment movement (eg taking out and putting away); group work (movement into pairs, small and large groups).
3. *Instructional management routines* – starting activities; defining boundaries of work area (whole group, small group and individual).
4. *Housekeeping routines* – record keeping; accidents; collecting valuables.
5. *Closure routines* – finishing the activity; leaving the work space.

These are all routines which trainees need to consider, experiment with and develop in order to organize their lessons, as well as to address teaching and classroom management standards and to appreciate and develop the essential association with those aspects of their planning standards. Observing other teachers and discussing with their mentor the most appropriate rules and routines for them to use and develop in the context of one or a series of lessons, are important components of understanding and developing these standards for the trainee. However, it is never straightforward: one has to consider constantly the complex evolving interrelationship between the teacher and the pupils both on a personal and a practical level.

A positive climate for learning

The climate in the classroom facilitated by the teacher will have a significant effect on the nature of the learning environment. Embroiled in the creation and maintenance of a positive learning environment are a number of interrelating factors. Kyriacou (1986: 101) makes the distinction between teaching qualities and tasks:

> In looking at effective teaching a useful distinction can be drawn between the general *qualities* of effective teaching and the component *tasks* involved. The qualities focus on broad aspects of teaching which appear to be important in determining its effectiveness, such as good rapport with pupils or pitching the work at the appropriate level of difficulty. The tasks refer to the activities and practices involved in teaching, such as planning a lesson or assessing pupils' progress.

As Kyriacou continues to point out, these are very much interrelated; however, the search for *qualities* is explicitly judgmental in character and may cut across a number of different *tasks* involved in teaching. With this in mind the next portion of this chapter will discuss issues related to the creation and maintenance of a good/positive learning environment.

What constitutes the best kind of classroom climate in terms of facilitating pupil learning? It has been described as one which is purposeful, task-oriented, relaxed, warm, supportive and has a sense of order (Kyriacou, 1991). The creation of such an environment influences the motivation of the pupils, creating a positive attitude towards their learning.

In terms of teaching skills, creating a purposeful and business-like classroom climate means that the teacher should not only be well organized and well prepared, but start lessons on time, keep lessons running smoothly and monitor pupils' work and progress (Mawer, 1995). It is the acceptance by the pupils of the teacher's organization and management of tasks, as well as their willingness to produce a positive effort in relation to the task, that characterizes the purposeful and task-oriented environment. This positive orientation is facilitated by the teacher establishing challenging yet realistic opportunities for success within the lessons. This gives learners the opportunity to build their self-esteem through productive, constructive and supportive experiences. Once again it is the teacher who is the catalyst for this in terms of planning interesting and meaningful experiences that take into account individual differences and in so doing allows for challenging yet realistically attainable learning experiences. Of course there is the other side of the coin in terms of a negative 'self-fulfilling prophecy' in which the teacher's prior knowledge and experience of a pupil may interfere with the kind of support that the teacher offers the pupil, which in turn influences the pupil's learning, initiating a negative cycle. In order to prevent this negative expectancy effect and retain a positive learning environment, teachers should try to keep their expectations flexible and current, adopting a present perspective rather than an 'historical' one. They can also avoid direct comparison with other pupils and instead concentrate on the individual's current understanding. The differentiation of activities allows all pupils to meet the demands of the task, as the teacher takes into account the potential learning difficulties of each pupil. Having set clear and realistic goals that the pupil can achieve, it is important that these outcomes are acknowledged and valued within the lesson.

Relationships

The type of relationship teachers establish with their pupils will influence the classroom climate. A positive climate is most likely to be achieved where there is mutual respect and rapport between the teacher and the pupils. It is important that the trainee is able to convey a sense of understanding and value of the pupil's perspective on an array of issues (academic, personal and social) to facilitate a caring and empathetic relationship. This has to be a two-way process where the pupils similarly reciprocate respect for the teacher's point of view. However, there are potential problems associated with a trainee attempting to create a rapport, not least being over-friendly with the pupils so that the necessary divide between teacher and pupil is blurred or lost. It is a difficult skill to achieve, but as Kyriacou (1991) points out, 'as an adult, and given your role (*teacher*), it is up to you to have a major influence in establishing such a harmonious relationship in the classroom.'

A sense of humour is another element of the relationship with pupils that can create uncertainty for the trainee, in that it is has the potential to be misinterpreted or get out of hand. A sense of humour is consistently cited as an important element in the teacher-pupil relationship (Capel *et al*, 1997; Kyriacou, 1991; Mawer, 1995), but it must be used appropriately. That is it should be used to complement strategies for behaviour management, for example to diffuse a situation or break the tension of a particular moment in the lesson. Humour must not be used too frequently or at the expense of pupils, as these have negative consequences with regards to over-familiarity and inhibiting pupil self-esteem, respectively.

Monitoring the class

Regardless of the fact that teachers may establish clear, challenging and reasonable tasks, there will be pupils who work to negotiate the boundaries of teacher expectations with a view to expanding their own terms. In an attempt to maintain the necessary 'dominance' in the relationship teachers need to monitor what the pupils are doing and assess their compliance with the task. Pupils are expected to be accountable for their work and adhere to the expectations of the teacher, but the teacher needs to deliberately monitor the learning environment in order to determine this. Effective monitoring of a class is achieved through good movement around the room and effective positioning. It is essential that teachers circulate around the class in such a way that they are able to see the entire class. This usually demands moving around the periphery. By keeping the whole class in view teachers are able to interact on a number of levels with individuals, pairs and small groups as well as the whole group, while at the same time being confident that if anything untoward was to happen in the learning environment (ie pupils being off-task or safety issues) they could pre-empt or quickly deal with them. Safety is a very important issue, especially if the fundamental nature of the activity is such that problems can occur (for example, an experiment or gymnastics lesson).

So, monitoring the class, along with the rules and routines that the teacher establishes and reinforces in lessons, is a significant classroom management skill. In addition to this there is a motivational issue. Just as the negative aspect of behaviour can be identified by teachers, so they should highlight the positive outcomes. Reinforcement of good work and application by the teacher is facilitated by good positioning and constant scanning of the class. Therefore, effective class monitoring is an important skill in preventative class management and keeping pupils on-task and safe. The potential sources of disruption or misbehaviour and monitoring techniques that might be employed to pre-empt or combat them are shown in Table 6.3.

Table 6.3 Matching the aspects of misbehaviour and its origins with potential monitoring techniques

Aspects of misbehaviour and its origins		Monitoring techniques	
Cause	Characteristics or origin	Technique	Characteristic
Boredom	Lack of relevance to activity Work too hard or too easy Demands prolonged concentration	Scanning	Frequently look around the room; sitting yourself where can see most pupils while you talk to individual pupils

Aspects of misbehaviour and its origins		Monitoring techniques	
Cause	Characteristics or origin	Technique	Characteristic
Excessive intellectual demands	Work is too hard or takes too much time	Circulating	Move around the work area, look at work, give praise or support, anticipate problems, ensure pupils are on task
Frustration	Work is too difficult or language is too hard. Other pupils can do it easily. Unable to contribute to class or group	Making eye contact	Address whole class and engage them; use eye contact for control; avoid interrupting flow of lesson
Low self-esteem	History of past failures causes lack of confidence. Easier not to do the work than fail again. Often feels 'picked on'	Asking questions	Target pupils; involve as many people as possible over the lesson period
Emotional difficulties	Unable to adjust to working with others; not valued at home, or even abused. Is a bully or sustains bullying from peers. Employs attention-seeking behaviours	Using space	Circulate among the pupils. When needed, use the whole room to separate pupils or groups from the main class
Lack of perceived pastoral structure in school	Unclear code of conduct and/or sanctions. Teacher does not apply rules fairly or consistently. May be construed as lack of care	Supporting	Give appropriate help, either motivational, by encouragement or academic by advice. Acknowledging the progress of pupils inhibits off-task behaviour
Teacher, school ethos	Pupil seen as a problem instead of the system failing the pupil. School unable to respond to pupil's needs	Changing activity	Alter the pace of work; signal changes by acknowledging those pupils who have yet to finish earlier work and ensuring they know what to do
Peer pressure	Some pupils may be influenced by other pupils with apparent credibility in the wider world; or who bully or offer inducements	Encouraging individuals	Ensure that all know that you are aware of their progress; encourage or praise good work for each pupil. Keep the individual in mind
Dislike of teacher	Teachers are disliked who are unfair, have favourites, apply rules arbitrarily or pick on people, do not prepare their lessons, arrive late	Acting	Insist on courtesies between pupils and between you and the pupil; confront disrespect. Address misbehaviour when it occurs or, if possible, prevent it. See scanning and circulating above. Remind pupils of rules and address violations

(Adapted from Turner, 1997)

The task for the trainee and mentor is to match the most appropriate monitoring techniques with aspects of misbehaviour and their origins so that they can attempt to incorporate them more effectively in their preparation and delivery of the lesson.

So far the emphasis has been predominantly on teaching *qualities*. However, if we turn our attention to teaching *tasks* we can identify the underlying interrelated aspect of a teacher's decision making. This will help illustrate for trainees and their mentors the significant principles underpinning their teaching.

Reflection and evaluation

Forming a continuous cycle underlying the teacher's decision making are three main groups: planning, presentation and monitoring, and reflection and evaluation (Kyriacou, 1991). Planning is a fundamental component of effective teaching and classroom management. Similarly the presentation and monitoring of lessons informs the teacher's decisions about the nature of the progression and interpretation of the learning context. In other words, the teacher's teaching skills involved in carrying out tasks of teaching will determine the extent to which pupils learn based on the three psychological conditions of attentiveness, receptiveness and appropriateness (Kyriacou, 1991). The whole notion of planning has been explored in detail in Chapter 5, so the focus of the remainder of this chapter will be on the reflective aspects teachers have to continue to develop if they are to enhance the quality of the learning experience for pupils.

Having considered a myriad of different interrelating aspects, both practical and theoretical, in an attempt to make the learning environment an effective one in the delivery of lessons, it is essential to evaluate and reflect upon the lesson's success in terms of class management: has it worked in achieving the desired learning outcomes? For many teachers, and especially trainees, the primary consideration when evaluating and reflecting on their lessons on a day-to-day basis will be whether their class management has been good enough to deliver what was intended in the way it was intended. However, there is the potential with such a focus to ignore the learning outcomes and concentrate solely on implementation. Therefore, the mentor and trainee must consider *both*, whichever they decide to focus on in the main. Reflection allows teachers to reconsider what is satisfactory and arrive at developmentally alternative interpretations that will make their teaching and the environment more sensitive to the learning of the pupil. As part of this there is the need to reflect upon the assessment and recording of the educational progress of the pupils. The formal assessment of learning in school (marked work, examinations, etc) provides a source of feedback on a pupil's academic attainment. It also forms a vehicle whereby the teacher can diagnose difficulties and problems that can then be remedied by feedback accompanying the marking, and specifically addressed in future lessons (Kyriacou, 1991: 128). Ultimately, when teachers have evaluated and reflected upon their teaching and its outcomes, those alterations and amendments which have been put in place themselves need evaluating and reflecting upon. It must be emphasized that teaching is intended to promote learning; if the priority of the lesson becomes class management then learning will not be the focus of the evaluation of the lesson:

> Class management tasks overshadow learning management. In such cirumstances, assessment is often confined to reporting attainment rather than to inform teaching. However, you need to assess if the lack of attention to learning strategies has caused the class management problems in the first place … The focus on class teaching because of class management priorities may reduce the opportunities to promote cognitive development. (Turner, 1997: 83)

The organization and management of lessons is only one portion of the whole framework for developing effective teaching. However, it is a fundamental portion which involves a myriad of factors that have to be considered and applied relative to the interrelationship between each individual teacher, the pupils they are teaching, the context, and the content of the lesson. The importance of thorough and accurate planning becomes clearly evident, but it must always be remembered that it is the management of *learning* that is most desirable, rather than the management of behaviour. Even though the latter may help facilitate the former, it is crucial when evaluating and reflecting upon their teaching that trainees and mentors constantly revisit the fact that it is the management of learning which is critical.

Task 6.1

Observe a series of lessons and try to identify what you think is misbehaviour. Discuss this with your mentor and try to establish how you might have anticipated, prevented or dealt with such behaviour.

Task 6.2

You should (assisted by discussions with your mentor, other departmental colleagues and the collation of departmental and school documentation) observe, record and reflect upon the different rules and routines established in a variety of situations within your department.

References

Brophy, J (1983) Classroom organization and management, *Elementary School Journal*, **83**, pp 265–85

Capel, S (ed) (1997) *Learning to Teach Physical Education in the Secondary School: A companion to school experience*, Routledge, London

Capel, S, Leask, M and Turner, T (eds) (1997) *Starting to Teach in the Secondary School: A companion for the newly qualified teacher*, Routledge, London

Cohen, L and Manion, L (1989) *A Guide to Teaching Practice*, 3rd edn, Holt, Rinehart and Winston, London

Department for Education and Employment (1997) *High Status, High Standards: Requirements for courses of initial teacher training*, Circular 10/97, DfEE, London

Fink, J and Siedentop, D (1989) The development of routines, rules and expectations at the start of the school year, *Journal of Teaching in Physical Education*, **8** (3), pp 198–212

Hardy, C (1996) Trainees' concerns, experiences and needs: implications for mentoring in physical education, in *Mentoring in Physical Education: Issues and insights*, ed M Mawer, Falmer Press, London

Kelly, L, Whitehead, M and Capel, S (1997) Lesson organization and management, in *Learning to Teach Physical Education in the Secondary School: A companion to school experience*, ed S Capel, Routledge, London

Kyriacou, C (1986) *Effective Teaching in Schools*, Blackwell, Oxford

Kyriacou, C (1991) *Essential Teaching Skills*, Stanley Thornes, Cheltenham

Mawer, M (1995) *The Effective Teaching of Physical Education*, Longman, Harlow

Siedentop, D (1991) *Developing Teaching Skills in Physical Education*, 3rd edn, Mayfield Press, CA

Turner, T (1997) *Learning to Teach Science in the Secondary School*, Routledge, London

7

Assessment, recording and reporting

Gill Nicholls

This chapter directs the trainee to aspects of assessment, recording and reporting that will need to be developed in order to reach the standards laid down in Circular 4/98 (DfEE, 1998a). The trainee is introduced to the concepts of assessment, including the types of assessment they will be involved in. These include discussion on SATs, GCSEs, GNVQs and A levels, as well the whole concept of formative and summative assessment procedures. Key terms used in assessment are considered, as are their implications in recording and reporting the assessments made. Assessment is examined and explained from the everyday classroom perspective, including marking and homework, to the wider perspective of statutory examinations. The trainee is then introduced to the importance of recording and reporting assessment to a variety of audiences.

Objectives

By the end of this chapter the trainee should have a clear under-standing of:

- the nature of assessment, reporting and recording;
- formative and summative assessment;
- key terms used in assessment;
- the nature of marking and the need for effective marking and pupil feedback;
- the key issues related to recording;
- the need to report to a variety of audiences.

Introduction

Assessment, recording and reporting have central key issues that relate to all areas of the National Curriculum and its Key Stages. Assessment has several forms and is needed for a variety of purposes within teaching and learning. It provides information on individual pupil progress, helps teachers address areas of weakness, and gives parents information about their child's progress.

Assessing pupils' work is not a new venture, but within the last five years greater emphasis has been placed on assessment in schools, both formally through Standard Attainment Tasks (SATs), GCSEs, GNVQs and A levels, and informally through teacher assessment.

This chapter will be divided into two parts: assessment, and recording and reporting. This will help focus on the specific issues within each topic. The chapter will first discuss assessment: what assessment is, the forms it takes, and the relevance it has to teaching and learning. There are tasks to help understanding of assessment within the context of the classroom.

Assessment

Promoting children's learning is a principal aim of schools. Assessment lies at the heart of this process. It can provide a framework in which educational objectives may be set, and pupils' progress charted and expressed. It can yield a basis for planning the next educational steps in response to children's needs. By facilitating dialogue between teachers, it can enhance professional skills and help the school as a whole to strengthen learning across the curriculum and throughout its age range. (Report of the Task Group on Assessment and Testing)

This quotation suggests that assessment of children's learning and progress is central to effective teaching and learning. Reactions to assessment are rarely neutral; they are frequently influenced by prior experience and exposure to the assessment process, either as pupils in school or as students in higher education or professional activities.

In recent years the teachers' role in assessment has become a central task, and a major influence on their professional activities. This has increased their workloads and required even greater organizational skills to allow assessment tasks to be conducted systematically and effectively.

As aspiring teachers it is essential to understand the range and purposes that surround assessment, and distinguish between the different procedures, namely 'formative, summative and diagnostic assessment'.

Formative assessment

This is an ongoing process that teachers are involved in at two levels: formal and informal. This reflects the way teachers absorb the information and evidence related to pupils' learning, and how they use it to inform their future lessons, whether this is the next task or series of tasks.

The aim of this form of assessment is to promote effective further learning by pupils. This is achieved in a variety of ways including:

- giving pupils helpful feedback;
- giving the teacher feedback;
- identifying pupils' future learning needs.

The main focus of this form of assessment is to identify errors, difficulties and shortcomings in pupils' work. It also informs the teacher of the nature of advice and information needed to improve pupils' future learning outcomes.

Without formative assessment teachers could not function effectively. However, formative assessment is less useful for those who wish to have definite information about pupils' progress. The main audience here is parents and teachers in other schools, providers of further education and training and potential employers. This type of audience requires a summary of achievement and progress, in order to have an accurate picture of the pupil's/student's learning. This is commonly referred to as 'summative assessment'.

Summative assessment

This form of assessment identifies the standard of attainment achieved by an individual at a given moment in time, normally carried out at the end of a period of teaching or instruction. This would include SATs, end of term exams and end of course assessments.

The outcomes of such assessments are typically grades, or percentages used on school reports of attainment, Key Stage levels or results from external examinations.

Formative and summative assessment in relation to the National Curriculum

It is important to remember that assessment within the National Curriculum has two distinct parts. (There is a debate as to the extent to which any assessment system can serve both formative and summative functions; see Gipps, 1994.)

First there is the detailed formative information that forms the basis of communication about individual pupils to other teachers. This is the descriptive part of national assessment. However, it is the summative assessment information that has to be published. This summative material is there for accountability and political purposes. It is there to evaluate and monitor school performance rather than individual pupils.

As a result of assessment being used for a variety of audiences, both national and individual, schools have become involved in a diversity of assessment practices. The most important are formative and summative. However, there are a number of key terms teachers should be aware of within the assessment framework.

Key terms of assessment

Norm-referenced assessment

In norm-referenced assessment all the pupils' scores are put into a graph and a certain percentage are assigned each grade (eg only 10 per cent will gain a grade A, 20 per cent a grade B and so on). Alternatively a cut-off point is chosen for passing, allowing a certain percentage to pass and the rest to fail. What this reflects is that the grade pupils achieve and whether they pass or fail depends partly on the performance of the other pupils.

Criterion-referenced assessment

In this type of assessment, tasks are designed to reflect whether or not a student can do a specific task, or range of tasks, as opposed to measuring how good or bad a pupil's performance is in relation to other pupils.

In criterion-referenced assessments levels of achievement or criteria of performance are set and pupils are marked or graded according to whether they reach the level of attainment. In this form of assessment there is no limit to how many pupils achieve a given level (see Gipps and Stobart, 1993).

Norm-referenced and criterion-referenced assessment and the National Curriculum

The National Curriculum assessment procedures within the norm-referenced/criterion-referenced continuum are confusing. The national criteria for assessment are encapsulated in the attainment targets as described in the level descriptors within the National Curriculum framework. The intention is that it should be a criterion-referenced system in which pupils' attainments are assessed in terms of national levels, which are determined with reference to statements of attainment.

Internal assessment

These are teacher-oriented tasks. They are devised, implemented and marked by the class teacher. Internal assessment is often used by teachers as part of their own teaching programme. These can be tests, homework projects or practical tasks. Internal assessment informs the teacher of continual individual progress.

External assessment

External assessment activities and tasks are devised by examiners outside of the school and are usually marked outside of the school. These include SATs, GCSEs, GNVQs and A levels. In some cases marking is then 'moderated', ie checked by external assessors for accuracy.

Informal/formal assessment

Informal assessment takes place as part of normal classroom life and practice. It is usually observational, where the teacher observes performance and makes notes for future reference. Formal assessment is made following prior warning that assessment will occur. This gives pupils the opportunity to revise and prepare for the assessment activities.

Continuous/terminal assessment

Increasingly continuous assessment is becoming a significant method by which pupils are assessed. It requires teachers/assessors to base the final assessment on the standard of attainment achieved on a variety of pieces of work over a long period of time. This technique is particularly relevant to GCSE and GNVQ qualifications. Terminal assessment is based on standards of achievement reached at the end of a course, module or programme of work.

Each of the types of assessment has to be used in the context of teaching and learning. It is important for teachers to realize and understand the rationale of each type of assessment so that the approach used matches the purpose of the assessment.

What purpose does assessment serve?

Assessment has many faces and can be used for a variety of purposes; however there are three fundamental reasons for assessment: feedback, progress and motivation.

Feedback

Feedback gives information about pupils' progress, which allows the teacher to evaluate how effective their teaching is, by assessing how well learning outcomes have been achieved. This then allows the teacher to correct misunderstanding, give remedial help if required, or stretch pupils who have been finding the work too easy. Assessment also gives direct feedback to pupils. It shows them where their performance is in relation to other pupils, as well as national standards, or expected standards. Feedback can direct pupils in their own improvement.

Progress

Assessment is a vital tool for recording and monitoring pupil progress over the short and long term. These records should help inform teachers of any decisions they need to make about helping in the future learning needs of pupils.

Records of progress are key lines of communication both for parents and other teachers. Records of progress should be key to teachers' long-term planning.

Motivation

This is a key factor in encouraging pupils to achieve what is expected of them. It makes pupils organize and learn the work that is required of them. Motivation can be intrinsic and extrinsic, and in many instances both. Positive feedback and success in assessment tasks are very effective mechanisms for future improvement and motivation.

Assessment has many purposes, which can be summarized as follows:

- record keeping;
- supporting pupils in their own learning;
- providing feedback;
- measuring what pupils know, understand, and can do;
- screening;
- providing information to parents and teachers;
- motivating pupils;
- diagnosing learning difficulties;
- measuring standards;
- informing future planning;
- informing teachers on their own effectiveness;
- deciding on pupil grades and levels of attainment.

Task 7.1

- Within your phase or Key Stage establish the types of assessment that take place within your school and evaluate the purposes for which they are used.
- Try to investigate and understand how the SATs affect teachers' assessment activities.

Assessing in the classroom

This can take many forms, but in the first instance a trainee will be involved in the following aspects:

- marking;
- everyday classroom tasks;
- homework;
- externally set tests and exams;
- teacher-based assessments.

Each form of assessment is important, but a clear view must be kept of the purpose or purposes of the chosen assessment. As trainees develop their teaching skills, so will their assessment techniques develop. The road to success is to set yourself achievable targets for learning the skills and techniques of assessment. Clear collective goals, derived from experience, practice and discussion with your mentors will be the most productive route.

Familiarization with recent documentation on assessment within the National Curriculum, such as the QCA reports on all Key Stage assessments and texts such as Broadfoot and Mortimore, will help you gain knowledge and understand the principles and practices of assessment, as well as tell you about the most recent changes in assessment procedures and thinking.

Teacher assessment has significant impact on pupils' daily lives as well as the teacher's own practice. The informal in-class, everyday assessment of pupils' work is as important as standardized tasks. What are teachers trying to do when they mark pupils' work and what are the essential elements of marking? The essential points about marking are:

- Marking takes up a great deal of teachers' time, so it is important to understand its significance in terms of assessing in the classroom.
- Marking work during and after lessons needs to be thorough, systematic and constructive, and the marked work needs to be returned to pupils in good time.
- Marking should give pupils informative feedback and satisfaction.
- Good marking motivates pupils to achieve more.

It is important to realize that marking pupils' work can have a profound effect on the way pupils perceive themselves and on their self-esteem. Even a simple mark out of 10 can influence a pupil's future performance. Pupils like having targets and goals to aim for and respond to; they also acknowledge praise and constructive criticism. All marking routines should aim to encapsulate the above points.

Task 7.2

Check the assessment policy for both the school and the department you are working in. Examine how your views and knowledge of marking fit with established policy.

Task 7.3

Discuss with your mentor the departmental assessment policy and examine how marking is used within the department. Establish which elements are essential for your training placement.

What can marking be used for?

Marking has two distinct stakeholders: the pupils and the teacher. Both should use marking as a means of raising achievement and attainment. From the teacher's perspective marking should:

- check pupil understanding;
- direct future lesson planning and teaching;
- monitor progress through the collection of marks;
- help assess pupil progress and attainment;
- set work of appropriate levels;
- have clear objectives about what and how you teach;
- inform pupils and parents formatively and summatively.

From the pupils' perspective marking should help them:

- identify carelessness;
- proof-read – make them check their work for spelling, punctuation, etc;
- in their draft work – pupils can become actively involved in improving their own work;

- identify areas of weakness and strength;
- identify areas that lack understanding and knowledge;
- become more motivated and value their work.

Marking should make the teacher focus on specific issues. We've identified two perspectives – that of the pupil and that of the teacher – and both elements need to work in harmony to create a positive environment for the pupils' learning. Marking provides the teacher with many vehicles for learning. Marking procedures involve a variety of skills and it is essential to understand and identify which skills are being used when marking pupils' work. For example marking can be used for:

- establishing whether work has been completed;
- identifying legibility, neatness and accuracy;
- checking that notes from the board or book have been completed accurately and added to;
- testing factual knowledge;
- checking accuracy in completing a recording of experimental or practical work.

Each of these examples focuses on outcomes; marking should also make the teacher focus on purpose. This means the purpose for which teachers set the work that is to be marked. Fitness for purpose is essential to good marking, recording and eventually reporting. You need to be clear whether the work being set is aimed at:

- checking that the work has been completed;
- establishing levels of understanding;
- judging progress in relation to a topic and concepts within the topic area;
- making an overall assessment of pupils' attainment over a long period of time.

These should guide you in what is marked, how the work is set and what use is made of the assessment outcomes.

Task 7.4

- With your mentor decide on a piece of work you are going to teach and mark.
- Identify how you will set, mark and report your assessments.
- Having completed the task, evaluate how effective you were in achieving your objective.

Marking is an activity that is public – all who have access to pupils' books can see what has been marked or ignored. This open scrutiny by parents, colleagues, mentors, senior teachers and Ofsted can give a quick judgement about the teacher's approach. It is always good practice to be consistent, systematic and constructive in the marking of pupils' work.

Using everyday classroom tasks for assessment

Assessment is both essential and integral to effective teaching and pupil learning. As discussed earlier there are many different ways to assess pupils' work. The everyday classroom task is an excellent way of collecting a variety of information about pupils. Conventional marking is just one form of assessment; observation, questioning and listening are also key components of the skills of assessment, all of which the trainee needs to practise and develop. Evidence of pupils' work can be collected from:

- oral work: reading, discussion, questions, role play;
- written work: drafts, notes, scripts, poems, investigations, experiment notes;
- design work: models, drawings, construction;
- physical skills: co-ordination and manipulative skills.

A broad range of examples of pupils' potential allows the teacher to gain evidence of progress from a wide variety of activities, and as a result report the extent of pupil achievement.

Task 7.5

With your mentor discuss and identify ways in which you can collect evidence from classroom activities you plan for your pupils.

Monitoring class work will produce evidence of learning. Both formal and informal classroom assessments are important as they allow teachers to make judgements about pupil progress and alter their style of teaching to facilitate learning. Feedback from pupils enables teachers to measure the effectiveness of lessons.

As a teacher there is a need to distinguish between monitoring informally through integrating assessment tasks into normal activities, and setting formalized tests. For example, is the teacher listening to a child read as a means of encouraging and estimating progress, or is it a means of predicting the pupil's reading level? Similarly in science investigations, is the teacher questioning to assess level or to help move pupils' thinking along in a positive way? In each case pupils need to know what the teacher is doing and why. The purpose of the assessment and monitoring has to be clear to teacher and pupil alike. Kyriacou (1992: 114) clearly states that:

> Skilful assessment of pupils' progress in meeting the National Curriculum targets depends very much on how well assessment tasks are integrated within normal class work without disrupting or interfering unduly with the normal progress of learning.

This is the key to successful monitoring of progress by teachers.

Homework

Homework is increasingly becoming a high priority in all phases of education. As this is an influential practice, it is important to identify the uses and purpose of homework setting. Homework has many functions, some more pertinent than others, depending on the phase and age group of the pupils. However, pupils of all ages should be encouraged to take their learning home to explore with parents and peers. Homework can be thought of as:

- promoting autonomous learning;
- promoting investigative and research skills;
- consolidating and extending learning;
- extending and challenging understanding;
- encouraging study skills;
- providing opportunities for independent private study;
- encouraging parental involvement in learning;
- extending the school day;
- developing pupils' organizational skills;
- providing feedback on learning difficulties.

Homework tasks in all phases of education are important in providing feedback about pupil performance and how future lesson planning may be directed. Homework can be a useful mechanism for pupils to learn how to organize their own learning through a variety of skills, such as researching, collecting material, memorizing spellings or tables. Homework should not just focus on the learning of new material, the revision of prior learning for tests, or routine tasks to reinforce learning – homework should also be creative, investigative and motivating. As a teacher it is important to understand the purpose of homework, and why the chosen tasks are set. This applies equally to the pupils. Pupils must not only understand the task set, but they must also appreciate its value and the worth of completing the task. For this to happen all homework must be marked and incorporated into the pupils' future learning.

When setting homework consider the following carefully, especially when working with very young and immature pupils:

- give very *clear and simple instruction* as to what to do and how it should be presented;
- say when it is going to be collected or needs to be submitted – when, where and to whom are essential elements;
- show where it fits in to the overall learning taking place;
- say how it will be assessed, including the criteria that will be used;
- indicate where it fits into the National Curriculum levels of assessment.

It is important to remember that if pupils are to learn from the tasks that have been set, they have to engage with the material or questions given to them. Homework should be planned into a lesson; it should not be thought of as an add-on activity. It should be well thought out and be an extension to pupils' learning.

Task 7.6

- Identify and plan a creative homework task for a specific age group of pupils.
- Devise a marking framework for the homework task.
- Discuss this and the outcomes with your mentor.

Task 7.7

Discuss with your mentor how you can collect a variety of homework tasks that will motivate and promote learning in your phase or age group of pupils.

Externally imposed assessment

Chapter 2 gave a clear explanation of the National Curriculum. Here the role of assessment is explained within the National Curriculum framework. It is essential that you have a clear understanding of what the statutory requirements for assessment are within a given phase of teaching. Each phase has a series of SATs – these are end of Key Stage formalized tests:

Key Stage 1: 7 years old, Levels 1–3.
Key Stage 2: 11 years old, Levels 2–5.
Key Stage 3: 14 years old, Levels 3–8.
Key Stage 4: 16 years old, GCSE.

Within the curriculum each subject has its Programme of Study (PoS) and the SATs assess pupils' knowledge, skills and understanding within each Key Stage to the levels indicated above. These are assessed through level descriptors. They provide guidance on the knowledge, skills and understanding required to reach each of the levels in each subject. In their assessment of pupils, teachers produce what they consider to be a 'best fit' of their pupils' work to the levels set out in the appropriate section of the National Curriculum. The School Curriculum and Assessment Authority (SCAA), now the Qualifications and Curriculum Authority (QCA) has produced many exemplars to help this process at each Key Stage and level for all subjects. The trainee should familiarize themselves with the QCA material and use it where appropriate in their planning and preparation of lessons and schemes of work.

Teacher assessment contributes to end of Key Stage assessment, but the main assessment of the core subjects – English, mathematics and science – is conducted through national tests. The key feature of the written tests are:

- markers are paid to score tests and these markers are appointed by external agencies;
- external agencies are used for moderation and quality assurance procedures;
- there is an appeals procedure with respect to re-marking;
- test results are reported to parents alongside teacher assessment.

Baseline assessment: key features

Baseline assessment was introduced in the 1997 Education Act (sections 15–18). The Act was put into effect by the Education (Baseline Assessment) (England) Regulations 1998, and applies to all maintained primary schools in England from the Autumn term of 1998/9. The circular dealing with baseline assessment is Circular 6/98 (DfEE, 1998b).

The circular sets out the legal requirements for baseline assessment of pupils on entry to primary school. All primary schools have to implement baseline assessment and the scheme they use has to be accredited by the QCA. All 4–5-year-old pupils have to be assessed by teachers within seven weeks of starting school.

The assessments have to cover the basic skills of speaking and listening, reading, writing, mathematics and personal and social development. Teachers should use the information collected from the baseline assessments to plan their teaching to match individual pupil's needs. It is hoped that over a period of time teachers and schools will be able to assess the progress pupils have made against the baseline.

Headteachers have the responsibility of discussing pupils' achievements on the baseline assessment. They are also required to pass the information on to the local education authority (LEA), which in turn passes the information on to QCA.

The information that headteachers have to transfer with baseline assessment includes:

- the pupil's family name and given name;
- the pupil's sex;
- the pupil's date of birth;
- details of whether the pupil attended school full- or part-time when assessed;
- the month and year when the baseline assessment was carried out;
- the outcomes of the assessment (split into the different elements of the assessment where available);
- those areas of the assessment in which the pupil was assessed in a language other than English.

Assessing at Key Stages 1 and 2: key features

Key Stage 1

All children in their final year of Key Stage 1 must be assessed. All pupils who are moving on to Key Stage 2 programmes of study in the next school year are regarded as being in the final year of Key Stage 1. Most of these children will be in Year 2 and have reached the age of 7 by the end of the school year; some may be older or younger because they have not been taught with their chronological year group.

The headteacher is responsible for ensuring that:

- all children for assessment at Key Stage 1 are identified;
- teacher assessment levels for the core subject attainment targets are recorded for all children;
- the overall subject levels based on those teacher assessments are calculated;
- all children take the appropriate Key Stage 1 tasks and tests;
- children judged as capable of reaching level 4 or above take the relevant Key Stage 2 tests;
- written reports are provided to parents on pupil progress.

(Modified from QCA Key Stage 1 document, pp 2–5.)

Key Stage 2

All children in their final year of Key Stage 2 must be assessed. Most of these children will be in Year 6 and have reached the age of 11 by the end of the school year.

The headteacher is responsible for ensuring that:

- all children for assessment at Key Stage 2 are identified;
- teacher assessment levels for the core subject attainment targets are recorded for all children;
- the overall subject levels based on those teacher assessments are calculated;
- all children working at level 3 and above take Key Stage 2 tests.

Teacher assessment is an essential part of the National Curriculum assessment and reporting arrangements. The results from teacher assessment are reported alongside the test results. Both have equal status and provide complementary information about children's attainment. The tests provide a 'snapshot' of attainment at the end of a Key Stage, while teacher assessment, carried out over a period of time, gives a more rounded picture.

Teachers are required to summarize their assessments at the end of the Key Stage for each eligible child. They need to show:

- a level for each attainment target in English, mathematics and science;
- an overall subject level in each of these subjects, which is calculated by aggregating teacher assessment and attainment target levels as set out in the appropriate documentation;
- the level descriptors in the National Curriculum which are used as a basis for judging children's levels of attainment at the end of each Key Stage.

The aim of an overall judgement of pupil performance requires the teacher:

- to base the judgement on knowledge of how the pupil performs over a period of time in many contexts;
- to take account of the pupil's strengths and weaknesses;
- to check against adjacent level descriptors to ensure the closest level is awarded.

Assessing at Key Stage 3: key features

It is essential that trainees understand the principle of the level descriptors within their given subject area. This will enable them to make effective judgements about pupil attainment, especially when used in conjunction with the exemplar material produced by QCA. Understanding the level descriptors should help in the planning of tasks appropriate to the pupils' abilities and attainment. Teaching and learning strategies should reflect the way the trainee addresses pupils' needs. The strategies should be varied and will increase as teaching skills are developed and improved. Some of the implications for teaching and learning strategies that require consideration within assessment are the types of assessment activities teachers give to pupils. These can include the following:

- practical activities;
- group activities;
- variety of homework tasks;
- timed tasks in class (written or numerical);
- school/class examinations;
- planned/investigative work.

At the end of Key Stage 3 only pupils attaining level 3 and above in mathematics and science and level 4 in English are required to take the written tests. Pupils are differentiated in these tests through tiered SATs papers. These exist in mathematics, which has four tiers, and science, which has two. The rationale behind tiered papers is to assess pupils within a limited range of levels. Overlap occurs within adjacent papers. Pupils who are considered as very able have the opportunity of taking extension papers in each of the core subjects. This allows a pupil to attain level 8, which reflects exceptional performance.

The final Key Stage assessment reflects both statutory SATs results and teacher assessment based on end of Key Stage level descriptors.

Task 7.8

Look at the level descriptors for your subject. With your mentor discuss and identify the knowledge, skill and understanding required for a given topic that you will be teaching during your school-based experience.

Key features of GCSE

The General Certificate of Secondary Education (GCSE) exemplifies the work of Key Stage 4. The end of Key Stage 4 assessment is the externally taken examinations of the various GCSE exam boards. The main features of the GCSE system include:

- a balance between course work and final examinations; the percentage of course work taken into account varies from subject to subject;

- differentiation through tiered papers: mathematics has three tiers, most of the other subjects have two tiers, one that covers grades G-C and the other that covers grades D-A;
- an exceptional performance grade of A*.

GCSE course work

This part of the GCSE is based on teacher assessment and it is very important for teachers to understand their role in it. All course work should be within the ability and attainment of pupils, it should allow for creativity and individuality, and it should be educationally valid.

Task 7.9

Within your subject area explore the use and assessment of course work at GCSE level.

Teacher based assessment

It has been stated earlier in this chapter that teachers are assessing pupils in a variety of ways all the time. But what is teacher based assessment and how is it functional in the classroom at all phases of education? Teacher based assessment can include:

- *Written assessments.* These can motivate pupils to study and learn in preparation for a formal test – these can be times tables, spelling, reading a short paragraph, fact tests, vocabulary or reasoning tests.
- *Observation based assessments.* These look at pupil performance. Practical skills such as art, drama, experimentation, etc can all be assessed by the teacher.
- *Communication based assessments.* Pupils reading aloud, speaking a foreign language, discussing and arguing about pre-researched work.

All assessment activities need to have purpose, clarity and a clear focus. There are several points that need to be considered prior to planning any assessment activity:

- Teacher based assessment over a long period of time should be varied to cover a large range of learning outcomes.
- The assessment task should actually assess what was intended to be assessed.

- Assessment should relate to intended learning outcomes appropriate to the National Curriculum requirements or as part of a particular course of study.
- All assessment tasks should be fair by way of assessing work covered, so that pupils have the opportunity to perform well.

It is important to realize that the nature of the assessment activity will determine the teacher's action in actually marking the assessment. If the pupil is expected to read aloud, the teacher is expected to listen. If a pupil performs a practical task the teacher is expected to observe. Hence the teacher's role in this type of assessment activity is crucial. The responsibility of assessing lies with the teacher irrespective of whether it is in the primary or secondary sector of education. Each phase of education has its statutory demands and it is the responsibility of trainees, with the help of their mentor and university/college tutor, to understand and be able to implement them within a working classroom situation.

Task 7.10

- Develop a teacher based assessment activity for a particular skill.
- Discuss this with your mentor.
- Attempt to conduct the assessment and evaluate your success.
- Reflect with your mentor.

If assessment tasks relate to individual pupils, the teacher's classroom management skills become essential. This is because, when a teacher focuses attention on one pupil rather than 'scanning' the classroom to make sure learning is taking place, the rest of the class needs to be kept on-task. When planning single pupil assessment activities consideration must be given to planning the nature of the task or tasks the rest of the class will be doing while you assess the individual pupil.

Essentials of teacher based assessment

- Do not over-assess – quantity of assessment is no substitute for quality teaching and quality assessment.
- Plan work or topic areas thoroughly so that assessment becomes an integral part of the planning routine rather than an add-on activity.
- Spend time developing assessment strategies and techniques. Don't rush a design of a test: a bad test shows nothing; a good test helps both teacher and pupil.

- Incorporate National Curriculum requirements into the planning of assessment criteria.
- Get a second opinion – show colleagues and mentors the assessment procedures you intend using. A more distanced view can help you focus on what you actually want to assess, rather than what you think you are assessing.

For further in-depth information about assessment and its implications to practice, see Gipps and Stobart (1993) and Sutton (1991).

Recording and reporting

Record keeping is a key feature of teaching and assessment. However, if this activity is to be completed efficiently and effectively some questions have to be addressed. Why do teachers keep records of pupils work, whom are they for, and what is their value?

A prime purpose of record keeping is to help monitor the progress of individual pupils and plan their future learning. Ofsted continually states the importance and need for teachers to keep good records of pupil progress. One of the many reasons for this is that they show that teachers have fulfilled their statutory responsibilities such as delivering the National Curriculum and monitoring pupils' progress through the framework of targets and level descriptors.

There are three main functions of record keeping, discussed below:

1. to monitor and plan ahead;
2. to inform others;
3. to demonstrate that these purposes are being properly followed.

Task 7.11

Investigate your school/department's recording policy. Identify all the records and reports you are likely to be involved in throughout your placement.

Thinking about good and effective record keeping requires an understanding of the usefulness of records. There are two areas that need to be addressed: the detail/quantity of information to be recorded, and how the information is going to be used. Records that are very detailed, dense and incomprehensible have little chance of being used.

The three main functions of good record keeping need to be recognized, understood and implemented throughout the trainees' teaching placement. Trainees should appreciate the importance of the three functions and monitor how they affect or change their practice.

To monitor and plan ahead

The type of information teachers collect and record should help the planning of future lessons and schemes of work. It should also help identify specific problems that individual pupils may have. Planning in this context requires teachers to build upon previous progress and ensure that they allow the pupil to progress in an adequate way by covering learning areas in breadth and depth. The trainees' own monitoring of pupil progress through their teaching placement should be given to the class teacher prior to leaving. These records will enable the class teacher to establish where the pupils are, the work they have covered and the nature of the progress the pupils have made. Passing on information is a key to monitoring the continuity and progression of learning.

The teachers' lesson plans and evaluations are a starting point for information gathering, followed closely by their mark book. All teachers keep a mark book of some kind in which they record marks, grades, comments and scores. How the trainee uses a mark book is key to accurate records and the monitoring of whole-class activities as well as individual pupil progress. Many approaches may be taken; an example is given in Table 7.1. Recording in this way provides a quick visual check on work completed, nature of the task, grade obtained, work outstanding through absence or incomplete work submitted, and a rough guide to overall progress.

Table 7.1   Example of pupil work record

Take a double page from a standard mark book for each class. List class names down the left-hand side. At the top of each column write the date and title of work set plus grading.

Pupil name	Date and title of task Grade/ID	Date and title of task Grade/ID	Date and title of task Grade/ID	Date and title of task Grade/ID	Other comments
John	2.4.98 fractions 9/10	10.4.98 decimals 7/10	18.4.98 algebra 5/10	26.4.98 end of unit test 6/10	appears to be struggling

This example is a starting point. As trainees progress, recording skills will develop and become more refined. This will be reflected by including targets for the pupils to aim towards as well as the levels they have reached as described by the National Curriculum assessment framework.

Task 7.12

Devise a record keeping journal that shows your understanding and progress in recording pupils' attainment.

To inform others

Records are kept not only to monitor progress of individual pupils but to inform a variety of audiences as to the work, progress and problems encountered when teaching a whole class as well as the individual pupil. There are three main areas in reporting that the trainee needs to be aware of:

1. Reporting to parents.
2. Reporting to pupils.
3. Reporting to colleagues/departments/the whole school.

Each requires different skills and use of evidence, but each type of report has to be informed by and based on data collected.

Reporting to parents

The parent has a key role to play in a pupil's learning and development, so reporting to parents has to be effective, meaningful and coherent. Schools normally offer three routes to obtaining information about their pupils' progress: written reports, parents' evenings, and individual meetings with the class teacher or tutor. Written reports are now a statutory obligation at the end of an academic year. Where appropriate these include Key Stage reports, which reflect the level achieved in each 'subject' area by the individual pupil. The report also reflects SATs results and teacher assessment, as well as a commentary on progress.

Task 7.13

With your mentor discuss and examine the school's policy of reporting to parents. Examine examples as a way of understanding how your school reports progress to parents.

Reporting to pupils

Children have the right to know how they are progressing. The teacher can achieve this in a variety of ways. Feedback is the key. After an assessment task, whether it be homework or a more formalized test, communicate to the pupils what they have achieved and attained, and what they need to do in order to progress further.

Reporting to colleagues

This is a skill that trainees will develop throughout their teaching career. When on placement trainees will need to keep a close record of the curriculum covered, including topic areas, texts used, exact areas of the schemes of work covered, homework set, extra activities covered, and test results and merit marks or stars given out. All this information will have to be passed to the class teacher when the placement has been completed. The information is an important record: it informs colleagues of problems that may have been encounter by pupils during the teaching of certain topics. The records should be specific with examples of where and how the pupil or pupils encountered problems. Trainees should appreciate that detailed records are also a means of monitoring their own practice in relation to pupils' learning difficulties or successes.

A framework for recording and reporting is summarized in Figure 7.1.

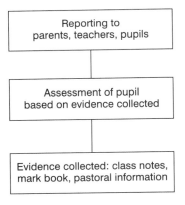

Figure 7.1 A framework for recording and reporting

Task 7.14

Ask to help with a parents' evening. With your mentor prepare a series of reports for a set of pupils; they should show both academic and pastoral progress.

References

Department for Education and Employment (DfEE) (1998a) *Requirements for Courses of Initial Teacher Training*, Circular 4/98, HMSO, London

DfEE (1998b) *Baseline Assessment of Pupils Starting Primary School*, Circular 6/98, HMSO, London

Gipps, C (1994) *Beyond Testing: Towards a theory of educational assessment*, Falmer Press, London

Gipps, C and Stobart, G (1993) *Assessment: A teacher's guide to the issues*, Hodder and Stoughton, London

Kyriacou, C (1992) *Effective Teaching in Schools*, Simon & Schuster Education, Padstow

Sutton, R (1991) *Assessment: A framework for teachers*, Routledge, London

Task Group on Assessment and Testing (TGAT) (1988) *A Report*, DES, London

8   Special needs in the 'mainstream'

Steve Alsop and Robin Luth

This chapter takes the trainee through the complex and often emotive subject of special educational needs (SEN). It shows clearly the role of the *Code of Practice* (DfEE, 1994) and how the more recent Green Paper, *Excellence for All Children* (1998) will affect schools and pupils with SEN. The chapter clearly demonstrates both ends of the spectrum, from pupils with physical and mental disabilities to the gifted pupil. Trainees are provided with suggestions and help in dealing with SEN in their classroom. What SEN are and who is responsible for them are explained, as are the roles of those dealing with SEN in the school. Trainees are given advice on the mechanisms for identifying and assessing SEN. They are also shown ways in which they can help improve access to learning for SEN pupils. The chapter concludes with some words of advice for the trainee.

Objectives

By the end of this chapter the trainee will have an understanding of and appreciation for:

- what special educational needs are;
- the fact that SEN includes gifted pupils;
- the *Code of Practice* (DfEE, 1994);
- the roles and responsibilities attached to SEN;
- the role of the SENCO (special needs co-ordinator);
- what the trainee can realistically do to facilitate learning for SEN pupils.

Introduction

Special educational needs (SEN) can be a highly emotive subject for both teachers and parents. Presently, over 90 per cent of pupils with SEN are educated in mainstream schools (Morris, 1998) and with the recent publication of the Government's Green Paper, *Excellence for All Children*, the commitment to further integration of children with significant sensory, cognitive and physical difficulties into ordinary classrooms is affirmed. It will be incumbent upon Local Educational Authorities (LEAs) to offer parents of a child with SEN a place in a mainstream school before other specialist placements are considered. Therefore, it is likely that a teacher entering the classroom for the first time will experience an increasingly complex environment, populated by many pupils exhibiting a variety of impediments, requiring a range of teaching styles and resources to ensure equality of opportunity and treatment.

Recent legislation, *The Code of Practice on the Identification and Assessment of Special Educational Needs* (DfEE, 1994), demarcates SEN as the responsibility of all teachers working within any school – not solely the responsibility of the Learning Support Department (LSD). The identification, assessment, planning and monitoring of pupils with SEN is therefore an important skill to be learned by any new teacher and one that will assume greater importance as the philosophy of integration gains momentum. So how does a newly qualified teacher gain the knowledge and understanding to cope with students with a complex and serious range of challenges that impede social, emotional and educational progress in the context of a busy and increasingly complex school environment? This chapter will attempt to provide helpful suggestions to teachers embarking upon their careers in an era which, paradoxically, is applying ever-increasing egalitarian expectations to those whose training in SEN is at best minimal.

In essence, what follows is an introduction to a complex and multifaceted area. The aim is to provide a clarification of the class teacher's role within the context of recent legislation and the new skills they need to acquire. The *Code of Practice* (DfEE, 1994) will be examined and the process of identification and assessment carried out by both the school and LEA and the role and responsibilities of the class teacher will be discussed with suggestions for teaching strategies. Following this a basic framework of approaches that will enable the class teacher to provide access to the school curriculum for all is suggested. As stated in the objectives, this chapter will help the trainee to become aware of the following:

- The recent legislation in SEN (in particular, the *Code of Practice*).
- How SEN operates in ordinary schools and the class teacher's role in SEN.
- The processes involved in the assessment of special needs.
- Ways of structuring lessons that are likely to succeed in meeting pupils' special needs.

What is a special educational need?

All children have particular needs – some individuals will prefer some topics, teaching styles and learning approaches more than others and all classrooms have a range of abilities. However, in the UK, the term 'special educational need' has a distinct definition: the DfEE defines a child as having a special educational need if he or she:

(a) has a learning difficulty that calls for special educational provision to be made;

(b) has a significantly greater difficulty in learning than the majority of children of the same age;

(c) has a disability that either prevents or hinders the child from making use of educational facilities of a kind provided for children of the same age in schools within the area of the LEA;

(d) is under 5 and falls within the definition at (a) or (b) above or would do if special educational provision were not made for the child. (DfEE, 1994)

This style of comparative definition can be traced back to The Warnock Report of 1978 (DES, 1978) and the subsequent Education Act of 1981 (DES, 1981). Prior to these reports, special needs pupils were seen as constituting only about 2 per cent of the school population – those, predominately, educated in special schools, units or classes. The Warnock Report broadened the definition of SEN and highlighted the 20 per cent (the famous one in five) of all school pupils who may at some time or another be in need of some form of special provision. This report was briskly followed by the 1981 Education Act that brought about changes in SEN responsibilities and procedures. LEAs and school governors were required to make provision for SEN and parents were included in the assessment processes and had a right of appeal. The Act re-emphasized the two groups of special needs pupils: the larger group, the 20 per cent who would have their learning requirements met within ordinary provision, and the smaller subgroup of these pupils (about 2 per cent of pupils) whose needs require special provision and for whom the LEA is obliged to provide a statement of needs.

The range of special needs is extremely diverse and any one pupil can exhibit a combination of needs. The National Curriculum Council has classified these needs into four broad groups (NCC, 1993):

1. Pupils with exceptionally severe learning difficulties.
2. Pupils with other learning difficulties, including mild, moderate and specific learning difficulties and emotional and behavioural difficulties (EBD).
3. Pupils with physical or sensory impairment.
4. Exceptionally able pupils.

Although these groups are useful as an overview, it is important to be cautious when generalizing about pupils' needs. It is inexact to assume that pupils will fall into any one of these groups as they are likely to exhibit a combination of special needs. It is also inappropriate to assume that because a pupil has a learning difficulty, he or she may not be in the superior range of intelligence. Many pupils, for example, who exhibit EBD are also formatively assessed to be in the high average or superior range of intelligence, as are students who present with specific learning difficulties (SPLD) in literacy acquisition. Similarly, a student who may be described as having moderate learning difficulties (MLD) may well evidence a variety of emotional and behavioural difficulties as a result of feelings of frustration and anger at not being able to complete classroom tasks. The labelling and categorization of students with SEN needs very careful interpretation; nevertheless, the groups shown above serve a purpose here for identification and our discussion of need.

Severe learning difficulties – profound and multiple learning difficulties

Students whose needs are best described in this category exhibit a profound combination of complex physical and cognitive handicap. These include pupils, for example, who have multi-sensory impairment (blind and deaf) as well as pupils who are severely autistic. These pupils may require 24-hour care and have mobility and ambulatory needs. It is usual that all of these students are statemented as soon as they are eligible and many, despite a philosophy of inclusion, remain catered for in special school with specially designed access and toilet facilities. Autistic pupils, for example, present a variety of social, emotional, behavioural and communication difficulties and many exhibit behavioural problems which preclude them from an inclusive education. However, some students with a condition named Asperger's Syndrome can progress very well in the inclusive, mainstream environment. Their intellectual skills are usually above average and they are well placed in the mainstream curriculum, although they will exhibit varying degrees of social and emotional needs. Asperger's Syndrome has received recent attention because of the extraordinary talents of Stephen Wiltshire, the teenager who has the ability to visualize and depict buildings in fine detail.

Other learning difficulties

This group is extremely wide ranging and in many respects the most difficult one to define. It includes pupils who, for some reason, are finding the curriculum difficult when compared with their peers. In some cases, a special need might be short lived, for instance, pupils who are unable to engage with the curriculum because they are suffering an emotional trauma after being bullied or following a family bereavement. Pupils can fall into this group for a host of reasons; in many cases there are combinations of reasons, which together pose a significant barrier for the learner. Here we focus on the needs of moderate, specific, emotional and behavioural difficulties.

Moderate learning difficulties (MLD)

Pupils whose needs are described as being in the MLD continuum display significant deficits in the acquisition of literacy and numeracy skills. The comprehension of written and spoken language presents difficulties for these children and they will benefit from a modified curriculum in terms of work load and concepts. Many of these pupils are in the low percentiles of cognitive functioning and may also evidence very poor self-esteem and other emotional and behavioural problems. Many students with MLD are placed in our mainstream primary and secondary schools and present a challenge to teachers in the sense of the correct presentation of curriculum materials and access to the curriculum.

Specific learning difficulties (SPLD)

Students with SPLD present a frustrating deficit in spelling, writing or number skills. This is the appropriate name for the condition labelled 'dyslexia'. Many 'dyslexic' students are in the high average band of ability and are completely frustrated by their inability to grasp simple spelling patterns or number bonds. Research continues into the particular causal factors of SPLD with retentive memory processing probably being to blame in the areas of aural and visual short-term memory. SPLD students need qualified teachers who understand their need for specially constructed teaching programmes. 'Dyscalculia' is now becoming a more useful term for 'mathematical dyslexia'. There are many students with SPLD in mainstream classrooms.

Emotional and behavioural difficulties (EBD)

With the current drive to include all of our students within mainstream setting, no other group is causing more controversy and debate in our schools and universities. The term 'emotional and behavioural difficulties' means many things to many people. People mostly relate to the 'behaviour' component of this group and visualize aggression, disruption, distraction and lesson-stopping aberrant behaviour with students who are rude, out of control and impossible to bargain with. They tend to forget that the 'emotional' component of the term describes a student whose emotional development may have been affected by terribly traumatic events or neuro-chemical conflicts which drive inappropriate behaviours in social contexts. Such students may have suffered multiple bereavement, physical and sexual abuse and are as challenged as any group in society. They are undoubtedly the most researched, with many books advocating psycho-dynamic and behaviourist responses to their management needs at both a group and individual level. There is no doubt that these students are difficult to teach; nevertheless they deserve as much empathy as any other child in need if not more as it can be hard to empathize with somebody who is intent on wrecking your lessons!

Trainees are frequently frustrated when dealing with students deemed to have EBD. The creation of good communication with more experienced colleagues and a whole-school behavioural management system go a long way to help sustain confidence in dealing with these students and in meeting their needs in a mainstream environment.

Pupils with physical or sensory impairment

Pupils with varying degrees of physical, visual and hearing impairment are frequently placed in mainstream schools. They will usually be statemented or on the way to being correctly assessed and supported by specialist teachers working on a peripatetic basis. They should also have access to an array of specialist resources that enable and facilitate their participation in the curriculum. It is important to carefully consider the physical learning environment for these pupils. For example, it is essential that trainees read the school records of all the pupils they teach to ensure that those children who wear audio aids or need glasses are correctly located in the classroom. Students with physical disability will need their access to the curriculum carefully planned to ensure that classrooms and other areas in the school are made fully accessible by wheelchair. Remember when teaching those students with such difficulties that you see the student and not the wheelchair and don't generalize about disability and intellectual performance. It is our experience that individuals with a degree of physical handicap in our mainstream schools won't let you! It is as important that the trainee recognizes and understands the needs of these pupils as it is to provide a suitable learning environment.

Exceptionally able pupils

These pupils are not defined as having a special educational need under current legislation; nevertheless, they pose a particular challenge in mainstream schooling. It is the class teacher's responsibility to provide activities that extend the abilities of these pupils.

Recent research suggests that many of these pupils are underachieving. A review by Her Majesty's Inspectorate (HMI, 1992), for instance, suggests that many exceptionally able pupils are 'insufficiently challenged' in many lessons. The phrase 'dumbing down' has been coined in the United States to refer to cases where teachers are found to provide activities that are beneath pupils' abilities. In some cases, these activities have been chosen to negate poor management techniques by keeping pupils occupied (McLaughlin, 1995). It is important that trainees can identify pupils with exceptional ability in their subject and nurture their talents. Trainees need to adapt the teaching and learning approaches in their classroom to cater for their advanced needs.

Task 8.1: An introduction to SEN in your classroom

Find out about the special needs of the classes you going to teach. If possible, talk to the class teacher, form teacher and a member of the LSD. Ascertain the particular needs of the groups and any additional SEN support if available. This information can be combined with your own experiences of observing the group. Find out if any pupils have special educational needs:

- What are these needs?
- Are any pupils statemented?
- Are there any pupils of exceptional ability?

Observe and reflect upon how the class teacher (and any additional support) meets the needs of these pupils.

Identifying and assessing SEN

Class teachers have a key role in the identification of special needs. It is the teachers' responsibility to voice the initial concern that may surround a pupil in their class in relation to his or her learning. The 1993 Education Act and the subsequent *Code of Practice on the Identification and Assessment of Special Educational Needs* (DfEE, 1994) provides a detailed analysis system for identifying, assessing, planning and monitoring SEN. The main thrust of this legislation is a five-stage model that places the school's internal procedures for identification and assessment in the first three stages and the LEA's procedures in stages four and five. The end result of the five-stage model usually results in the issuing of a statement of special educational need for the pupil and some extra resources that follow pupils into their school. Stage one is of particular interest to the trainee teacher and for this reason we will consider this in more detail. It is important to emphasize that the five-stage model presented below is primarily concerned with the identification and assessment of a pupil who may be evidencing some form of learning, social, emotional, sensory or physical difficulty in your class. The result of such a process helps in the planning and monitoring of an educational programme which, in part, is individualized to help accommodate the needs of that pupil within the classroom.

Stage one of the *Code* is the class teacher's responsibility and involves the initial registering of a concern about a pupil's learning. It is usually expressed by either a class teacher or form tutor and so has great relevance to 'mainstream' teachers. It could be that the student has difficulty in basic skills or completing work, or evidences some emotional or sensory difficulty. In any case some form of help should be offered and this usually means an increase in differentiated work-sheets or extra time given to complete tasks. The name of the student should be given to the school's special needs co-ordinator (SENCO) who may decide to contact the parents. In any case the expectation is inherent in the *Code of Practice* that teachers will attempt to begin to meet the individual needs of the pupil within their own curriculum delivery and lesson planning.

Stage two is the classroom teacher's and SENCO's responsibility. In this stage an individual education plan (IEP) is formulated. Concern is now increasing and the school SENCO becomes involved. The SENCO will draw up an IEP, which describes in detail the type and depth of special need and classroom strategies useful in meeting those needs. The SENCO will work alongside the class teacher, tutor, pastoral head of year and parents. Extra resources in the form of class based support teaching is not usually available in this stage but the more detailed assessment does help with planning for that pupil's needs.

Stage three is principally the SENCO's responsibility, with the involvement of outside agencies. After a preview of that student's needs, the SENCO is sufficiently concerned that there is a definite SEN that requires further detailed assessment. For this reason a range of professionals from outside of the school may be asked to come in and help assess and identify those needs. Some assessment, for example the student's GP or psychiatric services, may take place in the appropriate environment. The school's educational psychologist will undertake a proper assessment of the student's abilities. The SENCO will work closely with the class teachers and pastoral teachers to ensure that information is promulgated effectively. Parents are kept closely informed of the increasing level of concern about the pupil.

Stage four is the school and LEA's responsibility. Either the school SENCO or parent asks the LEA to begin a formal assessment of the student's needs with the hope that the LEA will issue a statement of special educational need which will bring some form of extra resource to the pupil. The LEA will usually ask for the following professional reports:

- school;
- parents;
- educational psychologist;
- medical;
- social services;
- other, for example speech therapist or physiotherapist.

Within 10 weeks the LEA must inform the parent whether it will or will not issue a statement. If the answer is positive, the statement has to be written and finalized within six months. Before 1994, it was perfectly possible for a student to enter a school at Year 7 and not receive the statement until they were in Year 10 or 11!

In *Stage five* the LEA describes the needs in a statement and allocates extra money to the pupil. The school must then implement and provide the extra support the pupil requires. Usually it is in the form of a support teacher specializing in literacy development or behaviour, or it might be a piece of enabling equipment like a lap-top computer, a hearing aid, or low-vision equipment.

Task 8.2: Understanding the *Code of Practice*

The *Code of Practice* (DfEE, 1994) contains more detail about the procedures involved in the identification of SEN. Study the code and make sure you are aware of your involvement and responsibilities, in particular, in stages one, two and three. Consult with your mentor and ask if you can look at the IEPs for the pupils in your classes. You will need to use these when preparing your lessons.

Special needs in your school

The arrangement for the education of special needs pupils varies between different LEAs and different schools. As a trainee it is most likely that involvement with special needs will be as a consequence of your subject teaching and any form-tutor responsibilities. All schools are required to have a SENCO and special needs policies, which are designed to support and meet the needs of both pupils and staff. The number of designated SEN staff will vary with the size and type of school as well as with the number of pupils on roll who have been identified as having needs. The SENCO will often participate in school INSET to clarify and improve the understanding of all issues relating to SEN within the mainstream spectrum.

They will also distribute the necessary paperwork that is used to identify, assess, plan and monitor the learning of all pupils with SEN. This might include the special needs register, copies of IEPs and any relevant psychometric testing data. In some schools this paperwork is widely available to all staff; in other schools information is more restricted.

To provide an illustration of the institutional structure of SEN provision, in the following sections we document two indicative case schools. The first school is a large inner-city comprehensive, the second is a one-form-entry first school.

School 1: SEN in an inner-city secondary mainstream school

Enford Grange is a large, inner-city comprehensive with a diverse multi-cultural mix. It has 1,200 pupils on roll arranged as a five-form entry. There are 345 pupils on the special needs register with 55 of those having a statement of SEN. Of the number on the SEN register some 200 are at stage two of the *Code of Practice* model and some further 96 are at either stage three or four. Many of the pupils who exhibit stage one are not formally identified and this presents challenges to the class teacher.

The LSD of the school has three full-time teachers, including the SENCO who is head of the department, and two SPLD specialists and seven learning support assistants who are on part-time contracts and deal solely with the needs of state-mented pupils. The LSD operates a tripartite system of intervention to help meet the needs of the students on the special needs register:

1. In-class support. The supporting of statemented pupils with either a teacher or a learning support assistant by on-task focusing and the modification of materials.
2. Withdrawal in groups for reading development. Some 60 students in groups of 10 are withdrawn for a corrective reading scheme four times per week to boost deficits in the acquisition of literacy skills.
3. Individual withdrawal for severe SPLD.

Some students with severe difficulties and demonstrating little ability in the area of comprehension of written or spoken language are withdrawn for very intensive work to boost basic classroom skills. These students are withdrawn four times a week, either individually or in groups of two.

The department can also draw on the expertise of various outside agencies that can offer specialist advice and materials for those students on the SEN register above stage three. These might typically include:

- educational psychologist (one visit every three weeks);
- educational social workers (one visit every three weeks);

- behavioural support teachers (as necessary);
- peripatetic teachers of the visually and hearing impaired (one visit per half term);
- referrals to child guidance clinics for students with severe behavioural problems;
- plus other satellite professionals including speech therapists, physiotherapists and occupational therapists.

The department primarily identifies and assesses pupils who may have a significant learning difficulty. It then disseminates that information to all other concerned staff within the school and advises on teaching strategies and materials to help meet the needs. Obviously with so many pupils on the register, the response in meeting those needs must be whole-school and all teachers must be responsible for planning and monitoring effective curriculum resources for all pupils. It is probable that within the school large departments such as the core National Curriculum departments will nominate one teacher to act as the SALT (subject area liaison teacher) and to liaise with the LSD.

School 2: special needs in a first school (ages 4–7)

The Cedars School is a one-form-entry first school with 150 pupils aged 4–7. There are 18 pupils on the special needs register with three pupils having a statement of need – two for visual impairment and one for EBD. Six pupils are at stage two and five at stage three/four of the *Code*. Special needs is co-ordinated by the science co-ordinator who receives an additional scale point for the SEN responsibility. The SENCO is allocated two hours timetable relief per week, which takes place during school assembly. The school operates a policy of inclusion and the SENCO addresses the needs of pupils by:

(a) liaising with staff, developing IEPs and providing any necessary INSET;
(b) co-ordinating the classroom assistants (parent helpers); and
(c) co-ordinating support from outside agencies.

The headteacher has used the revenue from the statemented pupils to employ three part-time helpers. Each class teacher has a regular meeting with the SENCO (two per term), usually after school, to review the progress of any pupils on the SEN register as well as discussing concerns about other pupils. The SENCO is in close liaison with the LEA and other outside agencies that may typically include:

- educational psychologists (two visits per term);
- educational social workers (two visits per term);
- behavioural support (once a week);

- medical and other health visitors (six visits per term);
- an LEA peripatetic teacher of the visually impaired (two visits a week); and
- LEA reading recovery support (five lessons per week for maximum of 20 weeks).

Task 8.3: Special needs in your school

Find out about SEN in your school. How does your school compare with the case profiles documented above? Acquire a copy of your school's SEN policy (and departmental policies if available). If possible, speak to a member of staff with responsibility for special needs. Find out about any pupils in your classes (or form group) with special needs and the support mechanisms that are available.

Special needs in your classroom

Under the 1981 Act, it is the responsibility of classroom teachers to provide access to the curriculum for all pupils:

> It is part of the teacher's professional role to recognize and develop the potential of individual pupils. All pupils should be encouraged throughout their school career to reach out to the limit of their capabilities. This is a formidable challenge to any school since it means that the school's expectation of every pupil must relate to their individual gifts and talents. (DES, 1981)

Trainees also have the responsibility of ensuring equality of opportunity in enabling their pupils, at any stage in the *Code of Practice,* access to the National Curriculum. It is especially important that curriculum planning for all students at stage one reflects an awareness and early amelioration of any problem you may feel a student evidences.

The key to promoting access to the curriculum is to consider individual needs and then structure the classroom environment to meet those needs. The more relevant information you can gather about the background and learning style of a pupil, the more you can plan effectively in preparing suitable curriculum resources for that pupil. It is essential that learning tasks are *differentiated* to match the needs of pupils. Differentiation is a complex topic and is closely associated with varying cognitive tasks and outcomes, for example, catering for children with different abilities and work rates. It is also important to consider learners' emotional, physical and sensory special needs, as these will also require differentiated tasks. A well-designed teaching activity will offer a challenging learning experience by which pupils can achieve success and remove any obstacles to their learning. Such a learning experience must build upon the learner's prior knowledge and be emotionally engaging and cater for any physical and sensory needs. Learners need to be able to progress at a rate governed by their cognitive ability and not be hindered by any other special needs.

A schematic representing four stages in planning for SEN is shown in Table 8.1. Successful planning is best achieved through the identification of needs and clear learning objectives, then using this information to provide differentiated lesson activities matched to the needs of the class and opportunities for clear assessment and feedback. With this approach, it should be possible to address the needs of all members of the class, including any with special needs. As noted by the National Curriculum Council (1989) 'What is good practice in relation to special needs is good practice for all'.

Task 8.4: A focus on differentiation

Consider the particular cognitive, emotional, sensory and physical requirements of your subject area. In what ways can you differentiate your subject teaching to provide access for children with SEN?

Ways of improving access for SEN pupils

In this section we suggest some ways of improving access to the curriculum for pupils with SEN. As previously noted, individual pupils often have a combination of needs so it is essential that there is consultation with the LSD or SENCO so that you are aware of pupils' needs. Some pupils will be accompanied in your lessons with a designated SEN in-class support. If support is available it is important that you utilize it fully. If possible, speak with the teacher in advance of the lesson and make long-term plans. The trainee and mentor should work together to meet the needs of individuals and classes – their presence and role needs to be included in lesson planning. Trainees should provide their mentor or SENCO with details of the lesson subject and structure prior to the lesson – they will offer invaluable advice; for example they will be able to give feedback about the appropriateness of the language level of work-sheets and handouts.

The following strategies are useful in meeting SEN. The list is not designed to be a recipe or panacea, but rather a collection of key points that could be useful in

Table 8.1   Key considerations when planning for SEN

Stages of planning	*Key considerations*
Identification of lesson learning aims and objectives	• Consult the National Curriculum PoS and identify the lesson's learning aims and objectives • Select subject matter that builds upon or extends pupils' current understanding
Identification of needs	• Identify the cognitive, emotional, physical and sensory special needs of individuals in the class
Planning for differentiated learning	Use the information gathered in the first two stages to select the most appropriate teaching and learning approaches to engage all in the curriculum. Consider: • the teaching style (How best can my teaching approach cater for the needs of all class members?) • the vehicle for teaching (What lesson activities are best to convey my lesson aims?) • the context for the subject (How can I make the subject both relevant and interesting?) • the physical learning environment (How can I ensure that physical and sensory impaired pupils have full access to my teaching?) • the social environment (How can I group pupils to create an effective learning environment?)
Assessment, monitoring and feedback of pupil performance	• How can I ensure that all pupils feel a sense of achievement? • How can I best assess the performance of all pupils (consult the NationalCurriculum level descriptors)? • How can I provide feedback to encourage all? • What are my indicators of a successful lesson?

lesson planning. In the case of statemented pupils, it is particularly important that the SENCO is consulted.

Pupils with SPLD (language and literacy)

One of the basic prerequisites for learning is that students can read and understand the language and the texts that are placed before them. However, research consistently suggests that teachers place texts and work-sheets before students which are written for those with reading ages far in advance of the students they are teaching (Jones and Charlton, 1996). It is not uncommon, for example, for some children at stage one in the *Code* to be asked to read work-sheets and books aimed at reading ages three, four or five years in advance of their actual abilities. The process of taking meaning from such texts is too complex and only increases the students' feelings of frustration and low self-esteem. Such perpetuation of failure leads to an increase in the chances of behavioural problems developing in the lessons. Trainees should discover the reading ages of those students who present literacy problems in their lessons and plan work that is appropriate for their abilities. It is then likely that the students will learn more effectively and the climate of the classroom will decrease the chance of any major disruption occurring.

As a new entrant to good classroom practice, the trainee must bear in mind that if students are off-task for any length of time this can lead to misconduct and be a distraction to other members of the class (see Chapter 6). Trainees should ask the SENCO to check the readability of their lesson work-sheets and any overhead transparencies. The SENCO can also show the trainee how to use a simple, diagnostic reading and spelling test – it can be quickly administered and will help the trainee immensely in catering for the individuals who may have significant and very significant reading deficits. Trainees will then contribute to an increasingly professional assessment of those students who are concerning them.

The following strategies can be used to adjust the linguistic demands of lessons and lesson materials:

- Reduce the length of paragraphs and sentences and simplify the language.
- Write sentences that are active rather than passive (the dog ate the cat rather than the cat was eaten by the dog) and avoid complex sentence structures (for example subordinate clauses).
- Present material in uncluttered format, with headings and subheadings and use illustrations.
- Print hand-written work-sheets or better still prepare them on a word-processor.
- Move from simpler to harder tasks and keep the learner active to maintain interest.
- Use numerical pointers to break up large sections of text. For instance, in a comprehension exercise structure the reading with indicators of the nature – 'read lines 1 to 10 and answer questions 1, 2 and 3'.

Remember that simplified text will often be longer than original text and any linguistic audits should be performed systematically rather than randomly.

Pupils with EBD (including social and communicative disorders)

Pupils with EBD may present with a variety of difficulties that range from very disrupting, challenging behaviours to silent and withdrawn behaviours, which can mask immense emotional upset. Students who present difficulties in either emotional health or aberrant behaviour do so for many and varied reasons and it requires a great deal of input and skill to meet their SEN.

Problems with concentration, distraction and tolerance to rules within the classroom are commonplace, and help to deal with such difficulties needs to be orchestrated within the school and involve the expertise of many outside agencies. Most schools will operate a system that utilizes a multi-disciplinary team involving professionals from education, health and social services. It must be remembered that while some of the students who have EBD will present the trainee with the greatest challenges in the classroom, they are also among the most deserving, in that their home environment and previous experiences are often the most adverse and difficult. In all cases, liaise with the school SENCO, as many of these pupils do benefit from a whole-school response and the trainees' experiences of them will usually be duplicated throughout the school in other teachers' classrooms.

The following points will help trainees cope with students who present such difficulties:

- Set firm and explicitly clear boundaries on the behaviour you expect.
- Ensure that students can succeed in the work that you set.
- Be more positive rather than negative at all times, as praise lifts self-esteem.
- Be consistent with your responses to behaviour that is unacceptable. Remember to reprimand the action and not the child.
- Try to find some individual time with the pupils to develop a more helpful relationship with them and decrease the anxiety they may be feeling about you as a new teacher.

Pupils with sensory impairments

Trainees need to be aware of pupils in their classroom who may have visual and/or hearing impairments. It is particularly important to be aware of the degree of these impairments as this will directly affect the ability of the pupil to function in your lesson.

Pupils' hearing or visual impairments will vary. For example, pupils can have selective hearing impairment and be sensitive to certain sound frequencies more than others (if high frequencies are lost then the higher notes of consonants will be difficult to hear; if low frequencies are lost then pupils may experience difficulties with the lower frequency vowel sounds). There are several types of visual impairment, usually classified in terms of functioning; these include totally blind pupils, pupils who can see contrasts and pupils who have difficulties in focusing. It is likely that some pupils in the class will be colour-blind and as a consequence may be unable to distinguish between reds and greens – this is an important factor to be borne in mind when using coloured work-sheets or recording a colour change in chemical reactions in science.

When teaching children with hearing impairment trainees need to consider the following:

- Make sure any hearing aid is worn and is functioning properly.
- Wear any additional microphones or communicators provided by the pupil – these can improve communication greatly (but remember to return them at the end of the lesson).
- Make sure that the pupil is sitting in a position where he or she is facing you and can see you clearly; remember to speak to pupils directly as much as possible.
- Make sure the pupil is looking at you when you are speaking. If a pupil is lip-reading, speak normally but make sure you do not obstruct your mouth and remember to repeat what classmates say during any class discussions.
- Use visual support to emphasize the key teaching points, for example, use the board or overhead to provide an overview of the lesson or give out a hand-out with the key lesson points at the start of the lesson.
- Try to improve the acoustics of the room, for example, by changing the seating arrangements or installing curtains.

When teaching children with visual impairment trainees need to consider the following:

- Make sure the visually impaired pupil is sitting close to the board and if there are any demonstrations ensure there is appropriate lighting available. (NB: take care as some pupils may be sensitive to bright lights.)
- Try to use specific and clear language particularly when giving instructions, and don't depend on gestures or other visual cues when teaching. Use big, bold and colourful visual aids.
- Visually impaired pupils will need more time to complete tasks – note taking etc, because of their disability. Pupils should not be expected to share texts.
- You should be familiar with any specialist equipment needed and have a working knowledge of its function.
- Good liaison with specialist support staff should be developed in order that work-sheets and texts can be enlarged or modified to meet the needs of the pupil.

Pupils with physical impairments

When dealing with pupils with a physical disability it is important to consider the pupil and not just the disability. If the trainee needs to address the disability this should be done in the context of the pupil. Many pupils with physical disabilities will be statemented; it is essential that you either read the statement or discuss the particular needs with the SENCO. In all cases, the key is to provide access to the curriculum – pupils need to be presented with tasks they can achieve. Particular needs will vary depending on the disability. For example, for pupils with wheelchairs the following considerations are essential:

- Make sure that there is space to move around the classroom and consider the suitability of any emergency exits.
- Check work surfaces to see if they allow access and are at a suitable height. Is there sufficient space for pupils to work collaboratively in groups? Is there sufficient space for a helper?
- Will pupils require moving in and out of the wheelchair? If so, take care and use an appropriate lifting procedure – for both your and the pupil's safety.

Task 8.5: The special educational needs of Terry and Carly

Case study: Terry

Terry is a Year 9 pupil who is causing you concern. He is at stage two of the *Code of Practice* assessment procedures and has great difficulty in remaining on-task for any length of time, is easily distracted by others in the room and is often mobile in any class in which he attends. He is above average ability but is reading some three years behind his chronological age and is very sensitive about this issue. He has supportive parents who value education. Terry has significant needs as identified by the school SENCO. As such he is one of 60 pupils from a cohort of 200 stage 2 pupils who receive a corrective reading programme. He is withdrawn four times a week from curriculum areas to receive help in reading. He is currently concentrating on developing better reading fluency and increasing his word attack skills in subject-specific language.

Imagine that Terry is a pupil in one of your classes:

- How can you best enable Terry to access your lessons and learning objectives?

- How can you best support the SEN teacher by increasing his linguistic skills?
- How can you best contain Terry's tendency to wander off-task and cause disruption?

Case study: Carly

Carly is a Year 5 statemented pupil who is visually impaired and has temper tantrums. She receives 15 hours a week of primary learning support assistant time and is visited every month by a peripatetic teacher of the visually impaired. She has tremendous difficulties with low vision and cannot read normal print. As a consequence, she has poor spatial awareness and difficulties with fine motor skills.

Imagine that Carly is a pupil in one of your classes and consider:

- How can you best enable Carly to access your lessons and learning objectives?
- How can you best support the SEN teacher by increasing Carly's spatial awareness and poor fine motor skills?

Final words of advice

When starting to teach it is easy to be overawed – trainees are concerned with their performance and ability to explain their subject and how the pupils will respond to their teaching. Special needs at this stage can appear daunting. Schools are very busy institutions with much day-to-day business going on, but more experienced colleagues will always answer questions concerning students who are causing you difficulty or whom you suspect evidence significant problems in learning in your classroom.

The development of good liaison skills with your mentor, other teachers, senior managers and parents will enable you to function as a better teacher and reduce the stress you may feel as a result of dealing with difficult students. So, learn to talk to others in order to understand and gather information about pupils who are of concern. Also, remember that one differentiated work-sheet completed on a computer can be saved and amended so that a reservoir of materials is developed and can be used again and again. Special needs pupils are often the most vulnerable pupils in school but they can also be the most rewarding to teach.

Further reading

In terms of recent legislation, we recommend that you read the *Code of Practice on the Identification and Assessment of Special Educational Needs* (see the references list).

The following books are of a general nature and are aimed at mainstream teachers; between them they provide a good introduction to SEN policy and practice:

Dyson, A, Clarke, C, Skidmore, D and Millward, A (1997) *New Directions in Special Needs – Innovation in mainstream schools*, Cassell, London

Farrell, P (1997) *Teaching Pupils with Learning Difficulties*, Cassell, London

Hegarty, S (1993) *Meeting Special Needs in Ordinary Schools*, Cassell, London

Jones and Charlton (1996) – see the references list

Montgomery, D (1989) *Managing Behaviour Problems*, Hodder and Stoughton, London

Smutny, J (ed) (1998) *The Young Gifted Child – Potential and promise: An anthology*, Hampton Press, London

References

Department for Education (1994) *Code of Practice on the Identification and Assessment of Special Educational Needs*, HMSO, London

Department for Education and Science (DES) (1978) *Special Educational Needs: Report of the committee of enquiry into the education of children and young people* (The Warnock Report), HMSO, London

DES (1981) *The School Curriculum*, HMSO, London

Green Paper (1998) *Excellence for All Children*, DfEE, HMSO, London

HMI (1992) *The Education of Very Able Children in Mainstream Schools*, HMSO, London

Jones, K and Charlton, J (eds) (1996) *Overcoming Learning and Behaviour Difficulties – Partnership with pupils*, Routledge, London

McLaughlin, M (1995) Re-building teacher professionalism in the United States, paper presented at The Re-thinking UK Education: What Next conference, Roehampton Institute, 5 April

Morris, E (1998) In. . . and out of the mainstream, *The Guardian Education*, 9 June

National Curriculum Council (1989) *Circular No. 5: Implementing the National Curriculum – Participation by pupils with special educational needs*, NCC, York

National Curriculum Council (1993) *Special Needs and the National Curriculum: Opportunity and challenge*, NCC, York

9

The inspection process

Kit Field

This chapter introduces the inspection process. It clearly shows and guides the trainee through the role of Ofsted and the implications of the inspection process on a school and trainees should they be involved in it through the course of their training. The trainee is taken through the requirements of an inspection, considering what is needed before, during and after an Ofsted inspection.

Objectives

By the end of this chapter the trainee will have an understanding of:

- the inspection process;
- the role of Ofsted;
- the nature and time line of an inspection; -
- the role of the school;
- the part played by a trainee/teacher in the inspection process.

Introduction

Little causes more of a stir and disquiet in a staff room than the mention of Ofsted (Office for Standards in Education). Teachers and other educators complain bitterly about the inspection system, regulated by Ofsted, for a whole range of reasons. Few deny the value of inspection by a body from outside the school, but the actual structure of Ofsted, the inspection process and methodology, the perceived positive and negative impact, the cost in terms of human and financial resources, and the regular changes of grading systems are all factors which contribute to the negative image.

The introduction of Ofsted fits into a period of 'audit explosion' (Power, 1997), which in a broad sense is popular. An open, public audit offers a degree of public control and a form of accountability. The birth of Ofsted happened also at a time when, Hargreaves (1995) claimed, teachers and local education authorities (LEAs) could not be trusted. Public accountability and quality control were of great appeal – particularly given the history of school inspections. Her Majesty's Inspectors (HMI) conducted inspections from 1868 to 1992 in order to provide evidence for the Secretary of State for Education to monitor and evaluate provision. The initial proposal that all schools would be inspected on a four-year cycle, thereby guaranteeing that 25 per cent of schools would be inspected annually, as opposed to the estimated 1 per cent of schools under HMI inspectors, represents a considerable improvement in terms of provision (Wilcox *et al*, 1993). The establishment of a new system of school inspection, under section 9 of the Education (Schools) Act 1992, does, superficially at least seem positive. The Ofsted catch-phrase and subtitle of its own corporate plan 'Improvement through inspection', also offers a very supportive and developmental ethos.

The stark contrast between this seemingly positive strategy and the operational stages of implementation has led to considerable disappointment and mistrust on the part of teachers. First, the appointment of Chris Woodhead was perceived by many as a political move. Woodhead's more negative stance does little to encourage teachers: 'When teachers teach better they will have greater public esteem, and their morale will as a consequence be higher' (Woodhead, 1998: 10).

Parsons (1997) also contrasts the concept of external auditing with LEA-sponsored self-evaluation schemes which had prompted the process of development planning based on a school's diagnosis of their own needs. DES publications (1989, 1991) encouraged a voluntaristic approach to school improvement along with management processes geared towards development, eg BS 5750 (now ISO 9000), Investors in People (IIP) and Total Quality Management (TQM). Hargreaves (1995: 119) has questioned the ability of schools to monitor their own performance given that teachers 'are not trained in the skills of inspecting and auditing, they lack a wider perspective and are inclined to parochialism'.

On the other hand, further criticisms indicate too great a detachment of Ofsted from practising teachers. Previously, contact with the LEA was on the whole well received. Indeed, many teachers still hanker after the personal touch, which some Ofsted inspectors have retained. It seems that teachers resent the failure of most Ofsted inspectors to offer guidance and to 'enter into proper dialogue with the inspection team' (OFSTIN, 1996: 7). The detachment is deliberate, Field *et al* (1998) claim. The DfEE privatized the inspection system by creating Ofsted. Ofsted contracts privatized inspection teams, which follow a strict framework. The Registered Inspector (RgI) reports to a school and Ofsted at the end of an inspection. These reports are public documents. The outcome is seen by many to be a weakness of the system. 'Inspection, it seemed, was something done to them (teachers), not something done with them in a joint search for improvement' (OFSTIN, 1996: 1).

Lonsdale and Parsons (1997) argue that this detachment, and the emasculation of the mediating potential of the LEA, have led inspectors to promote school improvement through threat and fear. Indeed Boothroyd *et al* (1996) question the whole notion of 'Improvement through inspection' when the end result can be 'possible school closure, destruction of professional lives and the negation of five years' school improvement work' (p 14).

The basis of an Ofsted inspection is a grading system (see later). Inevitably a process of aggregation takes place in order to provide an overall judgement on the effectiveness of a teacher, department/subject provision, and ultimately the school. Hargreaves (1995) claims that an individual school's report will give a far more favourable impression than the aggregated evidence that will contribute to the Chief Inspector's annual report. Woodhead's first annual report (Ofsted, 1993) states very clearly that his main priority is the raising of standards and improvement of quality, and that he would draw on the evidence accrued through school inspections in doing so. Inevitably, therefore, there would be a focus on the negative. Teachers' disappointment is entirely understandable when the focus has been on the minority of poor teachers and poor lessons, rather than the celebration of the majority of teachers' contributions. Fidler *et al* (1995) identified the information provided by inspections to the Chief Inspector as only one way in which inspection was intended to drive up standards. Inspection, they note, was intended to have a direct impact on each school.

Research has clearly shown that there has been a cost for schools and for teachers at a personal and professional level. The research by Boothroyd *et al* (1996) includes repeated references to stress to governors, heads and teachers, and they infer, also to pupils. Symptomatic of 'post Ofsted malaise' (Boothroyd *et al*, 1996: 4) is increased absenteeism, tired and exhausted teachers, and even a loss of purpose and low morale.

The financial cost is also enormous. An average cost of £20,000–£30,000 for a school inspection has caused serious questions to be asked. Funding has been made available by taking 'away from local authorities, (which is) part of the enormous price central government has had to pay for not trusting the educational service' (Richards, 1997).

A feeling of mistrust, and an awareness of the impact of an inspection have not endeared Ofsted to the teaching profession. 'Normal school life was disrupted for a period of at least three months' (Lonsdale and Parsons, 1997: 10).

The completion of an action plan to remedy faults found during the inspection requires school staff to focus on the negative, rather than celebrating success. This contributes to the sense of anti-climax and demoralization often mentioned after the completion of an inspection.

Ofsted inspections have been taking place since September 1994. The four-year cycle has been extended to a six-year cycle. The guidance for inspectors has been revised and amended on several occasions. All schools have now been inspected and at least know what to expect. Some have fed back positively on the experience. Lonsdale and Parson's research (1997) notes the value of the process as a means of emphasizing and prioritizing teaching and learning. Some have seen the report as a helpful tool to assist in the school's dealings with the LEA, and some valued the action plan as a vehicle for long-term development planning. Lonsdale and Parsons (1997: 8) commented that, 'Almost all headteachers felt there was some value in an objective process of inspection'.

The impact of an inspection is most forcibly felt in the cases of negative reports. There are three possible courses of action. First, a poor report can and should lead to reform and improvement by governors and teachers. Secondly, a poor report can lead to parents selecting an alternative school, thereby leaving the school to slowly 'wither away' (Hargreaves, 1995: 119). Finally, a school may be placed under 'special measures' or taken over by an educational association. Such schools are soon re-inspected to ascertain the effectiveness of implementing a stringent action plan.

Hargreaves (1995: 121) warns schools against attempting to 'mirror the Ofsted model' as a way of receiving a more favourable Ofsted report. Undoubtedly a positive inspection report does impress prospective parents, and in a climate of open enrolment, schools would be misguided not to use a report to attract more pupils. It is for these reasons that teachers must be aware of the inspection process, be ready to prepare themselves for an inspection, and to be able to present their strengths, without hiding weaknesses. In this way schools can build on success, rather than continue to conceal or cover up weaknesses.

There are three distinguishable stages to an inspection: the period of preparation, the week of inspection, and the subsequent preparation of an action plan. Teachers are subjected to regular inspection, where a non-negotiable, judgemental framework is applied. Too negative an approach is potentially damaging, and a 'take us as you find us' attitude is naive. It is worth bearing in mind that:

> Inspection carried out by skilled professionals can be a positive force, enhancing the performance of teachers, and thus the education of pupils, and improving public understanding. For those who do it well – the majority – inspection is a worthy occupation. (Laar, 1996)

Before the inspection

For many, the period before an inspection is when the actual inspection is won or lost. Ofsted selects schools for an inspection up to a year in advance, without specifying the exact dates. This allows the school to organize, prepare and collect documentation in advance, which Wilcox and Gray (1995) recognize to be an improvement on previous inspection systems. On the other hand, the account of the OFSTIN Conference (1996) highlights this aspect as a weakness in the system. The conference concluded that 'There are indications that the longer the existing pattern continues, the more skilfully schools will learn to "play the game", thus sustaining the system, but making it ever less effective' (p 9).

In terms of setting pupils a model for assessment, the conference report contains fears that by presenting the school in an over-prepared and unrepresentative fashion, it intimates that mild deceit is how adults go about evaluating their own performance.

On the other hand Ofsted itself (1995b) does recommend using the Ofsted Handbook as a tool for self-evaluation. Certainly the Handbook provides guidance and the criteria by which teachers will be assessed. Without doubt the provision of accurate information related to the categories by which a school is judged does provide the team of inspectors with a more positive frame of mind. Documentation may not exist, but its preparation from existing information is seen by many as a positive move. The report by Boothroyd *et al* (1996) on Ofsted notes that many teachers sensed a pre-determined agenda, 'a set of previously agreed expectations and issues' (p 11). The presentation of relevant policies and procedures will inevitably influence inspectors, a view supported by Field *et al* (1998) who claim that, through the analysis of Ofsted reports, negative aspects are often attributed to policy makers in a school. Indeed, Field *et al* go on to note that more attention is paid to the lack of policies than even to ineffective policies.

Schools are therefore well advised to begin to prepare the paperwork – which is a vast amount of work. Boothroyd *et al* (1996: 19) have attempted to quantify this:

> As for costs in terms of preparation, median values were: 40 staff days preparing documents, 10 days of the head's time on documents, £250 on reprographics and photocopying, 5 staff days on extra meetings of staff, zero on extra meetings with parents although some schools reported much more. Two staff days were reported as the median for extra meetings with governors and zero with the press, but with some schools reporting very large amounts (90 staff days).

Clearly, thorough preparation requires a considerable time commitment. It is hardly surprising that so much time is needed when one considers what will be reported on, as the guidance for inspectors makes clear:

- attainment related to national standards;
- progress in relation to prior attainment;

- attitudes, behaviour and personal development;
- teaching;
- curriculum and assessment;
- spiritual, moral, social and cultural development;
- leadership and management;
- staffing, accommodation and learning resources;
- efficiency.

Teachers, it seems, are in a no-win situation. Lonsdale and Parsons (1997) suggest that the process of preparation has a positive effect on those schools that do not have a tradition of development planning. However, members at the OFSTIN conference claim that the high levels of stress associated with the long lead into an inspection hit good teachers the hardest, as it is they who recognize and are aware of actual weaknesses the most.

The long lead in accelerates once the RgI has made contact with the school. The RgI is appointed by a privatized contractor, which has successfully won the contract for the inspection. The RgI assembles a team of inspectors from a register. All members of the prospective team must be trained and be in possession of an Ofsted number. Inspectors must have the expertise to cover the full curriculum, and also cross-curricular issues that impact upon the categories to be inspected. Most inspectors are not practising teachers. Many are former LEA officers, retired teachers, and/or experienced educators. The team must also contain a lay inspector who is not professionally involved with education but who has undergone training. The full inspection team therefore consists of sub-teams. Members of the core team, which includes the lay inspector, collate evidence and synthesize judgements on the whole-school issues. Members of the core team are likely also to be subject inspectors. Other subject inspectors obviously inspect their own particular subject provision, but also pass on evidence of and insights into whole-school concerns to the appropriate member of the core team.

It is not an uncommon complaint that inspectors are too far removed from the classroom. Indeed Boothroyd *et al* (1996: 7) note:

> For many of our correspondents the Registered Inspector or the composition of the inspection team, or both, proved unsuited to the school. The most common weakness was a mismatch of expertise and experience with the sector or subject being inspected.

The RgI should make contact, usually with the headteacher, to agree dates for the beginning and end of the inspection. Once the dates are agreed, an initial visit to the school is arranged. It is at this meeting that the composition of the inspection team should be discussed. Scrutiny of inspectors' CVs may lead to their position on the team being challenged. It is also normal practice for the RgI to meet with the staff of the school, to explain the inspection process and to discuss what information should be provided by the school. This meeting usually takes place approximately two to three months in advance of the inspection, leaving little time for documentation to be prepared.

The Ofsted Handbook (1995b) stresses categorically that 'On no account should inspectors issue additional forms to the school for completion beyond those prescribed by Ofsted'. Those prescribed by Ofsted are:

- a completed headteacher's form and statement;
- school prospectus;
- school development plan or equivalent planning document;
- copy of the last annual report to parents;
- minutes of meetings of the appropriate authority for the last 12 months;
- staff handbook;
- curriculum policies, plans and schemes of work;
- other policy documents that are available;
- a timetable of the work of the school for the period of inspection;
- other information the school wishes to be considered, including any documents about, and the outcomes of, any school self-evaluation activities.

Clearly the preparation of documentation is the responsibility of all teachers. Additional documentation will be required during the inspection, including attendance registers and samples of pupils' work, records and reports to parents.

At this critical visit the RgI will also negotiate with the headteacher a date and time for a pre-inspection meeting with parents. All parents are sent a standard questionnaire, which is returned in confidence to the RgI. Following an analysis of the questionnaire and a summary of the meeting with parents (which no members of staff may attend, unless they have a child or children of their own at the school) the general consensus is shared with the headteacher. The RgI seeks, through the questionnaire and the meeting, parents' views on attainment and progress, the attitudes and values promoted by the school, communications with parents, help and guidance available to pupils, homework, behaviour and attendance, the role of parents and the school's readiness to deal with suggestions and complaints.

Boothroyd et al (1996) question the validity of this consultation procedure. Research shows that proportionally few parents engage in the procedure and it is the validity of evidence based on a small and self-selecting sample that is questioned. They also question the naiveté with which information is interpreted.

The information collected and analysed by the RgI comprises the pre-inspection sections of a school profile, which is then circulated to the full team of inspectors. Along with the school profile is a brief commentary and copies of documentation relating to individual inspectors' areas of responsibility. At the same time copies of a PICSI report (Pre-inspection Context and School Indicator) are also made available. The purpose of this report is to enable inspectors to compare the statistical data contained in the headteacher's form with schools of similar type across the country. This facilitates the inspectors' responsibility to judge a school's performance in relation to national standards and norms. Wilcox and Gray (1995: 66) have questioned the usefulness of this exercise on the grounds that 'the PICSIs ... are not sufficiently developed. The headteacher's form is insufficiently imaginative'.

Members of the inspection team scrutinize the documentation forwarded to them up to two weeks in advance of the inspection. Subject inspectors use the information to begin to build a bank of evidence under each of the categories to be reported upon, and formulate questions that will help to clarify concerns and issues. The subject inspector will also make a provisional observation schedule with the intention of observing all teachers of the subject, across the age and ability range. The timetable is provisional as events may overtake plans (see 'During the inspection', below).

The subject-related paperwork conveys many messages to the inspector. The inspector will begin to ascertain whether subject aims and objectives contribute to whole-school aims; if teachers appear adequately qualified and trained; and if examination results meet with national norms. Schemes of work will demonstrate if National Curriculum requirements are met and policies on differentiation, equal opportunities and assessment begin to provide evidence of effective teaching. Expectations and methodology help to paint a picture of the subject provision.

At this stage the documentation does not provide answers. It does though help the inspector to form an opinion and to formulate questions. It is during the inspection that answers should emerge. Good inspectors will base their judgements on a range of evidence. Inspection is intense work for inspectors too. The criticism that inspectors do not always appear to have read the paperwork provided by the school in advance (Boothroyd *et al*, 1996) is in fact to challenge the professionalism of the inspector. Inspectors are bound by a code of conduct and schools are monitoring inspectors' conduct throughout an inspection. Any complaint must be supported by evidence, and consequently teachers do need to record any disquiet and concerns as they emerge.

During the inspection

During the week of inspection inspectors are required to complete the gathering of evidence and to provide answers to the questions formulated before hand. Ofsted's *Guidance on the Inspection of Primary Schools* (1995a) and its *Guidance on the Inspection of Secondary Schools* (1995b) list what is expected of inspectors. It is clearly stipulated that at least 60 per cent of inspectors' time should be spent observing. The subject inspector will spend between one and four days inspecting the subject, depending on the size of subject provision. However, teachers are not only observed in specialist subject areas, by specialist inspections. Particularly in a primary school teachers will be watched by a range of people, covering the full range of subject disciplines. Even at secondary level teachers will be watched during the form tutor period, personal social and health education assemblies and possibly in their own subject area for reasons pertaining to cross-curricular issues and concerns. Consequently when the modern foreign languages inspector leaves the school after three days, the modern foreign languages staff cannot relax.

Other duties for inspectors include the continuing scrutiny of documentary evidence, such as resources based within a subject area and in the library. Inspectors will note the impact of displays, will talk formally and informally with pupils and will observe pupils' work. During the evenings, through meetings with fellow inspectors, corporate decisions and judgements are made about the school. The overall picture is, at least in part, a collective judgement. Last of all, the subject inspectors will provide feedback to the subject leader and usually a member of the senior management of the school. This is usually in the company of the RgI too. Often on the Friday, the core team finally feeds back to the school's management team. After this meeting schools usually breathe a huge sigh of relief as the last inspector packs his or her briefcase and leaves the school site.

Observation

Observation is at the very heart of Ofsted inspections. Inspectors plan a schedule of observations, intending first of all to cover the full age and ability range. Fitzgibbon (1996) sees it as the most expensive part of the inspection in terms of the inspectors' time and stress for school staff. She criticizes the observation as 'amateurish' (p 19) as the inspector will draw unchallengeable conclusions about the effectiveness of lessons. She compares the process to the inspector of a business or industry, who would not permit a system that is 'based on opinion about how the business or industry should be run, not on sound research' (p 20).

In order to achieve the necessary coverage, whole lessons are not always observed. For this reason, it is in the teacher's interest to provide the inspector with a lesson plan, whether the inspector arrives at the beginning or end of a lesson. This plan should provide contextual detail such as the number on roll, number of boys and girls present, ability range and grouping and the identification of any pupils on the special educational needs register. Teachers should outline the content of the lesson and include clear objectives related to National Curriculum documentation. In this way the teacher can demonstrate easily the level at which a lesson is pitched, continuity and the range of activities, extending beyond the period of time the inspector is actually in the lesson.

The most contentious issue related to observation is that the inspector will grade the lesson under four categories: teaching, attainment, response and progress, on a scale of 1 to 7. A grade 1 represents excellence, and 7 very poor. Using a standardized pro-forma, the inspector will justify the grade, following guidance provided by Ofsted and an RgI. There are no strict criteria – the inspector is required to exercise professional judgement. Wilcox and Gray's (1995) research into inspectors' views demonstrates differences of opinion about the grading system. One inspector (p 65) feared that the system encourages a norm-referenced approach, particularly as there are no national standards to act as benchmarks for inspectors' judgements. A second commended the methodology, since once 80–100 observations and gradings have been achieved across the school, there is enough data available to discern interesting trends. Whatever the case, lesson observation is a skill, and all RgIs work towards a consistent approach within their team, often issuing guidance for subject inspectors.

Attainment is the easiest for inspectors to judge. They must assess whether the lesson and work achieved is in line with standards (in terms of National Curriculum levels) expected of learners of their age. The inspector should look for variations of performance by pupils in terms of gender, ethnic background and ability. Finally the inspector will grade this aspect. A high grade means pupils are performing above realistic expectations, and a low grade significantly below. It is important to note this use of national standards. Some schools (eg secondary modern) will almost inevitably receive a lower grade. It may be the case that some schools (eg grammar schools) could receive a high grade despite the quality of teaching.

The assessment of 'progress' can soften the blow! Inspectors have to gauge pupils' gains in a lesson, ie the reinforcement, consolidation or extension of skills, knowledge and understanding. Inspectors relate the lesson content to work covered previously, evident in exercise books, individual education plans (IEPs), through discussion and through comparison with other groups observed.

The perception of progress is inevitably linked to 'response'. Once again, a grade is given according to a range of factors. The inspector has to gauge pupils' attitudes, involvement, enthusiasm, application, concentration and perseverance. Their ability to participate in a range of activities (eg whole-class question and answer work, small-group work and individual work) is of course a very positive sign. Their relationship with the teacher is assessed as well as the group dynamics and interrelationships with fellow pupils. All of this culminates in a single grade.

All of the above rely on good teaching. Ofsted emphasizes the value of good teaching and the negative effect of bad teaching. Part of the role of Ofsted is to generate data that can be used to detect national trends. Hargreaves (1995) points out that Ofsted annual reports reveal that on average 20–30 per cent of lessons observed by inspectors are unsatisfactory. Teaching is seen to be the single most important factor. Inspectors seek, through lesson observation, evidence of subject knowledge, planning and preparation, clear objectives and appropriate content. Effective classroom management, pace, timing and differentiation are seen as contributory factors, as are effective classroom relationships, expectations and the ability to challenge and motivate.

Particularly good or bad teaching is exposed. Inspectors report to the RgI. Teachers receiving a grade 1/2 or 6/7 are informed of the grading. They must then be observed again, and following Ofsted's own guidance on *Reporting on Particularly Good or Poor Teaching: The Code of Practice* (Ofsted, 1996), if they receive a similar grade a second time, the inspector should complete a form justifying the grading. The teacher receives a copy, as does the headteacher. The form is to provide information, and is not to be used for disciplinary purposes. The more recent implementation of this practice involves the RgI adapting inspectors' grades (1/2 =1; 2/3/4 = 2; 5/6/7 = 3). This provides the RgI and the head with a whole-school teaching profile. Not surprisingly teachers are unhappy with receiving grades based upon very limited observation, and also resent the level of feedback received from inspectors.

Frustration at the lack of feedback is heightened by the fact that when it is provided, albeit informally, it is highly respected. Indeed Wilcox and Gray (1995: 7) sensed that the success of an inspection, in teachers' eyes, often hinged on the informal messages given out. Hargreaves (1995: 122) reiterates: 'in over half the schools, staff were disappointed that there was not more opportunity for discussion with inspectors after lessons'.

Scrutiny of documentary evidence

Having read schemes of work, and hopefully departmental handbooks, inspectors should be aware of the resources deployed. An examination of resources actually used in the classroom and readily available usually serves to confirm what is included in policies and procedures. Access to computers, TV and video, overhead projectors and other hardware is assessed. The number of textbooks and other materials are important factors, which may be linked to good or bad provision. As with observation, such scrutiny is all the more important when inspecting at primary schools when the provision of a particular subject may be through an integrated, project-work approach. Inspectors need to ascertain the extent to which particular resources contribute to the fulfilment of clear, subject-based learning objectives, whatever the mode of delivery. Inspectors do not grade such provision, but do make notes, copies of which are retained by the RgI.

Contact with learners is achieved in several ways. First, the scrutiny of pupils' work. Schools are asked to provide the work of at least three pupils per group, to represent the ability range. Inspectors look at the work from a subject perspective (does it meet with expected levels of attainment?) and from a cross-curricular point of view. Inspectors feel that the one evening devoted to this task is insufficient:

> Looking at pupils' work – you can do a fair bit as you go along. Getting a sample across the board is very valuable. In all honesty, though, the review of pupils' work is trivial and deserves a great deal more time. (Hargreaves, 1995: 68)

Talking to pupils formally helps to clarify issues that surface during the scrutiny of work. Again, inspectors are allocated to three pupils. Discussions centre around discipline, opportunities for cross-curricular and extracurricular activities, extension work and support. At primary schools inspectors listen to pupils read; at secondary schools more emphasis is placed on attitudes to homework. Again inspectors record, in note form, the essential points made.

Informal contact with pupils is also informative. Inspectors gauge pupils' attitudes to subjects and the school as a whole through contact in lessons and in corridors outside the classroom.

Feedback

Informal feedback to teachers after lessons is much valued. The feedback by the subject inspector to the subject leader is often seen as anti-climactic. Inspectors are always guarded. After an intense few days of gathering data, inspectors must present their judgements. The oral report must not differ in tone from the final written report. The RgI encourages inspectors to exemplify good and bad practice. School staff may challenge factual details, but not the inspectors' judgement. The inspectors' role is not to provide advice, but simply to report. The outcome of all this is that the oral feedback is very often a monologue, presented in 'Ofsted speak'. The inspector is compelled to translate numerical gradings into words, generating what Field et al (1998) have called 'scalar statements'. It is not difficult to relate the gradings to terms such as 'excellent', 'very good', 'good', 'fair', 'sound', 'unsatisfactory' and 'poor'. The final feedback to the senior management team differs little in tone. Through lengthy discussion, inspection criteria have been graded by the RgI seeking the opinions of all inspections. The feedback is therefore formal and closely structured by the gradings given. The grades are not revealed, however.

There is no doubt that the inspection week is busy and stressful. Inspectors try not to increase the stress levels beyond the inevitable. Rarely do inspectors enter the staff room, for example, and the Ofsted code of conduct emphasizes the need for courtesy and understanding. Nevertheless, it would be naive to suggest that all stress can be avoided. The best news on offer is that teachers can be prepared to the extent that they know what to expect.

After the inspection

The completion of the inspection week is often met with a sense of anti-climax. Memories of the inspection for heads of subjects centre around the feedback, which is inevitably relayed to colleagues in relevant teams. The outcome of the inspection will lead to several possible actions. At worst, the school will be called a 'failing' school, and will then be placed under special measures. A detailed action plan is required, and the school will be re-inspected. Headteachers can be replaced and governing bodies required to resign. At the very worst, a school can be closed or the school can be taken over and run by an authority, until such time it is felt to be back on course.

The usual procedure following the inspection is that after a period of five to six weeks the full report is produced by the RgI. A summary of the report is sent to all parents, and parents are informed that a copy of the full report is available from the school. The school may only charge for the cost of photocopying. The report is soon placed on the Internet (http://www.open.gov.uk/ofsted/ofsted/htm), and is therefore a public document. Schools use the report to issue a press release, which generally reflects the most positive aspects of the report. At school, the governors are responsible for the completion of an action plan, which serves as a response to the report. The action plan must be completed within 40 working days. Evidently, governors devolve responsibility to the headteacher, who consults with appropriate staff. Many schools – up to 19 per cent – employ a consultant to assist (Fidler *et al*, 1995). The consultant is often a member of the LEA support team, who has to read and interpret the report. Inspectors, whom many would judge to be in the best position to offer advice, are unsure as to whether they should do so. Ofsted inspections work on the principle that an audit is best performed by outsiders, and inspectors run the risk of breaking the code of conduct by engaging in consultation work.

The report

The report is the most lasting part of an inspection. Ofsted's guidance is clear (Ofsted, 1996: 36–37). The report and the summary should:

- be clear to all its readers – the appropriate authority, parents, professionals and the wider public;
- concentrate on evaluating rather than describing what is seen;
- focus on the educational standards achieved and the factors which impact on standards and quality;
- use everyday language, not educational jargon, and be grammatically correct;
- be concrete and specific;
- use sub-headings and bullet points where they help to make the message clear;
- use telling examples drawn from the evidence base in order to make generalizations understandable and to illustrate what is meant by 'good' or 'poor';
- employ words and phrases that enliven the report and convey the individual character of the school.

Field *et al* (1998) have analysed the language of Ofsted reports, and the results do not match up to the list of objectives above. The vast majority of sentences are 'scalar' in that they are verbal representations of a numerical scale. The report notes the percentage of lessons that fall into the categories of 'very poor', 'poor', 'sound', 'good' and 'very good' – the original five-point Ofsted scale. Terms such as these occur as often as once every 50 words in some reports. 'Qualitative' judgements – statements when the RgI attempts to explain the judgements through exemplification, noting causal factors and/or offering advice – are much more limited in number. The overall outcome is that the school's strengths and weaknesses are described. There are no suggestions to help the school remedy problems. Many commentators challenge the validity and reliability of the reports. The style of the report is that which measures output and performance. Maw (1996: 28) comments: 'validity and reliability cannot be subsequently checked for accuracy and fairness, because no record of events and observations exists in any other form other than evaluative'.

However, the report on Ofsted school inspections and their impact on school development, presented at the ECER/BERA conference in 1995 (Fidler *et al*, 1995) noted that two-thirds of schools are satisfied with their report, 12 per cent felt it was unfairly positive, and 21 per cent said it was too negative.

The report contains comments and judgements on each subject inspected and also on all aspects (see earlier) A copy of the report is sent to Ofsted, along with copies of the school profile (numerical gradings), subject profiles (numerical gradings), codes and grades from observation forms, and the headteacher's form. That which is sent to Ofsted forms part of a national database, providing evidence for the chief inspector. The policy of naming good and bad schools in the press is morally questionable, but difficult to negate on the grounds that the judgements are based on evidence. Little or no account is given to value-added issues. Performance is presented in terms of the relationship with national standards, and the report is the only publicly available document to support or challenge the judgement.

Action plan

Within 40 days the school has to produce an action plan, which must relate to the Ofsted report. Indeed the report contains 'key issues' and 'recommendations for action'. The task is not therefore onerous, albeit focusing on the negative shortly after the gruelling experience of an inspection. Lonsdale and Parsons (1997) discovered that three-quarters of issues contained within an action plan had already been identified by schools in advance of the inspection, and are contained within school development plans. Very often sensitive issues are 'to be kept under review', a tactic Lonsdale and Parsons see as fudging the issues. On the other hand, Lonsdale and Parsons also identify an 'empowering' report – one that can be used by the school as a lever with the LEA, as a means of prising out more resources. The action plan is therefore seen by some as a tool to implement plans that the school has wanted to introduce for some time.

On the whole 'action planning' is seen as positive, as a way of ensuring that inspections have an impact on schools and school development. Copies of action plans are sent to parents, thereby increasing the notion of accountability.

Conclusion

Ofsted inspections are here to stay. Teachers and academics criticize them fiercely. Whatever else, their purpose is clear and the procedures are transparent. The data generated is interesting, and teachers are required to understand how the information can be used to improve practice (TTA, 1998).

First it is important to know how to access a report. Any member of the public can ask for a copy from the school, for the price of photocopying. Copies are available on the Internet (http://www.open.gov.uk/ofsted/ofsted/htm), although users need Adobe Reader to download the files. For new teachers the reports can assist in forming a picture of the ethos and image of a school. The real use of the reports is wider-reaching than simply to absorb what they contain. Analysis of the headteacher's form and examination and test results gives a good picture of the level of performance. The PICSI report helps to place the school in context. The success of this document has led to the development of performance and assessment reports (PANDAs), which are now to be provided to all schools annually, rather than simply prior to an inspection. Self-evaluation systems, resulting in detailed school and subject development plans, and value-added systems all help to provide a full picture of a school's life.

The Ofsted report is simply one document among many that help to drive up standards. Alone it serves little purpose. Nationally speaking, a common,

Table 9.1 Table for locating information within the school

	Attainment	Progress	Attitudes, behaviour, personal development	Teaching	Curriculum and assessment	Spiritual moral, social, cultural	Leadership and management
Headteacher's form							
Subject handbook							
Subject development plan							
Internal assessment records							
Pupils' work							
Schemes of work							
Displays							
School curriculum model							
Timetable							
School policies							
Subject policies							
Extra curricular opportunities							
Inventory							
Records of subject expenditure							
Minutes of subject meetings							
Accounts of in service courses attended by subject staff							

standardized inspection system does allow for the comparison of schools, and the database does tend to throw up key issues. In this way the system is effective in that it provides the Secretary of State with an ongoing evaluation of educational policies. It is less the effectiveness of the policy which experts question, but the efficiency. Inevitably Ofsted's own question is thrown back at the system: is Ofsted value for money?

Task 9.1

Consider all the documentation available in school. How can the documentation generate evidence under each of the Ofsted categories?

- Use Table 9.1 to help you to locate information. Map out where you would expect to find details.
- Read the relevant information and note down how well you think the school provides for learners in each category.
- Read the school's Ofsted report, and compare your judgements to those of the inspection team.

References

Boothroyd, C *et al* (1996) *A Better System of Inspection*, OFSTIN, Hexham

Department for Education and Science (DES) (1989) *Planning for School Development*, HMSO, London

DES (1991) *Development Planning: A practical guide*, HMSO, London

Fidler, B, Earley, P and Ouston, J (1995) *Ofsted School Inspections and Their Impact on School Development*, a report of ECER/BERA Conference, September, Bath

Field, C *et al* (1998) Ofsted inspection reports and the language of educational improvement, *Evaluation and Research in Education*, **11**, pp 125–29

Fitzgibbon, C (1996) Ofsted's methodology, in *A Better System of Inspection*, ed C Boothroyd *et al*, OFSTIN, Oxford

Hargreaves, D (1995) Inspection and school improvement, *Cambridge Journal of Education*, **25** (1), pp 117–25

Laar, B (1996) Ready for inspection, *Times Educational Supplement*, p 24, 18 October

Lonsdale, P and Parsons, C (1997) Inspection and the school improvement hoax, in *School Improvement After Inspection*, ed P Earley, Paul Chapman, London

Maw, J (1996) The handbook for the inspection of schools: models, outcomes and effects, in *Ofsted Inspection: The early experience*, J Ouston, P Early and B Fidler, David Fulton, London

Ofsted (1993) *Handbook for the Inspection of Schools*, HMSO, London

Ofsted (1995a) *The Ofsted Handbook: Guidance on the inspection of primary schools*, HMSO, London

Ofsted (1995b) *The Ofsted Handbook: Guidance on the inspection of secondary schools*, HMSO, London

Ofsted (1996) *Reporting on Particularly Good or Poor Teaching: The Code of Practice*, HMSO, London

OFSTIN (1996) Improving School Inspection: An account of the OFSTIN conference, New College Oxford, July, Oxford

Parsons, C (1997) The shame of Ofsted: not improving but policing, *Improving Schools*, **2**, pp 38–42

Power, M (1997) *The Audit Society*, Oxford University Press, Oxford

Richards, C (1997) The high price of inspection, *Guardian*, p 7, 3 June

TTA (1998) *National Standards for Qualified Teacher Status*, Teacher Training Agency, London

Wilcox, B and Gray, J (1995) The Ofsted inspection model, *Cambridge Journal of Education*, **25** (1), pp 63–73

Wilcox, B, Gray, J and Tranmer, M (1993) LEA frameworks for the assessment of schools: an interrupted picture, *Educational Research*, **35**, pp 209–19

Woodhead, C (1998) *Chief Inspector's Annual Report 1998*, DfEE, London

10 Working with parents

Tricia David

The aim of this chapter is to introduce the trainee to the concepts and issues relating to 'working with parents'. It identifies the key role parents have to play in their children's education from nursery to post-16. Primarily the chapter deals with recent changes in legislation and how these affect the teacher and trainee. Issues such as learning from birth, educating the under-5s, transition points in schooling and teacher-parent partnerships are discussed. It is a key chapter in helping the trainee to acquire a rounded knowledge of working with parents.

> **Objectives**
>
> By the end of this chapter the trainee will have an understanding of:
>
> - the need to work and closely liaise with parents;
> - recent legislation affecting parents' rights;
> - parent-teacher partnerships;
> - transition points in schooling;
> - growing and changing: life phases and transitions in learning.

Parents: the primary educators

Despite the fact that pioneers such as Margaret McMillan, who opened nurseries in highly disadvantaged areas of Bradford and London almost a century ago, promoted the view that parents needed to be informed about their children's health and about the education process, it was not until after the publication of the Plowden Report (CACE, 1967) that the key role and influence of parents and families began to be truly recognized by teachers and schools. A further catalyst had been the impact of the pre-school playgroup movement, founded in the early 1960s, since (usually) mothers who had been engaged in their children's early learning through participation in playgroup sessions and courses no longer accepted a role defined by teachers – outside the school premises and on the school's terms. They wanted to know what went on in classrooms, how their children were learning, and how they could help them at home. Further, some research carried out for the Plowden Report demonstrated the importance of parental influence on children's school attainment and when educational priority areas (EPAs – see publications by Eric Midwinter, eg, for further information) were set up to provide support for children and schools in areas of disadvantage, one key element was deemed to be the enrolment of parents as helpers in classrooms, as fund-raisers, and as members of supportive networks for other parents. In other words, parents gained recognition as the 'primary' educators of their children. However, the meanings and development of home–school partnerships have continued to be very mixed, and parents continue to feel sceptical about their ability to influence what happens in schools.

It was to be another 20 years before the then Secretary of State for Education, Kenneth Baker, in setting out his proposals for the very first UK National Curriculum in 1988, told parents at the Annual General Meeting Conference of the National Confederation of Parent Teacher Associations (NCPTA) that he was handing power over to them through his Education Reform Act. At that time, the assembled parent representatives shunned his proposal, saying they wanted partnerships not power. As has subsequently been observed, parents continue to have little power over the education system, so one might argue they were simply being delegated the role of 'policing' schools rather than actually engaging in decisions about what their children should be taught and how. In England at least, power over the content of the curriculum, and some might even argue pedagogy too, has become more centralized. Where others among our European partner countries are involving as wide a membership of the population as possible in debates about schooling, values and childhood (for example Spain and Sweden), we seem to have submitted to being told what must be done and how – as can be seen from the recent imposition of the literacy hour and arguments about whether or not this innovation is mandatory.

However, the ability to forge strong home-school links is clearly seen as an important attribute of well-trained teachers, particularly those qualified to work in the early years and primary sectors. Circular 4/98 (DfEE, 1998b) includes in the standards that must be met in order to be awarded Qualified Teacher Status (QTS) relating to phases 3–8 and 3–11, a requirement to:

demonstrate that they. . . have a knowledge of effective ways of working with parents and other carers (p 11);. . . manage, with support from an experienced specialist teacher if necessary, the work of parents and other adults in the classroom to enhance learning opportunities for pupils (p 14).

In addition all trainees for primary and secondary teaching must:

> demonstrate that they:. . .
>
> 1. recognize that learning takes place inside and outside the school context, and
> 2. understand the need to liaise effectively with parents and other carers and with agencies with responsibility for pupils' education and welfare. (p 16)

Thus it is no longer permissible to assume that knowledge of and some experience in working with parents can be left until newly qualified teachers have a few years' teaching under their belts and teachers in partnership schools will, according to Annex D Circular 4/98, be required to offer training appropriate to such demands.

Schools already have a statutory duty to:

- report to parents on their children's progress;
- enable parents to participate in the statementing process if their child is deemed to have special educational needs at that level and to inform parents of all decisions about the child's progress whatever the level of special educational need diagnosed (see Chapter 8 of this book and DfEE, 1994);
- ensure they have access to copies of inspection reports on the school, as well as other information documents about the school's policies and curriculum;
- hold an annual meeting at which parents may ask questions and make comments about the school's approaches.

Parents are also represented on each school's governing body. In the case of voluntary and private nursery settings, parents may be on a management committee, but this is not a statutory requirement. Thus all schools should be able to help trainees gain an understanding of the basic aspects of home-school liaison. However, what many headteachers, teachers and early childhood educators (ie those who work in the voluntary and private or independent pre-5 sector) have tried to do is to encourage partnerships with parents in a variety of ways, because they acknowledge the enhanced progress children can make when their parents are able to support their learning as a result of being well-informed. Additionally, close liaison between children's families and staff can help the teachers learn about children's existing knowledge and experiences, since each child's home will form the unique central core of an 'ecological niche' (Bronfenbrenner, 1979; Bronfenbrenner and Morris, 1998) in which that child's learning process will have begun. Parents and children co-construct their own worlds and their own meanings: parents are not a homogeneous group, even within a particular community. Each home will have its own culture and shared understandings and to teach appropriately, in ways that will ensure each child is able to access what is being taught, practitioners need to be able to see from the child's point of view, or as it is often put: 'to start where the child is'. Starting in a different 'place' will render teaching pointless, as learning is either boringly repeated or too difficult and off-putting.

In this chapter I will present information about the practices intended to support a child's entry into formal education and how parents can be key players throughout the child's educational career. I will use the term 'parent' to mean those adults with the major parental responsibility for a child, though it may be that several people, for example, grandparents, step-parents, carers, nannies and child-minders share this role. Prior to the 1989 Children Act, parents were seen as having rights over their (birth) children, but this Act recognized children's rights by insti-tuting the concept of parental responsibility and laying down the expectation that professionals (such as teachers and social workers) would always involve parents (those with parental responsibility) in decisions about their children, even in cases (now relatively less frequent) of children being taken into care, and work together to provide support for them, as the Act requires (see Chapter 8).

Making human sense: learning from birth

During the last 20 years we have begun to recognize the ways in which dependence upon (or collusion with?) developmental psychologists, whose methods caused the underestimation of what babies and young children are capable of achieving (Deloache and Brown, 1987), confirmed low expectations not only of small children themselves but of those who worked with and cared for them, at least in terms of their intellectual stimulation. The whole attitude to provision of nurseries as 'edu-care' settings demonstrated how unimportant the early years of life and learning were deemed to be. As a result parents who wish to or must continue employment outside the home after children are born continue to undergo crises and heartache as they attempt to ensure their children are happy, stimulated and safe with carers who will provide a continuous service. It seems strange that, were parents told when their children reached the age of 11 that their child would have to attend a number of different institutions year on year, they would be horrified. Yet this is accepted almost without question in relation to under-5s, exemplifying indoctrination to the effect that under-5s do not learn or do very much and so can be treated almost like parcels, being left to be 'minded'. However, we now know that during the first five years brain growth is at its most rapid and more is learnt during this phase of life than at any subsequent stage.

Babies' propensity for wanting to 'making sense' of the context in which they find themselves and their preparedness for language are factors which led contem-porary researchers (eg Trevarthen, 1992) to conclude that human beings come into the world 'programmed' to be social learners. Children are learning from birth (and probably even before that). As educators we cannot afford to waste children's precious time before 5 by giving them meaningless tasks – or after 5 by failing to build on what they already know and can do. Children, like the other participants in the process (the parents, teachers and headteachers) bring to their admission to nursery and reception class a rich history of varying experiences (Barrett, 1986). The same is true of each successive transition. The more we can help all pupils use their previous learning to make sense of and exploit the next learning situation, the faster and more confident will be their settling-in and progress.

Educating under-5s

The new Labour Government, while adopting different strategies from the previous government for achieving the expansion of nursery education, has continued the push for every 4-year-old whose parents wish them to attend nursery to be offered a place. In fact, most 4-year-olds are found in the reception classes of primary schools in the academic year in which they become 5. Many such classes are on the one hand being seen as part of the expansion of 'nursery provision' but on the other many are still operating as if they are providing for older children, failing to ensure the kind of approaches, staffing ratios, space and equipment that would be available in a nursery. Parents at first reported that in some cases they were told that their child could not be guaranteed a place at the school of their choice if they did not transfer their child from a local nursery or play-group/pre-school to the reception class at the start of the academic year or term determined by the school. Others still find that schools impose a part-time regime on children who have already settled well in a nursery for full days.

Naturally children need a period of time to adjust to and become familiar with a new setting, but some schools have been overly rigid in imposing this pattern on families, sometimes creating great difficulties for working parents, particularly working mothers whose families may rely on their incomes. What happens to children during the rest of their day, and the difficulties faced by some parents because of school hours and lack of 'out of school' care facilities, have not generally been high on the agendas of schools because other demands (such as the curriculum, assessments, inspections and the mass of paperwork) have taken precedence.

The Government's directives to local authorities to set up nursery partnerships and early years forums, which should review both education and care provision in the area, are a positive move forward which will hopefully lead to greater co-ordination of services to suit both children and parents (DfEE, 1998a).

Meanwhile, most under-5s' services which are receiving funding under nursery partnership schemes are using the *Desirable Outcomes for Children's Learning* (SCAA, 1996 – currently being revised) as the basis of their curriculum planning. The six areas of learning delineated by the *Desirable Outcomes* are:

1. personal and social development;
2. language and literacy;
3. mathematics;
4. knowledge and understanding of the world;
5. physical development; and
6. creative development.

These 'areas' are thought more appropriate for thinking about young children's learning than 'subjects' in the National Curriculum, but they are linked to subjects and aspects of the curriculum for 5- to 16-year-olds in the *Desirable Outcomes* (SCAA, 1996).

Although the statements about the six areas detail 'goals for learning' at the time of entry to school (SCAA, 1996: 1) and the document itself indicates that 'compulsory education begins the term after the child's fifth birthday' (p 1), these same statements form the basis for assessments of children in their first term of reception class (when many are just 4) and the basis for the curriculum in most preschool settings inspected according to regulations set up through the Nursery Education and Grant Maintained Schools Act 1996. Despite the fact that the *Desirable Outcomes* were not intended to be 'the curriculum', the latter is hardly surprising, since the criteria for nursery inspectors' judgements are breakdowns of the same statements (Ofsted, 1998a).

Having said that, the advantages of such documentation are that practitioners and parents can debate the *Desirable Outcomes* and appropriate pedagogy for achieving them, while the nursery inspection reports offer parents greater insight into the teaching and learning process in the early years than has been available in many institutions in the past. In addition, parents must be informed that a nursery inspection is to take place and the inspector must solicit the views of parents about the provision. In a section headed 'Common features of good practice', the *Desirable Outcomes* document states:

Each setting has a statement, shared with parents... which outlines the aims, objectives and content of the curriculum, how it is taught and how children's progress and achievement are assessed, recorded and communicated to parents and the schools to which children will progress... Children's progress and future learning needs are assessed and recorded through frequent observation and are shared regularly with parents. (SCAA, 1996: 6)

Then in a section on 'Parents as partners' (SCAA, 1996: 7), effective home-nursery liaison is advocated and parents' knowledge and skills, as well as that of educators, are acknowledged. Staff in nursery settings are expected to recognize the parents' fundamental role in their children's education and to enter into partnerships based on mutual respect and shared responsibility.

So far, the main focus has been on the education of 4-year-olds during this first phase but developments for 3-year-olds are now in progress, as are better and more comprehensive care facilities for children under 14, which include plans for children from birth to 3. Further initiatives, such as 'SureStart' projects, are intended to promote early learning and to help parents encourage their children from babyhood.

Some key points need to be recognized:

- children are learning from birth, so all nursery partnerships will have to ensure that those who work with all young children are properly trained to provide for their learning in ways appropriate to their age/stage and cultural context;
- continuity in relationships and learning is an essential ingredient in the achievement of higher standards (Whitebrook *et al*, 1990), so parents need to be partners with educators and all involved need excellent lines of communication. Further, frequent changes of carer and educator will be counterproductive – nursery partnerships need to attempt to minimize the number of transitions during this phase and to ensure parents are enabled to act as the link persons with the best knowledge bases about their own children.

Parents as link: transition to primary school

There are few, if any, schools which do not now arrange several visits for children and their parents to familiarize them with the reception class and its staff in the term before children are admitted to primary schools. For some more fortunate children the transition from pre-school or home to primary school will be even smoother, since they may be attending an 'early years unit', where nursery and reception teachers work closely together and children aged 3, 4 and 5 spend part or all of the day together.

When this is not the case, parents too will be 'new' to a school and may have strong feelings evoked by memories of their own school days. For some these will not have been happy and successful, whereas for most adults who become teachers, school will have been a positive experience. That some parents are afraid to ask for help with their children's learning has been confirmed by government-sponsored research in which mothers from poorer families are found to understand the importance of a good education for their children but have little confidence in their own ability and feel too intimidated by schools and teachers to seek help. (The research was carried out by the National Campaign for Learning, a charity jointly funded by the DfEE and British Industry; Ghouri, 1998.) Thus, once again, teachers need to try to put themselves in the shoes of the other people – this time, parents.

Reiterating the principles set out in the *Desirable Outcomes* (SCAA, 1996) primary and secondary schools, like nurseries, need to consider whether their approach to parents is:

- welcoming;
- respectful;
- based on shared responsibility;
- explicit in its recognition of parents' role in their children's education;
- clear in demonstrating that dialogue is a two-way process;
- encouraging collaboration;
- using parents' and other family members' expertise to support learning in and out of school;
- ensuring parents are enabled to contribute to their children's achievements and assessments;
- stimulating and informing the continuation at home of learning begun at school.

From the school's point of view, it is also important parents gain accurate and fair information so that they may make informed decisions about choice of school (where that is possible). Sources of information include: other parents; inspection reports and league tables; and pre-school providers, so teachers, and especially head-teachers, need to think carefully about how these sources garner and interpret their information and how much they are able to influence the information passed on by providing evidence which is positive. In some areas, schools communicate to parents from linguistic minorities through interpreters of local minority community languages, either by recruiting teachers and support staff from those communities or by enlisting the support of 'experienced' bilingual parents and using media such as video with footage of school life, having voice-over in different languages.

Teachers must also be aware that some parents will be at pains to hide the fact that they are illiterate, so messages and information must be communicated verbally from staff to parents and through parent networks. The use of videos of school life, displays with photographs of learning activities and cartoon booklets for the children starting school (rather than printed), are all examples of strategies that are positive ways of engaging young children themselves as well as parents with such learning difficulties.

One of the most recent innovations to practice in reception classes is the QCA (Qualifications and Assessment Authority) baseline assessment scheme. Early years teachers have assessed young children's learning according to curriculum-related criteria for many years (see for example Tyler, 1979) in order to diagnose any learning difficulties and to plan for future learning. What is different about the QCA scheme is that assessments are largely focused on literacy and numeracy, with some items on personal and social development. The reasons for this are that a) literacy and numeracy are seen as paramount in the education process; and b) numeracy in particular is one of the few areas which is reliable in a statistical sense and which can be assessed on school entry and again at the end of Key Stage 1 in order to derive a 'value-added' score for a school – that is, how much progress the children have made while attending the school.

The problem with baseline assessment is that it may end up producing a top-down pressure on parents and pre-school educators, who in their turn may put pressure on young children to achieve high scores in a narrow test. Parents were already convinced their 4-year-olds needed more formal teaching in nursery (David, 1992) as a result of the testing at the end of Key Stage 1. Baseline assessment is likely to be similarly misinterpreted by parents unless educators and teachers convince them of the long-term benefits which are derived from a play-based, child-directed curriculum in the pre-school. Each year, the evidence from American High/Scope research indicates that such a curriculum has long-term advantages over formal, didactic teaching of such young children, in terms of their ultimate educational achievements, later emotional stability, employability and qualifications, avoidance of crime and teenage pregnancy (Sylva, 1998).

Parents' roles in (and out) of schools

It is of course easy to acknowledge in theory the importance of parental involvement in their children's education. In practice, some teachers find true partnerships more difficult to achieve. Perhaps one of the main difficulties for teachers arises out of the fact that all parents have themselves experienced schooling during their own childhood and they therefore bring with them a preconception of what a teacher should be like and what teaching and learning in school should entail. Similarly, most teachers come to the work with preconceptions based on their own experiences. Younger trainees may remember their parents being involved in their pre-school setting and primary school and maybe as representatives on a PTA committee. However, lack of life experience and confidence may mean that they are not ready to involve parents in certain types of partnership until they have been teaching for a while. Mature students who have children of their own may have been pre-school supervisors, classroom assistants, or voluntary helpers in such settings, so they may be much more confident about engaging parents in a variety of ways. However, what actually happens will also depend on the expectations of the headteacher and other senior staff and the level of support for new teachers and trainees in this respect. If senior teachers act as competent and assured role models in their interactions with parents, newly qualified teachers and students have much more chance of becoming competent and assured themselves.

In the past, it was suggested that our education system offers parents three types of involvement in schools:

1. school-focused (usually fund raising; membership of the governing body for some);
2. curriculum-focused (helping with homework; helping in the classroom);
3. parent-focused (parents are seen as the primary educators and are given support and knowledge by the school) (Torkington, 1986).

Certainly the efficacy of some types of parental involvement and some roles allocated to parents in the past have been questioned (see David, 1990; Edwards and Knight, 1994).

The publication of the *Parent's Charter* (DES, 1992) by the previous government (and note the position of the apostrophe indicating perhaps that each parent is a single entity) reiterated their new 'role' as the consumers of education – despite the fact that the children are supposedly the beneficiaries and despite a teaching force which was by and large unhappy and unfamiliar with the notion of education as a commodity.

Teachers need also to be aware of parents' previous experiences and understandings of the proper relationship between parents and teachers. For some, this will mean a relationship that is socially distant and quite formal (Bastiani, 1997). Further, teachers are paid to do work in school and some parents may resent being asked to take on roles as unpaid help. Suschitzky and Chapman (1998: 94) propose one thinks of two types of parental roles: one is active involvement as a helper or fund-raiser; the other a partner in children's learning. Edwards and Knight (1994) and Bastiani (1997) claim that parent-school relationships are determined by the aims of the school and will be evident in its ethos. So, for example, if dialogue with parents is claimed to be important, the school will have in place structures to ensure that sufficient time is allowed for such dialogues. It is in the ethos that one can also detect whether issues of power have been addressed. If parents are seen as people who have to be 'educated' because they are perceived to be deficient, rather than experts on their own children and on other areas of knowledge they may be able to share with the school, a form of cultural supremacy will be operating which may 'resonate of colonization and ultimately lead to alienation' (Edwards and Knight, 1994: 114).

If one makes a list of what we expect of a 'good parent' and then list alongside it what we expect of a 'good teacher', one often finds it is the emphases and intensity rather than the actual responsibilities which differ. As the US early years expert Lilian Katz has commented, parent-child relationships are 'hot' – because parents invest such a lot in their children in many, many ways, whereas teacher-child relationships are 'cooler', less intense, because a teacher must 'invest' in a larger number of children over a shorter period of time (Katz, cited in Pugh and De'Ath, 1989). Teachers who claim that the parents at their school are not interested in their children's education because they do not come into the school or attend parents' evenings might ponder this and ask themselves if there are invisible barriers preventing some parents entering the school and how they might remove them.

Perhaps most of all, teachers need to recognize the ways in which parents, particularly mothers, act as mediators of their children's learning about the external world. As Pollard remarks in the conclusion to his research study:

> the notion of 'parents as consumers' does not recognize the vital role that mothers and fathers play in supporting children's identities, self-confidence and learning. The danger is that it can create detachment and division.
> (Pollard with Filer, 1996: 308)

In a review of the inspections of voluntary and private nursery provision, Ofsted (1998b) claims from evidence of inspection reports that:

> In 72 per cent of institutions there are good links with parents and carers. . . Parents and carers in general, are encouraged to contribute to assessments of children by sharing observations of their children's learning at home. Encouraging parents to engage more with their children's education is an objective that should be given greater attention in many institutions.
> (Ofsted,1998b: 14)

Since it is in these earliest years that the pattern for home-school partnerships can be laid, it seems somewhat worrying that almost one-third of the early years settings inspected under this framework did not successfully engage parents. During the next 12 months (1998–1999) each local authority nursery partnership will be required to plan the ways in which a qualified teacher will be involved in every nursery receiving funding under the scheme. It seems urgent, therefore, that part of such a teacher's brief should be to ensure that training and support relating to parental involvement is offered, possibly encouraging pre-school playgroups with special expertise in the area to share this with their colleagues.

Growing and changing: life phases and transitions

As children move through the education system they are also entering different life phases. The period of 'middle childhood' relates well to what is now called Key Stage 2 and it is during this phase that children become even more peer-oriented and independent. Depending on how schools in an area are organized, it may be that some children change from one school to another during this phase and having been confident 'elder pupils' they suddenly find they are 'the babies' again. How the school handles this transition, whether it can be seen as a happy 'rite of passage' or a stressful jolt, will depend on more than just parents and teachers. Older children can be enlisted to 'mentor' new pupils and the hidden curriculum of a caring school can be reinforced by – again – 'standing in the new child's shoes'. Just as at the start of nursery and reception class, familiarization visits, videos and so on, can help, but it must be remembered that it is often the case that as the children get older the school premises get bigger and more complex, with more groups moving around and more opportunities for bullying. Ensuring parents and children know they can talk to sympathetic senior or pastoral staff if they have any anxieties is vitally important.

Teachers' partnerships with other adults

In Chapter 8 the teacher's responsibility relating to the Children Act 1989 is discussed. One aspect of dealing with inter-professional liaison which must be thought through concerns school records. Parents are entitled to access to their own child's records, with the exception of confidential records kept to log cases of suspected child abuse. School personnel need to be clear about who does have access to these records and how long they are to be kept after a case has been dropped. Some of the professionals with whom teachers will be liaising during child protection investigations have Codes of Conduct requiring them to maintain confidential records, meaning they cannot share all the information they hold. At present teachers have no such code, although it seems likely that the General Teaching Council could institute a professional code of ethics. Meanwhile, teachers need time to debate such issues and in training to be provided with models of appropriate professional conduct whereby information on children and their families is treated with great respect.

It is difficult to find sufficient time to include training in inter-professional liaison in Initial Teacher Education (ITE), but the standards (DfEE, 1998c) do require that NQTs qualifying for work with young children can demonstrate an understanding of the roles and responsibilities of other agencies and all must understand their responsibility to protect children from abuse. Information about the great range of roles and agencies involved in the care of young children can be found in David (1994) and in Solity and Bickler (1993). A useful assignment for trainees can be to investigate the role of a worker from a different type of setting or service and to focus on the areas of overlap – for example, if investigating the work of a speech therapist, the trainee could explore the ways in which speech therapists and teachers approach and provide for language development and how they can work together.

In particular trainees need to understand the roles and responsibilities of all those involved in the assessment and provision for children with special educational needs (see Chapter 8), especially the ways in which the child's parents should be supported and given a voice.

However, perhaps the most important area which requires attention during ITE is general training in teamwork, since this is at the root of all effective collaborations both within the classroom, where a teacher may work with a team including nursery nurses, classroom assistants, parent and governor volunteers, advisory teachers, a variety of students, tutors from FE and HE (to name but a few) and more widely. Similarly, whole-school teams include more than the class teachers, since kitchen, caretaking and cleaning staff, dinner and supervisory staff, as well as classroom assistants, peripatetic specialists, governors and others are also part of the team. This means that even in a small primary school the team can be larger than is obvious, so team leadership requires thought and training.

Rodd (1994) suggests that effective team leaders:

- use their personalities to lead by example, stimulating a team culture;
- are innovative, improve team morale and productivity, and so make things better;
- ensure constructive relationships are established and maintained;
- foster self-esteem and confidence in team members;
- coach team members to improve performance.

Rodd also lists the features characterizing such team leaders: adaptability; energy; people-orientation; quality consciousness; being united (they clarify common purpose and promote co-operation); entrepreneurship; being focused; and informality. These features are imbued with particular values and attitudes and moving teams on systematically, step by step, involves setting achievable goals; clarifying roles; building supportive relationships (including developing trust); encouraging active participation using the skills and talents of individual team members; and monitoring team effectiveness.

School teams and inter-professional teams set up to deal with particular events must however beware of building so strongly that they exclude the very people they are working for and with – the children and their parents, who should in any case be seen as team members too.

Beyond the standards

The standards for gaining Qualified Teacher Status provided in Circular 4/98 are the basic criteria with which all must comply. In developing parent partnerships, teachers and headteachers may go beyond these standards by challenging their own and trainees' assumptions about parents. Parents are not a homogeneous group yet it is likely they all need support in raising and educating their children at some time. Few now live among their extended families and the school can be the centre of their community network. As the African proverb has it – 'It takes a village to raise a child.'

Task 10.1

Obtain the school's policy document for dealing with parents and outside agencies. Discuss with your mentor the implications of these policies with special reference to your teaching phase.

Task 10.2

Establish what policies the school has for pupils in transition. This can be from reception to Key Stage 1, Key Stage 1 to Key Stage 2, Key Stage 2 to Key Stage 3, Key Stage 3 to Key Stage 4 or from GCSE to A level.

Discuss with your mentor how such transitions are dealt with, both from a parent/pupil perspective and as a member of staff.

References

Barrett, G (1986) *Starting school – An evaluation of the experience*, AMMA, London

Bastiani, J (1997) *Home-school Work in Multicultural Settings*, David Fulton, London

Bronfenbrenner, U (1979) *The Ecology of Human Development*, Harvard University Press, Cambridge, MA

Bronfenbrenner, U and Morris, P (1998) The ecology of developmental processes, in *The Handbook of Child Psychology Volume I: Theoretical models of human development*, ed W Damon, Wiley, New York, pp 993–1028

CACE (1967) *Children and their Primary Schools* (The Plowden Report), HMSO, London

David, T (1990) *Under Five – Under-educated?*, Open University Press, Milton Keynes

David, T (1992) What do parents in Britain and Belgium want their children to learn?, paper presented at the OMEP International Congress at the University of North Arizona, August

David, T (ed) (1994) *Working Together for Young Children: Multi-professionalism in action*, Routledge, London

Deloache, J S and Brown, A L (1987) The early emergence of planning skills in children, in *Making Sense*, ed J Bruner and H Haste, Cassell, London

Department for Education and Employment (DfEE) (1994) *The Code of Practice on the Identification and Assessment of Special Educational Needs*, DfEE, London

DfEE (1998a) *Excellence in Schools*, The Stationery Office, London

DfEE (1998b) *Requirements for Courses of Initial Teacher Training*, Circular 4/98, DfEE, London

DfEE (1998c) *Teaching: High status, high standards*, DfEE/TTA, London

Department for Education and Science (1992) *The Parent's Charter*, DES, London

Edwards, A and Knight, P (1994) *Effective Early Years Education*, Open University Press, Buckingham

Ghouri, N (1998) Mum's too afraid to ask, *Times Educational Supplement*, p 4, 4 September

Midwinter, E (1996) Simply switch the future, *TES*, 7 June (4171), p 22

Ofsted (1998a) *Guidance on the Inspection of Nursery Education Provision in the Private, Voluntary and Independent Sectors*, The Stationery Office, London

Ofsted (1998b) *The Quality of Education in Institutions Inspected under the Nursery Education Funding Arrangements*, Ofsted, London

Pollard, A with Filer, A (1996) *The Social World of Children's Learning*, Cassell, London

Pugh, G and De'Ath, E (1989) *Working Towards Partnership in the Early Years*, NCB, London

Rodd, J (1994) *Leadership in Early Childhood*, Open University Press, Buckingham

SCAA (1996) *Desirable Outcomes for Children's Learning on Entering Compulsory Education*, DfEE/SCAA, London

Solity, J E and Bickler, G J (1993) *Support Services: Issues for education, health and social services professionals*, Cassell, London

Suschitzky, W and Chapman, J (1998) *Valued Children, Informed Teaching*, Open University Press, Buckingham

Sylva, K (1998) Too formal too soon?, Keynote address, Islington Early Years Conference, 9 July

Torkington, K (1986) Involving parents in the primary curriculum, in *Involving Parents in the Primary Curriculum*, ed M Hughes, Exeter University Occasional Papers, Exeter

Trevarthen, C (1992) Infants' motives for speaking and thinking in the culture, in *The Dialogical Alternative*, ed A H Wold, Oxford University Press, Oxford

Tyler, S (1979) *Keele Pre-school Assessment Guide*, NFER, Slough

Whitebrook, M, Howes, C and Phillips, D (1990) *Who Cares? Child care teachers and the quality of care in America*, Childcare Employee Project, Oakland, CA

11 Professional requirements

Gill Nicholls

The aim of this chapter is to examine the issues related to the professional requirements of a trainee, and how they may be addressed and developed in school through their teaching practice and beyond through continual professional development. The trainee is introduced to the concept of the professional, what it is to be part of a profession and how these impact on gaining qualified teacher status (QTS).

Objectives

By the end of this chapter the trainee should have a clear understanding of:

- the professional requirements of a trainee as found in Circular 4/98 (DfEE, 1998a);
- what it is to be professional and part of a profession;
- establishing effective working relationships across the school;
- the importance of personal presentation and conduct;
- professional responsibilities in relation to school policies and practices;
- the importance of informal learning through after-school activities;
- awareness of the role of school governors.

Introduction

The aim of this chapter is to examine the issues related to the professional requirements of a trainee teacher, and how they may be addressed and developed in school through their teaching practice and beyond through continual professional development.

Becoming a teacher requires many skills and attributes, as suggested in Chapter 1. Towards the end of the initial training period, more emphasis will be put on the professional requirements made by the teaching profession. These fall into two distinct areas. The first relates to professional duties such as pay and conditions of employment, legal liabilities relating to race, sex and health education, safety and the Children's Act of 1989. The second area relates to professional issues directly related to the trainees' day-to-day responsibilities and commitments. These include:

1. Establishing effective working relations across the school.
2. The importance of personal presentation and conduct.
3. Understanding professional responsibilities in relation to school policies and practices.
4. The importance of informal learning through after-school activities.
5. Awareness of the role of school governors.

These five issues are discussed in this chapter.

The training process requires in-depth understanding of the nature of the world the initial teacher trainee is entering and developing in. It requires taking on considerable responsibility and professionalism. What are the implications of these on the trainee? What is meant by being a professional and demonstrating professionalism in the work of the teacher?

Whether teaching is classified as a 'profession' is an endless debate. However, it is important to establish what is required by a professional and the implication this has for a new teacher. A 'profession' is said to have certain characteristics, including:

- a substantial body of knowledge which the professional needs to acquire;
- a lengthy period of training prior to joining the profession;
- a profession is self-governed and publicly accountable.

These elements need to be considered in the context of the school and the teaching environment in order to help trainees understand their commitment and responsibility to the teaching profession. It requires trainees and newly qualified teachers (NQTs) to:

- reach a certain standard and competence in both training and knowledge base;
- continually develop their classroom skills as well as refine the nature of their professional judgements;
- have high personal standards of achievement, involvement and reflection as a means of becoming an effective teacher.

These areas span the whole of teachers' professional education, whether trainees or experienced teachers. For initial teacher trainees, it is essential to understand how these affect their development. Circulars 10/97 (*High Status, High Standards:*

Requirements for courses of initial teacher training) and 4/98 break down these broad categories under several headings, all of which have to be taken into account before QTS can be obtained. Each area of development will be considered individually.

Establishing effective working relationships across the school

Establishing successful working relationships within schools is essential to good training and future long-term development. Every teacher is a member of several different groups and teams within a school. These include year teams, subject departments, sport groups, peer groups and academic groups as well as friendship groups. Teaching can often be a lonely profession, so it is important for the trainee to become involved within the school by becoming a member of one or more groups of people.

Working with colleagues, whether formally or informally, is an essential part of training and becoming a professional. As an individual within a group it is important to know what contribution can be made, and the value of that contribution. The nature of an individual's interaction within a group falls into five main categories:

1. sharing in common activities;
2. promoting a cause or idea;
3. gaining power or status;
4. establishing friendships and gaining a sense of belonging;
5. understanding that working in groups is part of one's job.

Working together with other teachers is a skill that develops and grows with time.

Teacher leadership is crucial to successful teaching and professional development. As Fullan and Hargreaves (1995: 35) state:

> Teacher leadership, defined as the capacity and commitment to contribute beyond one's own classroom, should be valued and practised from the beginning to the end of every teacher's career. There are few more basic things to fight for.

Trainees and NQTs can and should make an important contribution to any established groups. They bring with them new and fresh ideas, frequently challenging traditional approaches. These types of challenges are good for the group and the development of those involved. For the new teacher it is a case of trying to understand when to make suggestions and when it is better to be seen but not heard. Working at group relationships is a very important part of the trainee's training and personal development.

The importance of personal presentation and conduct

Personal presentation and conduct have a considerable impact on the way teachers are perceived and develop. Raymond *et al* (1992) suggest that:

> the link between personal and professional dispositions makes it important for teachers to have opportunities to examine their own personal commitments, histories and teaching styles. Discovering and making explicit the roots of their commitments, understanding the personal grounds that underlie their professional work, being clearer about the types of educational contexts ... assist in the process of teacher development.

This description applies to all levels of professional development. What is important for trainees is to understand the impact personal presentation and conduct may have on the way their teaching develops. It is about recognizing the importance of being professional, and understanding the needs of pupils and colleagues alike. This is a large responsibility when starting out on a teaching career.

Being professional starts with the way trainees present themselves to the teaching community and school as a whole. It reflects the commitment and views the trainee holds regarding education, teaching and learning. It is important that trainees are aware of the school ethos and code of dress, as well as the nature of conduct expected by the headteacher of the staff generally. They need to familiarize themselves with the working practices and principles of the school, such as starting times, staff room rules, expectations about playground duty and duties in general, register taking and accessibility to senior staff such as the headteacher. All these will reflect your style and approach to the teaching profession.

It is also essential that trainees realize and appreciate that they will be a role model for pupils, irrespective of the pupils' age. Even the very youngest pupil will observe the way a teacher dresses, talks, looks and reacts. Personal presentation at this level is a starting point to development.

The way in which trainees conduct themselves is equally important to the nature of being a professional teacher. Joining a group of established professional teachers is not always easy. Trainees should be prepared to integrate into the life of the staff room and the school. Becoming part of the group may take time, but understanding the dynamics of that group and where one can slot in is part of the trainee's professional development as a teacher.

Professional personal conduct is not restricted to the staff room or in front of the senior management: it stretches into the classroom. It is essential that the trainees' conduct in the classroom is nothing less than professional. Mutual respect is the key to success. Pupils will judge teachers on their behaviour and interpersonal skills. If a teacher continually shouts at the pupils, the pupils will undoubtedly respond in a similar manner, causing a noisy and disruptive classroom; if the teacher is continually late to lessons, the teacher cannot expect pupils to be on time. These are the key elements to be aware of and there is a need to consciously develop good practice throughout the teaching placement and beyond. Courtesy and respect for colleagues and pupils constitutes good professional conduct.

Understanding professional responsibilities in relation to school policies and practice

All teachers and trainees have professional responsibilities, which will vary from school to school. However, trainees need to be aware of the types of responsibilities that exist within the education system, and particularly those that are expected of them throughout their training placements. These can be divided into three types of responsibilities: personal, professional and contractual. Many of the personal responsibilities have been outlined above; the remaining two need further consideration and discussion.

Professional responsibilities

These relate to the way teachers and trainees take responsibility for their colleagues and their pupils. It is a question of maintaining the highest quality of work they are capable of. This will include lesson planning and preparation, marking of pupils' work, reporting and recording pupils' work, as well as considering the staff they work alongside and who are involved in the trainees' school based training. It is the trainees' professional responsibility to explore and find out about the school's policies and how they directly affect their work as a teacher in the school. The trainee needs to be aware of the school's policies on assessment, discipline, bullying, pastoral care, special educational needs, after-school activities and school uniform. In order to gain QTS trainees have to take responsibility as professional teachers to familiarize themselves with the nature of these policies and how they are implemented within the school.

Contractual responsibilities

Teachers have a variety of contractual responsibilities and duties. The trainees' contractual duties will be negotiated between the university/college, the school and the individual trainee. When qualified those who choose to be employed in state schools in England or Wales will be governed by the DfEE's *School Teachers' Pay and Conditions* document (1998b). This is issued under the School Teachers' Pay and Conditions Act of 1991. They will also be subject to statutory responsibilities and duties. These have been established by the government through legislation; the main features are set down in the *Ofsted Handbook for Inspection, Part 6. The Statutory Basis for Education* (1997). Trainees will be involved with a considerable number of legislative areas; the most important at this stage of development include:

- pupils' spiritual, moral, social and cultural development;
- behaviour and discipline;
- attendance;
- subjects of the curriculum and other curriculum provision;
- assessment, recording, and reporting;
- equality of opportunity;
- provision of SEN;
- teaching and non-teaching staff;
- resources for learning.

It is important to understand the context in which these issues are assessed and developed within a school, whether it be through direct professional development or through school-defined policies. All schools are subject to Ofsted inspections and trainees will be responsible for the pupils they teach. It is therefore in the trainees' interest to have a working knowledge of these issues. The training period is a key time to investigate, explore and consider the effect legislative procedures can have on an individuals' professional development.

In addition to this as a trainee and a teacher there are legal responsibilities arising from the following legislation and guidance:

- the Race Relations Act 1976;
- the Sex Discrimination Act 1975;
- Sections 7 and 8 of the Health and Safety at Work etc Act 1974;
- teachers' common law duty to ensure that pupils are healthy and safe on school premises and when leading activities off the school site, such as educational visits, school outings or field trips;
- what is reasonable for the purposes of safeguarding or promoting children's welfare (Section 3(5) of the Children Act 1989);
- the role of the education service in protecting children from abuse (currently set out in DfEE Circular 10/95;
- appropriate physical contact with pupils (currently set out in DfEE Circular 10/95);

- appropriate physical restraint of pupils (Section 4 of the Education Act 1997 and DfEE Circular 9/94);
- detention of pupils on disciplinary grounds (Section 5 of the Education Act 1997);
- the progression from SCAA's *Desirable Outcomes for Children's Learning on Entering Compulsory Education* to KS1, the progression from KS1 to KS2 and from KS2 to KS3.

These are the Acts and recommendations of which trainees need a working knowledge and understanding. During trainees' periods in school they should with the help of their mentors and senior staff familiarize themselves with the basic issues related to these Acts.

Task 11.1

Select one of the above Acts or sections of an Act and identify the central issues of concern. Discuss these with your mentor and reflect on the impact they may have on your present and future practice.

The importance of informal learning through after-school activities

The need to understand and be aware of the importance of informal learning is clearly set out in Circular 4/98. It states that initial teacher trainees must demonstrate that they:

> recognize that learning takes place inside and outside the school context, and understand the need to liaise effectively with parents and other carers and with agencies with responsibility for pupils' education and welfare.

Chapter 10 gives a clear explanation of the implications of working with parents.

All schools are involved in the process of information exchange, whether it be between pastoral and academic staff, parents or members of external agencies such as the social services. Each has a procedure and this may well be different in every school. The important point is that trainees should acquaint themselves with the procedures in place. They need to know what to do with information that is gathered about the pupils in the school. Systems that are in place need to be adhered to and respected.

There are many areas of a child's life that are brought into school. It is easy to forget once inside the classroom the impact life outside of school may have on a pupil. Taking the register is a good way of getting to know your pupils. Absence notes are more than an administrative procedure: they can give considerable insight into a child's life outside of school.

Task 11.2

Consider the following absence note, then discuss with your mentor the various options you have for dealing with such a situation:

James will be absent from school for the next week. I am going into hospital next week for surgery, and as I have no one to look after the younger children, James will have to take over.

Yours sincerely,
Gill Brown

How a teacher reacts to a pupil in such a situation, or any sensitive situation is crucial. Awareness of home situations is a very important part of a teacher's role As a teacher you convey powerful messages to your pupils, their parents and colleagues, all of which can affect future relationships. Trainees often come across situations such as pupils' suffering a bereavement in the family, or a break-up of the family home. In such cases trainees should always seek expert help from their mentor or senior teachers, and at the same time watch and learn from the way they deal with the potential problems and passing of information.

In learning the art and craft of dealing with moral and social issues that may affect a pupil's progress, speak to the pastoral head of the placement school. Become aware of how to deal with potentially sensitive areas and which of the agencies can or should be used to help pupils.

After-school activities are another means by which pupils learn, whether it is being involved in school sports, play, music or a chess club – they all form a vital part of education. Being a trainee teacher is an ideal opportunity to gain an understanding of the importance of the learning that takes place in 'informal settings'. These are very powerful learning zones and can profoundly influence a child's development. A good example here is that of the child who has excellent computer skills and can gain information easily and actively from the Internet.

Task 11.3

Identify areas of informal learning that a group of pupils in one of your classes are involved in. Reflect on their responses and identify how this may affect your teaching.

Awareness of the role of school governors

As a trainee teacher it is unlikely that you will have any real contact with school governors. It is however a requirement to understand what their role is and how they operate within the school structure.

There are different types of governors within any governing body, including teacher governors, parent governors, nominated governors, and co-opted governors. The headteacher can choose whether or not to be on the governing body, but has the right to attend meetings in any case. Minutes are taken at all governor meetings and are available for inspection by any interested party. Teacher governors are elected within the school by ballot, and are there to represent the interests of the teachers and to relay back to the staff decisions etc from the governing body.

Parent governors are nominated and elected by parents, usually by ballot. Parent governors are very important as they represent all the parents of the school. Their role is to bring parent-related issues and problems to the attention of the governing body. Their opinions are crucial as it is their children who are at the school.

Nominated governors are usually nominated by political parties through the LEA. Their role is to give an overall perspective to school governance. Usually, major political parties are represented.

Finally, co-opted governors are chosen to fill gaps in the expertise of the school's governing body.

Following the 1988 Education Act governors have had an increasingly important role to play in the running of schools, both primary and secondary. The roles and responsibilities of school governors are wide and varying and include:

- school policies on issues such as sex education, uniform, special educational needs, the curriculum, budgets, appointment of staff, and health and safety aspects of the school generally;
- maintaining relationships with staff in the school, parents, the community and the LEA;
- helping to maintain good standards within the school.

Governors can and often do delegate a great deal of these responsibilities to the headteacher, who in turn regularly reports to the governing body. Governors' roles within schools can vary: some schools allocate governors to departments, while others appoint governors to particular areas within the school, for example special educational needs or the curriculum. Whichever approach schools take, governors generally work with the staff with the aim of giving pupils the best learning opportunities possible within the school. Governors are not paid members of staff, yet they hold considerable power and are now trained to fulfil their duties. A key person is the chair of governors. Some governing bodies take a high-profile approach to governance. They will be seen around the school, visiting classrooms and being actively involved in day-to-day school issues. Others take a more discrete approach to their work and appear to be in the background. Whichever approach is adopted governors' policy decisions can have a considerable effect on teaching practices and learning outcomes in schools. All trainees should be aware of the role the governing body has in their placement school.

A significant function of the governing body is to regulate the conduct and discipline of staff, and to dismiss where necessary. All governors' roles and responsibilities are covered by regulations and codes of conduct. These can be obtain from the professional teaching bodies.

Task 11.4

Establish how your school's governing body operates, and whether specific governors are responsible for given areas within the school structure.

References

Department for Education and Employment (DfEE) (1994) *The Education of Children with Emotional and Behavioural Difficulties*, Circular 9/94, DfEE, London

DfEE (1995) *Protecting Children from Abuse: The role of the educational service*, Circular 10/95, DfEE, London

DfEE (1997) *High Status, High Standards: Requirements for courses of initial teacher training*, Circular 10/97, DfEE, London

DfEE (1998a) *Requirements for Courses of Initial Teacher Training*, Circular 4/98, DfEE, London

DfEE (1998b) *School Teachers' Pay and Conditions* document, HMSO, London

Fullan, M and Hargreaves, A (1995) *Developing Planning for School Improvement*, Cassell, London

Ofsted (1997) *Handbook for the Inspection of Schools: The statutory basis for education*, Ofsted, London

Raymond, D *et al* (1992) Contexts for teacher development: insights from teachers' stories, in *Understanding Teacher Development*, ed A Hargreaves and M Fullan, Cassell, London

SCAA (1997) *Desirable Outcomes for Children's Learning on Entering Compulsory Education*, SCAA, London

12 Continual professional development

Gill Nicholls

This chapter aims to inform the trainee of two distinct areas within professional development. The first section deals with applying for a teaching position, constructing a CV and preparation for interview. The second deals with the concept of professional development from both a personal and institutional point of view. Trainees are directed to construct their own action plan for future development.

Objectives

By the end of this chapter the trainee will have a clear understanding of:

- the need to apply for and secure a first teaching position;
- how to apply for a teaching position;
- how to construct a CV;
- how to prepare for interviews;
- what counts as professional development;
- the need to plan future development.

Applying for and securing your first teaching post

Securing your first teaching position will be one of the most important steps in your teaching career. As such it needs careful planning and preparation. You will need to consider several issues prior to application. These may well include:

- *Where you want to work.* You may want to return to your home area, or you may wish to remain in the area that you have trained in. What you must realize is that the more flexible you are the more opportunity there is for employment.

- *What age range you want to teach.* You may wish to teach only a particular Key Stage; this will restrict the types of vacancies you can apply for.
- *What type of school you want to teach in.* You may wish to teach in a primary, middle, or secondary school; equally important to you may be your desire to teach in a denominational school. These types of decisions will direct you where to look for teaching positions.
- *Where teaching jobs are advertised.* The majority of teaching positions are advertised in the *Times Educational Supplement,* which is published every Friday. *The Guardian* also has a comprehensive job section, published every Tuesday. For those who wish to teach in specific schools, teaching positions are also advertised in religious and ethnic newspapers, such as the *Jewish Chronicle, Catholic Herald, Universe, Methodist Recorder, Asian Times* and *The Voice.* The Catholic Education Service also produces a weekly vacancy sheet. Most Local Education Authorities (LEAs) produce lists of vacancies that are sent directly to schools and departments of education in higher education institutions.
- *What information is available to help applicants.* There are several sources available, including *First Teaching Appointments Procedures,* published by the Association of Graduate Careers Advisory Service (AGCAS). The teaching unions also publish useful information that will help to produce a solid application.

Application procedures

The first thing to note with applications is that if you are thinking of applying for a job in Scotland or Northern Ireland the procedures are different. Further information for such applications can be obtained from the Scottish or Northern Ireland Office. Within England and Wales applications can be specific to schools or open to LEAs. Open applications allow you to apply directly to the LEA asking them to consider you for a suitable teaching position. If you are thinking of applying in this way, or seeking to be considered for what some LEAs call 'teacher pools', your letter of application needs to state clearly the type of school you wish to teach in, the locality within the local authority area in which you wish to teach, your subject preference and subsidiary teaching subjects. These types of opportunities are becoming rare. More frequently schools advertise their own teaching vacancies in the publications mentioned above. In these circumstances specific applications need to be made directly to the school.

With specific applications schools may suggest you visit them prior to application. It is good practice to take up such an offer. The merits of doing this are two-fold: it suggests to the prospective school that you are genuinely interested in the school, and it gives you the opportunity to see the school in working conditions. The thing to remember on these types of visits is that there is no such thing as a truly informal contact with a school prior to application. The school is observing you just as you are viewing the school.

Making the application

Your letter of application and application forms are often the first point of contact between you and the school you have chosen to apply to. It is important to realize that if your application is not read you stand very little chance of being selected for interview. Many applications are reject immediately due to:

- poor presentation – illegibility, typing errors, too much information on one page;
- spelling mistakes – these include the name of the headteacher and the school, poor grammar, general spelling mistakes, careless use of English;
- failing to address points stated in the job description – the main issue here is answering questions inappropriately or not addressing issues at all.

The letter of application is where you market yourself: it is your way of telling the headteacher and governors what you can offer the school. You are ultimately trying to persuade them to interview you.

A good letter of application takes time and planning. You need to research the school and find out what it is actually looking for in a newly qualified teacher (NQT) in your chosen subject and age range. You will also need a well constructed and formatted CV. Allow yourself plenty of time to structure your letter of application and your CV. These are vital to your success in securing an interview.

Applications for teaching positions are mainly in one of two formats: that specified by the LEA or that specified by individual schools. Some LEAs have set application forms which require careful completion; these are often accompanied by a statement of support and your CV. Applications direct to a school often require a letter of application and your CV. Make sure you are clear about the type and format your application has to take. The following points will help you plan and construct both your letter of application and your CV.

Letter of application

Most important here is be positive and enthusiastic in your writing. Focus on what you think makes you a good teacher and suitable for the particular position you are applying for. Unless otherwise requested in the job advertisement, it is better to word-process your letter of application and your CV. Do not write an essay: aim to be concise but informative. One side of good quality A4 paper is sufficient, with a maximum of two sides.

Preparing your CV

Your CV should present the basic information that would normally be incorporated in a standard application form. The following details should appear on your CV:

- Name.
- DfEE number.
- Date of birth.
- Marital status.
- Schools and colleges attended. Give information about your schooling post-11.
- Qualifications. List these starting with your GCSEs and A levels, followed by your university education/courses and degree. PGCE students should include information on the content and class of degree.
- Other qualifications. These may be sport, music, first aid, etc.
- Teaching experience. Give details of your teaching practice schools, including names and dates of attendance. You may wish to include here any teaching you have been involved in outside of your specific training, such as coaching a sport, teaching English as a foreign language, reading schemes in adult education, helping in play groups or nursery schooling.
- Other work experience. Give concise details of any previous work experience you have had. This is particularly important if you have changed career.
- Interests and activities. This section should tell the school something about you and your personal interests. Don't just list them – indicate their relevance to teaching and being a teacher, for instance youth club leader, scouting or guiding.
- Other information and additional skills. Give details of any specific qualifications you may have obtained, for example computing expertise, musical qualifications, driving licence, foreign languages, being bilingual.
- Referees. Choose your referees with care. In a first job it is expected that one of your referees is from the college or institution in which you have trained. The second referee is ideally the headteacher or head of department from one of the teaching institutions in which you have been training.

Task 12.1

Draft a CV and a letter of application. Discuss it with a senior member of your school, or your personal tutor at college. Taking account of their comments, reconstruct your application and CV.

This task will help you to be prepared for any vacancy that arises.

Preparing for the interview

The interview is crucial to obtaining a teaching job. The interview is where you need to convince the headteacher and governing body that your are the right candidate for the job. You should have briefed yourself about the school, its catchment area, its Ofsted report, the standards achieved in the school, its sporting and after-school activities, its overall ethos, and parental involvement. This type of information will help you answer interview questions appropriately. It will also help you ask questions of the panel regarding aspects of the school you wish to know about. Make sure you are aware of the information you gave in your letter of application; it is always wise to re-read the letter prior to an interview.

You may be asked to teach a lesson while on interview. You should plan for this very carefully and ask for help and guidance from your mentor and your college tutors.

If you secure a teaching appointment at your first interview this is excellent, but be prepared to be rejected. Try not to be too disappointed; reflect and learn from your experiences. If a debrief is offered, take the opportunity if possible: you will gain a great deal although it may seem painful at the time. It is the only way to discover what requirements if any you did not meet. In this way you can take the experience and the learning to your next job interview.

What is essential is that you have planned well, prepared in advanced, and are determined to succeed.

Professional development

This section introduces the concept of professional development and how trainee teachers can understand its meaning and take responsibility for following their early development through to their future careers. Professional development and its role in keeping teachers up to date and informed are given high priority in Circulars 10/97 and 4/98. The former document states that it is important that the trainee teacher:

> understands the need to take responsibility for their own professional development and to keep up to date with research and development in pedagogy and in the subject they teach. (Circular 10/97: 13)

What counts as professional development?

This is a term that is often used very loosely, and taken to cover all learning undertaken by teachers throughout their career. It can take the form of private research through reading, external courses, long-term higher education, or a short course. You will find that teachers often refer to 'INSET' (In-service Education and Training) rather than 'professional development'. The terms are frequently used interchangeably.

There are many reasons for considering professional development as an important part of your training and future learning. Throughout your training you have been developing skills, knowledge and pedagogic practice. Now that you are reaching the end of this initial period you have to consider which areas you still need to develop and how. The most important reasons for looking to your future development may include:

- extending your experience in a particular direction, eg special educational needs, or acquiring specific subject knowledge;
- developing your professional knowledge and understanding in certain areas, eg baseline assessment, Key Stages 1, 2 and 3, SATs, pupils with severe learning difficulties, gifted pupils;
- extending and developing your teaching skills in a particular subject area;
- advancing your subject knowledge beyond its present level through taking a higher degree;
- extending your knowledge of teaching very young children or post-16 pupils;
- acquiring and developing your skills in writing school/departmental policy;
- developing your pastoral care skills.

Whatever your reason for your choice of development, you will find that even when you concentrate on one area, you develop a number of other skills at the same time. Reflecting on what and how you have developed and learnt is a key to your long-term future development as a teacher.

As you move from trainee to NQT you will find that professional development falls within two categories: personal development and institutionally-led development. It is important for you to realize that the two are inextricably linked, and that overall teacher and school development cannot occur in isolation from each other. This has more recently been written about as the 'learning school', one which takes the view that:

> if schools are about promoting the learning of pupils in a changing world and learning is worthwhile and not about a static or bounded process, then the learning of education professionals throughout their careers is essential. (Craft, 1996: 11)

This suggests that as teachers it is important to accept the fact that we have to continually learn in order to cope with the increasing demands for change within the teaching profession. It is therefore necessary for you to know what professional development means for you as you start your teaching career.

What is professional development?

Continual professional development will be a significant part of your teaching career; it will be one in which you explore existing skills, knowledge and responsibilities and endeavour to maintain, enhance and transfer these skills to a variety of situations that occur in teaching as a whole and to you as a teacher.

Professional development is about enhancing and extending your knowledge, pedagogy and experience. It is a way of enhancing your effectiveness as a teacher, gaining promotion and developing a career. This can be achieved by considering your starting point and where you want to go in the future. Professional development involves self-review, target setting and individual planning. Most NQTs will start from their career entry profiles (CEPs) (see Chapter 11). You will have completed a CEP by the end of your training period. The CEP will have concentrated on four specific areas of competence:

1. subject knowledge and understanding;
2. planning, teaching, and class management;
3. monitoring, assessment, recording, reporting and accountability;
4. other professional requirements.

Your first school will expect to see development in all areas of competence from your CEP. What you need to appreciate is that it is your responsibility, with the help of your school, to be involved in professional development.

Your CEP is the starting point of your planning for future development. Evaluating your situation is key. Consider the following points when discussing or planning your future needs:

- What areas of development arise from my CEP?
- What other areas do I want to develop?
- What is my preferred style of learning?
- What personal areas do I want to develop to help my career path, eg pastoral, curriculum, or administrative?
- What do I want from my appraisal in terms of specifying development needs?

A combination of all these factors will influence the context of your future professional development. Figure 12.1 summarizes the interplay of issues that should help you plan your professional development.

Figure 12.1 Establishing your future needs

Task 12.2

Consider your final reflections from teaching and determine what you feel your developmental needs are, both immediate and long term. Set yourself some targets. These can be taken to your new job for discussion.

References

Craft, A (1996) *Continuing Professional Development*, Routledge, London
Department for Education and Employment (1997) *High Status, High Standards: Requirements for courses of initial teacher training*, Circular 10/97, DfEE, London
Department for Education and Science (1969) Black Papers, HMSO, London

13 Induction for newly qualified teachers

James Williams

This chapter aims to focus the trainee's mind on the requirements, expectations and statutory demands of a newly qualified teacher (NQT). It explains the most recent demands from the Department for Education and Employment (DfEE, 1999) as to the arrangements for induction of the NQT. These requirements commence from May 1999. Clear direction is given to trainees regarding the induction period, what this entails, and the expectations of schools from the NQT in their new school.

Objectives

By the end of this chapter the trainee will have an understanding of:

- what it is to be an NQT;
- the aims of the induction period;
- roles and responsibilities during induction;
- the induction standards;
- what is meant by unsatisfactory progress.

In April 1998, the TTA was asked to provide the government with recommendations on arrangements for induction for NQTs. From May 1999, all those who gain qualified teacher status (QTS) must successfully complete an induction year. The TTA was tasked to produce a set of arrangements that were rigorous, manageable and supported teachers during their transition from trainee to fully qualified teacher. It was recognized that attaining the qualification to teach was no guarantee that this would automatically lead to continued effective professional practice. DfEE Circular 13/98 (DfEE, 1998a) announced that funding for this new and important initiative would also be made available within a school's standards fund. In particular, it stated that 'the level of funding will allow schools to meet the statutory requirement. . . from 1999. It will enable LEAs and schools to provide the necessary help and support to the NQT' (DfEE, 1998b, para B7).

The government's 1997 White Paper, *Excellence in Schools* (DfEE, 1997) outlined its commitment to providing training and support for new teachers. This supported the widely available but varied provision in LEAs and schools. For the first time, the government gave access to funding, with guidance on the nature of NQT induction. With the publication of the Green Paper in December 1998, this commitment to support for new teachers was further strengthened, and the government recognized that support for new teachers underpinned the professional development that all professionals have a right to:

> Professional development starts when a new teacher first enters school. . . The government will provide the necessary funding to guarantee all new teachers a reduced teaching load and a programme of support to ensure that they have the time to consolidate and improve their performance. (DfEE, 1998b, para 120)

The notion of an induction year is neither new nor unwelcome within the profession. The probationary year for teachers, abolished in 1992, was not considered by many to be a quality experience for many new teachers. As a mechanism for support and continued professional development it mostly failed to deliver. The provision of quality induction or probation in many LEAs depended on local commitment to fund a locally devised programme. Its abolition did not encounter much opposition. It is now recognized that a quality induction programme is a crucial step in the recognition of teaching as a valuable and valued profession. We must provide a professional approach to the treatment of new entrants to the profession. In other professions, such as law and medicine, a professional approach to induction enhances the status of that profession. The induction year must be viewed as a similar process for teaching.

Under the Teaching and Higher Education Act 1998, induction for NQTs is statutory. The award of QTS will still be conferred upon the successful completion of initial teacher training (ITT). However, this award will not be fully confirmed until the successful completion of the statutory induction year. Should teachers fail to complete their induction year they will no longer be eligible for employment as teachers in a maintained or non-maintained special school. This will apply to all NQTs awarded QTS from May 1999. The General Teaching Council (GTC), which the government intends to establish in 2000, will maintain a register of qualified teachers. All serving teachers will be required to register and all NQTs who are awarded QTS will be given a provisional registration. Failing to successfully complete the induction year will mean that provisional registration will not be converted to full registration.

The consequences of failing the induction year are severe. To continue with a career in teaching in the state sector, a teacher failing the induction year must complete a full PGCE once more. It is anticipated that the number of teachers failing to meet the standards laid down for successful completion of the induction period will be a small minority of those qualifying. There will be an appeals procedure, initially through the Secretary of State, but subsequently handled by the GTC.

The aims of the induction period

The initial guidance on induction arrangements has five broad aims:

1. To build upon the knowledge, skills and understanding developed in ITT.
2. To provide a foundation for long-term continuing professional development (CPD).
3. To build upon the areas of development identified in the NQT's career entry profile (CEP).
4. To ensure proper support is offered to NQTs making unsatisfactory progress.
5. To put in place rigorous assessment procedures for the induction year.

Early in 1999, guidance issued by the Secretary of State for Education in Circular 5/99 informed headteachers and LEAs about the implementation of this new statutory requirement. In addition it is planned that support materials will be issued to help exemplify the requirements.

In order to fulfil the stated aims of induction, it is important to set out the roles and responsibilities of those involved in an NQT's induction period. Although the induction period is statutory for those seeking employment in the state or maintained sector, it is not statutory for NQTs who enter teaching for the first time in the independent sector. Switching from the independent sector to the state sector for anyone who qualifies after May 1999 will mean that they must complete an induction year, regardless of the number of years' experience they have. For those who move to the state sector but who qualified before May 1999, there is no requirement to complete an induction year. The government is, however, urging the independent sector to implement an induction year.

Roles and responsibilities during induction

Various bodies and individuals will have particular roles and responsibilities during the induction period. Successful induction will require all concerned to carry out their role professionally. The headteacher, the induction tutor, the NQT, the LEA (the 'appropriate body') and the school's governing body all have a part to play in ensuring successful induction. Tables 13.1 to 13.5 summarize the roles and responsibilities of the various bodies and individuals involved in setting up, monitoring, assessing and reporting upon the induction programme for NQTs.

Table 13.1 The roles and responsibilities of the headteacher during NQT induction

Headteacher

Role	*Responsibility*
• To designate staff responsibilities	• To prepare staff for their roles during the induction period • To assign staff to act as induction tutors for each NQT in the school
• To develop the induction programme	• To ensure that an appropriate induction programme related to the NQT's CEP is available
• To agree the NQT's timetable	• To ensure that the NQT's timetable is no more than 90% per cent of a substantive teacher's full timetable
• To provide rigorous and fair assessment of NQTs	• To ensure that induction tutors' assessment is fair and rigorous
• To provide independent assessment of NQTs failing to make satisfactory progress	• To observe the teaching of any NQT deemed to be at risk
• To collate assessment meeting reports	• To ensure that reports of any assessment meetings are forwarded to the appropriate body
• To make recommendations to the appropriate bodies	• To inform the appropriate body of any NQT who satisfactorily completes the induction period • To inform the appropriate body of any NQT who fails to satisfactorily complete the induction period
• To maintain NQT records	• To liaise with other schools and obtain/pass on records of NQTs who move jobs during the induction period • To liaise with other schools/appropriate bodies where NQTs are employed part-time
• To inform the governing body of induction arrangements/progress	• To ensure that governing bodies are aware of the induction programme and the progress of any NQTs

Table 13.2   The roles and responsibilities of the induction tutor during NQT induction

Induction tutor

Role	*Responsibility*

• Day-to-day monitoring and support	• To implement the school's induction programme
	• To act as a source of advice
	• To observe NQTs teaching
	• To report and feedback on observations to:
	  – the NQT
	  – the headteacher (where appropriate)

• Be trained for the role of induction tutor	• To attend INSET deemed necessary by the headteacher
• Apply induction assessment criteria	• To be familiar with induction assessment requirements • To apply induction assessment criteria rigorously and fairly
• Implement the NQT's CEP action plan	• To translate the NQT's CEP action plan into an achievable programme given the circumstances present within the school
• To enable full and proper support	• To ensure that there is an appropriate breadth of experience for the NQT • To arrange for additional support and experience outside the NQT's school if necessary
• Record keeping	• To maintain accurate records of the NQT's progress
• Assessment activity recording	• To ensure that assessments of NQTs are undertaken according to induction guidelines and keep formal records of their outcome

Headteachers have the responsibility for ensuring that a high quality induction programme is available for all NQTs employed by their school. This includes a number of management-specific issues such as preparing experienced staff for their roles as induction tutors, ensuring a fair but rigorous assessment of NQTs and other more administrative issues such as notifying LEAs of when NQTs join and leave the staff. The main role of the headteacher is, however, to make a recommendation to the appropriate body as to whether or not an NQT has successfully passed the induction year.

The induction tutors' role in supporting and monitoring the work of NQTs is vital. It is clear from a summary of their roles and responsibilities as set out in Table 13.2 that they must be accessible and approachable. In most cases, particularly in

Table 13.3   The roles and responsibilities of the NQT during induction

Newly qualified teacher

Role	*Responsibility*
● Take part in the induction programme	● To actively participate and monitor own work in relation to the induction standards
● Aid target setting	● To use the CEP to negotiate short, medium and long term targets for professional development
● Monitor the support, assessment and guidance given	● To raise professional concerns over the induction programme if necessary through the appropriate channels
● Understand the purposes of induction and the standards related to them	● To be familiar with the induction standards and the programme for induction

large primary schools or in secondary schools, the induction tutor will be the NQT's line manager. In practice this will mean a department head in the secondary setting, perhaps a subject co-ordinator in a large primary. In the case of a school with a small staff complement the headteacher may be the only suitable person to take on this role.

The governing body has the responsibility for overseeing the establishment of induction within a school. The appropriate body will be the LEA for all maintained or non-maintained special schools. Should independent schools wish to implement an induction programme for NQTs they may request that an LEA acts as their appropriate body.

NQTs have a duty to fully participate in the induction process and to monitor their own progress in meeting the induction standards. Should NQTs feel that the induction programme is not meeting their needs it is their responsibility to make this known to the headteacher.

Induction will last for a minimum of three terms and may, under exceptional circumstances only, be extended. This does not, however, have to be a continuous period and neither does it have to be within the same school.

The monitoring and support programme

Each NQT should be provided with an induction programme by their school that is to a large extent tailored to their individual needs. These needs will be directly related to the NQT's CEP. The CEP, introduced as a means to smooth the transition

Table 13.4 The roles and responsibilities of the appropriate body during NQT induction

The appropriate body

Role	*Responsibility*
● Maintain a list of NQTs for whom it acts as the appropriate body	● To collect information from headteachers of NQTs employed and the term of induction that applies ● To maintain a list of supply NQTs who are employed for a minimum of one term or more
● Liaison with other appropriate bodies	● To exchange details of NQTs employed part-time in more than one appropriate body's area
● Identify a named contact	● To ensure that a named contact is made known to schools and induction tutors with whom issues about provision can be raised
● Decide on satisfactory completion of induction	● To act on the recommendation of the headteacher as to satisfactory completion of induction ● To act on advice that NQTs are not making satisfactory progress and respond to the headteacher's notification of this ● In exceptional circumstances, to offer an extension to the induction period ● Where there is disagreement between the headteacher's decision and the evidence produced to support this, to reject the headteacher's decision and substitute its own
● Liaison with the General Teaching Council (GTC) and DfEE	● To inform the GTC of those NQTs who have satisfactorily completed induction ● To inform the Secretary of State for Education of those who satisfactorily complete induction ● To inform the NQT of whether or not it accepts the headteacher's recommendation ● To inform NQTs of the post-induction process ● To maintain records until the GTC informs that NQTs have moved from provisional to full registration
● Quality assurance	● To ensure that induction programmes are appropriate and of high quality ● To ensure that headteachers and governing bodies are aware of their roles and responsibilities ● To consult with headteachers and others on the form that quality assurance should take ● To provide advice and guidance on how schools may meet the induction guidance arrangements

Table 13.5 The roles and responsibilities of the governing body during NQT induction

The governing body

Role	Responsibility
• Oversee induction arrangements	• To ensure that appropriate and adequate induction programmes are available in their school
• Liaison with the appropriate body	• To seek guidance on the nature, range and appropriateness of induction arrangements for NQTs
• Oversee the roles of individuals with responsibility for induction	• To seek guidance on the extent and nature of the roles of individuals responsible for the induction of NQTs

between ITT and full-time employment concentrates on the strengths of the NQTs, identified during their extensive teaching experience, and looks at those areas still in need of further development.

It has been recognized that many NQTs will not have gained full experience in all of the situations that they may encounter in teaching. At the start of an NQT's first job, meeting with those responsible for NQT induction is important. In some situations, eg in a small primary school where the headteacher necessarily acts as the induction tutor, it may be necessary to provide experience for an NQT in other schools. In a rural setting where there may be a small group of schools with NQTs, a local cluster arrangement for the provision of quality induction may be appropriate. Due to the size of secondary schools and their staffing structure, headteachers are unlikely to act as induction tutors and this role is envisaged as being part of the subject leader's role.

Although the intention is to provide an individualized programme for each NQT, there will be some generic elements common to all NQT induction programmes. These will include the designation of a person to look after the NQT, regular observation of the work of the NQT, observation of experienced teachers either in the school or at another school if this is deemed appropriate, a professional review of the NQT's progress, and professional development.

Observation of the NQT's work must be carried out regularly. In order for observation to be of benefit it must be clearly targeted. During the ITT programme, trainees will have benefited from observation by their school-based mentors and, in many cases, these observations are moderated by the ITT institutions that provide support and training for mentors. Targeted observations where the observer and the trainee or, in the case of induction the NQT, have discussed in advance the nature of the observations and what the focus is, eg class management, effective questioning, differentiation issues, etc, lead to the most productive evaluation of a teacher's work. Over the induction year, observations may be made by a wide variety of individuals apart from the induction tutor – senior school staff, staff with specific responsibilities such as subject co-ordinators, year heads, LEA advisory staff or the newly-created advanced skills teachers.

During ITT trainees spend time observing experienced staff. Once trainees qualify they are rarely given the chance to repeat this valuable exercise. The induction year proposals address this by specifying that an induction programme should allow NQTs to observe experienced teachers with a view to gathering evidence on what constitutes good and effective practice. In small schools this could be a problem. Schools are encouraged to allow NQTs to observe teachers in schools which may have been identified as demonstrating effective practice.

The professional review of progress will be ongoing. In a feasibility study the TTA found that at least one meeting per half term was required to ensure that NQTs were given appropriate support. This does raise issues about the time constraints under which schools operate. It is clear that in future, schools which plan to fill posts vacated by experienced staff will have to look carefully at the feasibility of appointing someone who will need to complete induction. Associated with the teaching load which will have to be absorbed by other staff there is also the knock-on effect of releasing induction tutors to conduct regular review meetings and allowing them to complete the paperwork associated with the induction process. Any review discussions will have as their focus elements of the evidence being gathered about the NQT's progress and the progress of the NQT's pupils. In any system of observation and review, target setting as the basis of the next stage of induction should be the norm.

The professional development of all teachers is important, but in the case of NQTs this aspect is helped by the inclusion of professional development needs as a component of the CEP. In ensuring that NQTs begin their professional development as soon as they are appointed, schools should provide all newly appointed staff with details about the specific post they have been appointed to and as much information about the school as possible. A common complaint among both NQTs and experienced staff is a lack of information about their new post. School brochures, examination results and other publicly available information may be easy to get hold of but, of use to the NQT and, for that matter an experienced teacher, is information on school policies, teaching sets, examination statistics, curriculum and staff structure and, where appropriate, schemes of work.

A key part of professional development is access to high quality in-service training; NQTs will have this during the course of their induction year. In addition many networks have been established by LEAs, ITT institutions and commercial companies to cater for the needs of NQTs, which will also be available during induction training. Many schools have in place general induction arrangements and these will be enhanced with the new induction year.

Assessment requirements

The guidelines relating to induction, which all schools have been issued with, set out the formal assessment requirements. In addition they list the induction standards that all NQTs must meet. These standards aim to build on the standards for QTS that all NQTs will have met and, in addition, supplement those standards by focusing on the notion of professional practice.

In essence there are two criteria upon which NQTs will be judged when headteachers are making decisions about whether or not an NQT has successfully completed induction:

1. That the NQT has continued to meet the standards for the award of QTS on a consistent basis during his or her employment.
2. That the NQT has met all of the induction standards.

During the induction year, the induction tutor and headteacher will gather evidence on the NQTs' progress and there will have been at least three formal assessment meetings between the NQTs and the induction tutor or headteacher. The assessment meetings should have a clear focus. The first meeting should look at the NQTs' performance in relation to the standards for QTS and whether or not they are meeting these standards consistently. This will take into account evidence from formal observations of the teachers' performance in the classroom and their integration into the school as a community. The second meeting will look at the NQTs' progress towards meeting the standards for induction and the third meeting will determine whether or not the NQTs have met all of the requirements of induction. The current proposals are that the meetings should be held termly, or pro-rata for those employed on a part-time basis.

The end of the induction period is seen as the start of a teacher's continuing professional development. By the end of induction new targets for professional development will be set and the NQT will be integrated into the school's appraisal system, new arrangements for which will be set in place by the government.

In any process of assessment there must be evidence that contributes to that assessment. Induction is no different. The NQT's induction tutor will gather evidence. This will take the form of observation reports written by the induction tutor or any other experienced teachers who see the teachers teaching as part of the school's monitoring and support programme. In addition, notes of any pre- and/or post-observation meeting will be collected and evidence on the progress of pupils for whom the NQT has responsibility will be reviewed. This last aspect may be one of the more demanding areas. Clearly teachers who assume responsibility for a group must also take on board the responsibility for ensuring some form of positive achievement as a result of their teaching. Exactly what form this achievement may take is not specified due to the wide variations between cohorts of pupils in different circumstances, eg inner city vs suburbs, and the problems associated with baseline testing and the calculation of value-added in respect of pupil achievement. We may well find that the criteria surrounding the evidence of pupil progress as a means to assessing NQTs' progress differ from school to school and year to year.

The induction standards

The induction standards set out specific criteria that must be met. In essence they follow the standards for QTS, covering planning, teaching and classroom management. Where they differ is that they extend the QTS standards by focusing on their applicability within an employment situation. NQTs then, will be asked to look at their pupils and set targets relating to their individual progress, and plan effectively to allow all pupils to achieve their full potential taking account of their individual needs. NQTs will also be expected to secure a good standard of behaviour by setting appropriate rules and high expectations of discipline, pre-empting inappropriate behaviour. Their planning must also meet the needs of pupils with SEN.

In common with all teachers, NQTs will be assessed on their monitoring, assessment, recording and reporting on pupils. This involves developing the skills to make accurate assessments of pupils' performance in subject areas and liaison with parents/guardians and others.

As a member of the school community their integration and performance as members of the staff will also be monitored. This will involve the active implementation of school policies, the effective liaison with and deployment of support staff and a degree of reflective practice, setting targets for their own professional development.

Unsatisfactory progress

The induction arrangements have been put in place on the basis that few NQTs should be in danger of failing to complete their induction period satisfactorily. One of the problems with the old probationary year was the granting of extensions to those who were clearly unsuited to teaching. The granting of an extension to the new induction year is set to be the exception rather than the rule. As this is the case, failing to pass the induction year is a serious matter. In effect failure will mean removal from the register of qualified teachers. The consequence of this is that anyone who wishes to continue teaching in the state sector will be required to register, follow and pass a PGCE course once more. As induction is not a requirement for the independent sector, 'failed' NQTs would be eligible for employment in this sector, but it will be difficult to persuade any potential employer that they have the necessary skills to carry out the job well. Failure in the induction year will lead to the termination of employment as a teacher.

It is envisaged that any doubts as to the progress of an NQT would be identified early on in the induction year. The first indications should be noted at the school level with the induction tutor and others charged with giving appropriate support for a struggling NQT. This will also have to be notified to the appropriate body in the termly report to them on NQT progress. This report will identify the weaknesses, the agreed targets set for the NQT in relation to the induction standards, the support planned for the NQT and the evidence base for the decision made by the headteacher. As soon at it becomes apparent that an NQT may fail to meet the induction standards the headteacher and the appropriate body have the responsibility to ensure that the assessments made are accurate and well-founded, that the weaknesses have been correctly identified, that appropriate targets were set and that a proper support programme was put in place. In addition, the headteacher must observe the teaching of any NQT deemed at risk of failing. Any NQTs who fail their induction year may appeal against this decision. At present the appeal is made to the Secretary of State for Education, but once the GTC is established, the appeal will be heard by them. Should the appropriate body feel that the headteacher's decision is incorrect, based on the evidence supplied, it may overturn the decision.

Conclusion

Support for NQTs and attention to their continued professional development are long overdue. The consequences of failure are severe, but with the rigorous assessment of trainee teachers and the procedures currently in place for ensuring that they meet the current standards for QTS, induction should be seen as part of a continuum of career progression. With the standards for subject leaders, advanced skills teachers and headteachers now coming on stream, that continuum is set to provide a fresh new challenge for entrants to the teaching profession that sees teaching as a true profession and not just another job.

Task 13.1 (During ITT)

Using any evidence you have so far, in the form of observation reports on your teaching and formal and informal interviews with your school and/or ITT-based mentor, develop a strategic plan to deal with any weaknesses identified.

At this stage your weaknesses may be related to classroom management, subject knowledge or the core activities of lesson planning. Your strategic plan should contain the following elements:

1. The identified weakness.
2. The evidence for that weakness.
3. An action plan to deal with the identified weakness.
4. Specific performance indicators that will identify if the weakness has been successfully overcome.

Task 13.2 (At the start of induction)

Arrange a meeting with your line manager to discuss specific support available for NQTs. This may take the form of a generic induction programme or it may look at the availability of INSET for NQTs. Set the agenda for the meeting to include the following items:

1. The school's generic induction provision.
2. The INSET budget and its management – ie whether it is devolved to departments or bid for from a central fund, and who is responsible for it.
3. Where details of available INSET (LEA, ITT and commercial courses) are held within the school.
4. The process of application for subject-specific and generic INSET.

References

Department for Education and Employment (DfEE) (1997) *Excellence in Schools*, HMSO, London

DfEE (1998a) *The Standards Fund 1999–2000*, Circular 13/98, DfEE, London

DfEE (1998b) *Teachers: Meeting the Challenge of Change*, DfEE, London

DfEE (1999) *The Induction Period for Newly Qualified Teachers*, Circular 5/99, DfEE, London

Index